Education's Prisoners

Studies in the
Postmodern Theory of Education

Joe L. Kincheloe and Shirley R. Steinberg
General Editors

Vol. 325

PETER LANG
New York • Washington, D.C./Baltimore • Bern
Frankfurt am Main • Berlin • Brussels • Vienna • Oxford

KEN MCGREW

Education's Prisoners

SCHOOLING, THE POLITICAL ECONOMY, AND THE PRISON INDUSTRIAL COMPLEX

PETER LANG
New York • Washington, D.C./Baltimore • Bern
Frankfurt am Main • Berlin • Brussels • Vienna • Oxford

Library of Congress Cataloging-in-Publication Data

McGrew, Ken.
Education's prisoners: schooling, the political economy, and the
prison industrial complex / Ken McGrew.
p. cm. — (Counterpoints: studies in the postmodern theory of education; v. 325)
Includes bibliographical references and index.
1. Prisoners—Education. 2. Criminals—Rehabilitation. I. Title.
HV8875.M44   365'.6660973—dc22   2007043350
ISBN 978-1-4331-0175-5
ISSN 1058-1634

Bibliographic information published by **Die Deutsche Nationalbibliothek**.
Die Deutsche Nationalbibliothek lists this publication in the "Deutsche
Nationalbibliografie"; detailed bibliographic data are available
on the Internet at http://dnb.d-nb.de/.

Front and back cover images by Ken McGrew

The paper in this book meets the guidelines for permanence and durability
of the Committee on Production Guidelines for Book Longevity
of the Council of Library Resources.

Printed in the United States of America

To my grandmothers
and to the other wonderful teachers I have known

Table of Contents

Acknowledgments

I would like to thank the following people for their influence on my thinking related to this project: Michael Apple, Andreas Kazamias, Herbert Kliebard, Gloria Ladson-Billings, Stacey Lee, Pamela Oliver, Daniel Pekarsky, Thomas Skrtic, Clifton Tanabe, Gregory Tewksbury, and Terry Williams. Anja Chimileski served as a research assistant in preparation of the manuscript. I would also like to thank the professionals at the Juvenile Court who accommodated my research and shared the insights they have developed over many years of service. Finally, I must thank the young people who trusted me with their stories and were my co-investigators.

Chapter 1

By Way of Introduction

During the years of 1998 and 1999 I served as a volunteer and conducted critical-ethnographic research, at a county juvenile court and detention center in Wisconsin, in a community I refer to here as Coldville. As I approached the research, I expected to write a theoretical treatment of the relationship between the political economy, education, and the prison industrial complex in the United States. It was my intention to use historical and theoretical analysis within the tradition of critical theory both to document and explain the complicated relationships among these social phenomena and institutions. Such research is valuable because too little scholarship has addressed the ways that increasingly punitive laws, racially and economically disproportionate law enforcement, and massive increases in incarceration are affecting public education and the lives of many of the young people with whom teachers work. Like Bill Ayers (1997), "I was beginning to see a straight line between failing schools and burgeoning youth jails" (p. xv).

I hoped to demonstrate persuasively that the diversion of resources towards incarceration and away from schools and communities was creating a structural situation in which young people from poor families, for a myriad of complex reasons, are increasingly more likely to spend a great deal of their lives in jails and prisons. Worse yet, I would argue, this trend was becoming functional in society in general and to the economy specifically, creating jobs and profits for some segments of society at the expense of others. Ultimately, in the tradition of the work of Paul Willis (1977/81), I would describe the double-edged sword of student resistance that represents their rejection of the false promise of educational opportunity, holds revolutionary potential, and yet tends to trap them in their structural roles of school failure and incarceration.

My conception of the problems of school failure and incarceration are substantially unchanged, and that conception of these social problems informs this book. I continue to view educational failure and incarceration as the likely, though not inevitable, results of structural inequalities in society, which in turn are functional to capitalist production and the maintenance of class hierarchies. While conducting the fieldwork for this book, I attempted to provide an avenue for young people to tell their own stories and to engage in a debate with the scholarly literature that so often theorizes about them. My commitment to enter into dialogue with my informants about theory, however, has led me to raise questions about the usefulness of resistance theory, for reasons that will become clear later.

Population in the Study

The Juvenile Detention Center had 18 beds for boys and girls who typically ranged in age from 13 to 16 (17-year-olds are prosecuted as adults in Wisconsin), but could be younger than 11. Most of the young people were 15 or 16 years of age. In 1998, 1,035 juveniles were referred to the Juvenile Court (primarily by police). In 1999, 1,318 juveniles were referred to the court. Roughly 25 percent of the young people referred were "outright released" to a guardian or to themselves (if 15 years of age or older), depending on the nature of the referral. Another 12 percent were held in a non-secure shelter home or custody situation. Some young people were already under a court-ordered placement and were returned to this placement, unless they were alleged to have engaged in a serious criminal act. Unlike at many detention centers, these young people were to be given a determination by the court at the earliest possible time as to whether or not there was a safe place to which to release them and whether or not they were a danger to themselves or others; the court favors releasing them whenever possible. Despite this policy, in 1998, 503 of the young people referred (74 percent of those not outright released) were held in the detention center. In 1999, 528 of the referred young people (57 percent of those not outright released) were held at the detention center (Annual Report).

Most of the young people who were held in detention were there for a short time. The annual report from the juvenile court does not indicate the average length of stay in the detention center. I would estimate the average length of stay to be two weeks, though some young people were held only until a guardian could come for them or until after the initial hearing. Given the length of time that young people stayed in the detention center, the young people with whom I spent the greatest amount of time and with whom I developed the most trust tended to be those held for longer periods of time. This typically meant that they were awaiting trial, or that they were deemed a risk to release, or that the court felt there was not an appropriate environment to which they could be released. Young people who were held for shorter periods of time are represented in my data and their voices speak prominently at times. In general, however, the focus of the research and the primary population I worked with were the young people who were there for longer periods.

About 70 percent of the young people referred to the juvenile court were boys. Despite their low numbers in the community (4 percent of the population), around 40 percent of the young people referred were African-American, with other ethnic minorities accounting for almost 10 percent of referrals. Of those young people actually held in the detention center, and not outright released, around 45 percent were minority male and 12 percent minority female. White boys were 30 percent of those held, and White females around 11 percent. I was not at the center every day, so my notes cannot establish the exact demographic breakdown of children held there, nor the length of their stays, but my notes do convey impressions of what typical days were like. In my notes from one such typical day I observed:

> 13 boys: 1 Caucasian, 11 African A., 1 Latino.
> 4 girls: 1 Caucasian, 1 Latina, 1 African A., 1 out sick.
> 11 boys new to me. 2 girls new to me.
> 1 boy back after being released a month ago.

So it can be shown that my population, or those young people actually held in the secure facility, were disproportionately Black and male. The annual reports do not organize the data to reveal average length of stay by race and gender. My observations revealed that in the detention center white skin was rare, especially among those held for longer periods of time. Although I was unable to track this to any degree of certainty, youth of color did remain in detention for significantly longer periods of time. Girls of color were held for only slightly shorter time periods than the boys of color.

The young people in my study also tended to be from families with some of the lowest incomes in the community. The Juvenile Court does not track family income related to the young people referred. I chose not to ask very direct questions about income or whether families were on welfare given the emotional pain that is often associated with poverty and being on welfare, and because I wanted to preserve my developing relationships with my informants. From my conversations with the young people, however, I was able to determine that most of their families survived on very low incomes. Some young people would volunteer this information directly. I also knew the neighborhoods in the community in which they lived, which tended to be home to people of color and low-income families (due primarily to discriminatory housing practices in the community, as rents were only slightly lower in these neighborhoods than in the rest of the community). My research took place at the time of the welfare changes under the policies of Governor

Thompson's administration as well as those of President Clinton (see Fine & Weis, 1998). The families in my study tended to be working poor, welfare recipients, or families forced into the underground economy when they were forced (directly or indirectly) from the welfare rolls.

Around half of the young people of color that I met reported moving to Coldville from Chicago or other large cities associated (in the minds of most people in Coldville) with Black criminality. Their parents, as I was informed by young people and their parents alike, had made the move in hopes of providing them with access to better schools and safer neighborhoods with fewer negative influences. The way that young people of color are viewed in Coldville is very much related to this migration. Not only were they viewed as being different and other, they were also considered outsiders and a drain on the community's resources. Poor people of color had been ghettoized into several small and neglected neighborhoods, where they were under constant surveillance by a disproportionate concentration of police. Many White members of the larger community, despite the liberal reputation of Coldville, expressed to other White people a strong disdain for the communities of color amongst them. I have heard these comments frequently, from strangers and acquaintances alike, and can report that these views were commonplace. It is likely that this attitude influenced policy decisions, policing strategies, hiring decisions, and jury deliberations. Coldville is a racist community. It is a polite racism, a quiet or unspoken racism carried out by White people who do not want to think of themselves as racist, but it is a racism that has resulted in racially biased per-capita arrest and incarceration rates that top the nation (Beck, Karberg, & Harrison, 2002). The young people in my study come from the families whose members fill these prison cells and these detention cells.

This is not a study of all young people, or even of most young people, in Coldville. It is instead a study of young people in Coldville whose families live in its economic margins, ghettoized by income and race, and who face myriad related problems at home and at school. These are the young people one finds at the detention center.

While at the center I spent hours on end with my informants, having meals together, cleaning up together, engaging in conversations, interviews, and educational activities. I also benefited from the guidance and insights of the professionals who have dedicated their lives to helping young people like those whom I came to know. In the pages that follow I report on the life histories of the young people whom I met at the juvenile court. I describe their behaviors and mannerisms. I capture their descriptions of their hopes and dreams. I allow them to tell us what *they* think about the lofty questions that scholars have often asked *about* them. They tell us how they experience mainstream curriculum and instruction. They teach us about the impact of the economy on their lives and the stark options that they see for themselves in the present and the future. At times they reveal the pain and worry that they carry around inside them; which is often hidden behind a mask of bravado. They tell us about the racism that they experience in their daily lives, the profiling and violation of rights perpetrated against them by the police, and about how unfairly they are treated in the justice system. They reveal their complex relationships with issues of sexism, class, and race.

Working in the Field

The detention center space was too small for the number of young people who were routinely held there, both on a short- and long-term basis. Young people were routinely shipped out to detention centers in neighboring counties when the center ran out of beds. The layout of the space was also problematic. There were two wings of cells in which young people rested and slept, separate for boys and girls. Showers were located in each of the wings. I never entered either of the wings. There was a small room surrounded by lockers and storage closets that also held a foosball table and a weight lifting machine. There was a computer room, a kitchen, a central desk area for the staff, a general use room and a television room. All of the rooms were small. The general use room held five plastic tables with plastic chairs. It served as the dining room, recreation room, and classroom. This room had windows looking out on the street below. I was told that the cells also had windows. The center staff and directors had been advocating for a better space for some time.

One consequence of the layout of the center was that having the young people in more than one of the rooms at the same time required at least one member of the staff to be observing each location. Given other administrative duties, including paper work and food dispensing at meal times, there was seldom enough staff supervision to allow for more than two of the rooms to be occupied at the same time. Most of the time spent outside of the cells, which were called "rooms" at the center, was spent in the general use room. On one of the walls of the general use room the artwork and writing of young people were often present. On a board dealing with abstinence, for example, a young person had spelled out the following sentence with block letters: "keep that thing in your pants and keep the legs crossed." At the back of the room a schedule and the rules of behavior were displayed.

There was seldom enough staff coverage for the young people to use the exercise equipment, much less to exercise on the roof. As a consequence of the crowded conditions and bad acoustics, normal conversations in the general use room could seem quite loud. The staff were often forced, therefore, to require the young people to sit quietly at the tables. They were also, at most times, not allowed to look out the windows. These rules were in place for reasons of safety and to preserve the nerves of the staff in what would otherwise become a loud and chaotic environment. For the young people, who were unable to exercise, laugh, or otherwise blow off steam, sitting quietly could seem an unfair requirement. These factors combined to create most of the conflicts between the young people and staff, which were actually fairly rare. While at the research site I assisted the staff in a variety of capacities by running discussion groups, serving as an educational assistant, or simply supervising a room. I believe that being able to help in these ways mediated the additional demands that my presence at the center placed on them in their attempts to accommodate the needs of the study.

It would be a mistake to give the impression that the detention center was a dreary or unfriendly place. Unlike other detention centers in surrounding communities (as they have been described by the young people and staff members alike), most of the staff at this facility were genuinely committed to providing a safe and supportive environment for the young people. There were few exceptions to this general observation. I attribute the positive environment at the detention center to the example of the directors, the teacher, and two senior members of the general staff, whose genuine concern for the young people was obvious to myself and the young people. The directors of the center continued to believe in rehabilitation, the concept of adolescence, and juvenile justice. The senior staff concerned themselves with what I saw as their unstated goals of treating all of the young people under their care with respect, concern, and even affection. The young people would even refer to some of the staff with familiar and affectionate names, like "Gramma." The climate at the center, for the most part, was very humane. Despite what the young people might have done or what might have been done to them before coming to the center, once there they found a stable environment that many of them confessed to enjoying, with the exception of the loss of some freedoms.

A typical weekday at the center consisted of meals, showers, school, phone calls home, occasional visits, and free time. Free time activities could include exercising, playing foosball, writing letters, watching television, participation in evening group educational programs, or playing cards or board games. Weekends did not include school. Sundays were generally relaxed and allowed for more free time. Evening educational programming took a variety of forms, depending on who was present in terms of staff, interns, or volunteers such as myself. This programming was often replaced with more free time. Each activity I was involved in allowed for opportunities to engage in informal conversations with groups and individuals, with both the staff and the young people. The presence of volunteers and interns provided a needed distraction to what could be a monotonous routine, as did the constant arrival and departure of young people who were not held for longer periods pending trial.

I was pleased to be able to serve as a volunteer at the center at the same time I was conducting the fieldwork. This allowed me to help the overworked staff and to give something back to the young people and staff for the time they spent with me. It also gave me insights into and opportunities for interactions and conversations that I might otherwise never have had, or else would have observed from the outside rather than as a participant observer. The multiple roles that I had in the center, along with the physical layout, made the research process complex and difficult at times. I had to choose carefully what I asked and said given who was able to overhear a given conversation. My duties as a volunteer sometimes precluded me from engaging in more detail around a topic with one or more of my informants. This happened, for example, when there was not enough time to delve deeper into a conversation, or when I might not have entirely supported the policies of the center, but was obligated to enforce them nonetheless.

My role in the detention center was complex. I took the role at times of researcher, volunteer, staff, teacher, and confidante. I am white, male, and educated, and was perceived by many of the young people as being wealthy (compared to many of them I was). I wore casual dress clothes, shirt tucked in, and a belt at all times at the research site. This, at least initially, would make me stand out in appearance from both the young people and the staff. Some informants were receptive to talking with me right away, others were completely uninterested in talking with a researcher, and others would only speak with me once one of their peers had made introductions or had vouched for me: "he's ahright." Then the population would cycle out and the process would begin anew. Eventually I was at the center long enough to see particular young people return to detention on some new or related charge.

I was able to benefit from the structure provided by the staff without, for the most part, having to exercise authority myself. When I was running an educational activity or group discussion the conversation would often be an important source of data. For the most part the young people wanted to participate in these conversations. If one or two of the participants were having a bad day for some reason and were inclined to disrupt the discussion, and if I could not persuade them to reconsider their participation, I could count on the staff to remind them that participation in educational activities was mandatory. Because the staff took on this role for me, I benefited from the rules without having to be viewed by the young people as necessarily endorsing those rules. This arrangement gave me access to conversations that would have been less likely to occur otherwise and helped me to avoid straining relationships with my informants.

Because of my shifting identity at the center and because of the staff handling discipline issues, I was afforded the opportunity to reveal more of myself to the young people than the staff could. I was able to have conversations with the young people, not as a peer, but not quite as an authority figure either. I was able to engage with groups of young people and individuals. I could tell them what I was thinking about an issue and I could ask them if they thought I was on the right track. In fact, the young people were free to disagree and challenge me when they felt the need. Engaging around these points of agreement and disagreement helped me to understand their thinking in ways that simply asking questions could not.

This style of interaction is similar to the approach that I use in the college classroom. And like in all classrooms that are informed by the work of Paulo Freire, I listened carefully to the ideas and perspectives of the young people while I also tried to influence them at times, not by means of authority but with reason. In the classroom, I try to get my students to question their own assumptions and truly consider other perspectives. I try to teach them to weigh and sift competing evidence and points of view. My interactions with the young people in the detention center were not quite the same as when I teach on the college level, in part because I did not want to shape what they were telling me, and I did not want them to tell me what they thought I wanted to hear. So at times I held back my views even when asked. When a young person expressed the idea that she was incapable of learning or that he had nothing better to look forward to in life than selling drugs, I felt compelled to try to persuade him or her otherwise. The data gained from these sorts of interactions is, in my view, very rich. But it is not pure, not gathered without interference from the ethnographer. It is information gathered in the attempt to respectfully persuade my informants. It yields a special sort of knowledge; knowledge of how young people can and cannot be persuaded to believe in their own potentials and futures. When they could not be persuaded, these conversations still helped me to understand why they held the views that they held. At its best, this book is a record of my attempts to both listen and speak, and then to try to make sense of what was learned.

The Community Context

I have followed political trends in the community, including the allocation of public resources, housing policies that ghettoize people of color and poor people into particular neighborhoods, and patterns of policing and prosecution, all of which had a direct impact on the circumstances of my informants. I felt, as the research progressed, increasingly compelled to document local struggles and conditions. National and international changes in the economy as well as the growth of the prison industrial complex in the United States have resulted in patterns that are consistent across the country, but in a given community these forces always play out in particular ways. It is conceivable that the community in which I lived and conducted my research could have demanded different approaches to teaching, housing, policing, and prosecution. The life of this community, the struggles for access to community resources among interest groups, and the impact on the lives of my informants are not unusual, but they are particular. This study tells the story of my informants as well as the story of the community in which they lived.

The local community became central in my analysis, both during and after the fieldwork. In attempting to address the research questions that I began with, as well as others that developed in the field, I considered the extent to which the young people I had come to know were in their current situations because of their own and their families' choices, because of larger social forces, because of educational practices, or because of the policies and attitudes in the community.

I have had an ongoing debate with myself as to whether I should name the city and or the state in which the fieldwork was conducted. The obvious benefit of concealing such information is to better protect the identities of one's informants. There are additional benefits to doing so. In her ethnography *Unraveling the "Model Minority" Stereotype* (1996), Stacey Lee addresses this question when she writes of her own research that:

> I use pseudonyms for the school and city as well. Although people familiar with public high schools on the East Coast may be able to identify the school, I use a pseudonym to shift the focus away from this particular school and to redirect the focus toward public schools in general. I want to stress that it would be unfair to isolate the school for any "blame." The findings – "positive" and "negative" – were only discovered because Dr. Levine gave me access to the school and the teachers and students allowed me into their lives. While particular events and people are unique to this school at a particular historical moment, I want to stress that the questions and concerns raised by the data speak beyond the school. (p. 10)

This was an ethical and theoretical dilemma. I felt that it was unclear the extent to which my data speak beyond the local community. I suspected that there was some truth to the notion that the stories of my informants had a great deal in common with the stories of other young people from similar backgrounds across the nation. At the same time, I increasingly came to believe that the attitudes and choices of local citizens, politicians, prosecutors, judges, and police officers contributed substantially to the struggles of these young people.

Although I had great respect for the administration and most of the members of the staff at the center where I conducted my fieldwork and found them to be exceptional in their efforts to treat the young people under their care in a dignified manner, I felt that some actors involved with my informants deserved to be criticized and named. Naming the community became all the more tempting when I considered, as Lee stated above, that efforts to hide research sites are largely symbolic. There were consistent allegations made by many of my informants of violations of their rights and even torture by police officers. I felt that the local community needed to address the allegations and that I needed to do justice to the promise I made to the young people to accurately convey what they had told me, not only to a national academic audience, but in their own city where it might actually do them some direct good. If true, many of their allegations would warrant discipline or even criminal prosecution. My dilemma was compounded by the need to protect my informants. It was further complicated by my personal need to preserve access and complete my research.

In the end I have decided to name the state, Wisconsin, which, under the leadership of Governor Tommy Thompson, had been at the forefront of efforts to curtail social services and to incarcerate people of color disproportionately. I will not name the local community, which I refer to as Coldville. I will, however, refer to specific local events and conditions that could be easily identifiable to anyone familiar with this community. I will not disclose the names of my informants nor will I testify against them.

Reasons for Using a Critical-Ethnographic Approach

My motivation for conducting an ethnographic study began with a sense of obligation to and solidarity with poor people. As Jay MacLeod writes in his critical ethnographic study of aspirations among low-income youth, *Ain't No Makin' It* (1987/1995):

> If we are to understand what we see on the streets, if we are to make sense of the
> forces that act upon these boys, and if we are to generalize from their experiences in

any meaningful way, we must situate our work in a broader theoretical framework
by letting theory inform our data and, ultimately, by allowing our data to inform our
theory. (p. 10)

Neither my own nor my participants' perspectives exist in an intellectual
void. They are theoretically informed (whether or not they realize it or have
read theory), and therefore, I determined, one aspect of the study must be to
make explicit the underlying theoretical assumptions upon which I, the participants, and other scholars build our respective understandings of social
phenomena. Critical ethnography is an approach well suited to sorting out
the complex relationships between the subjective and objective.

It is necessary that I should give some description of what I mean when I
refer to this ethnography as critical research. Critical ethnography is ethnography conducted by scholars who hold particular assumptions about the nature of society under capitalism and other systems of economic exploitation.
Critical theory has its roots in Marxism and neo-Marxism, though it is politically aligned with broader struggles against exploitation and oppression
throughout history. The traditions of scholarship that have come to be called
critical theory developed and evolved with history, academic debates,
changes in the political climate, and political struggles in the academy.

Critical theory refers to a cluster of traditions of inquiry with a strong
family resemblance. Within this universe, there have been a number of attempts to define the term, but no definition has won the day (for a brief over-
view of some of the developments in critical research see Apple & Weis
1983, chapter 1, or MacLeod 1987/95, chapter 2). For my purposes, it will be
useful to work within the definition offered by Phil Francis Carspecken and
Michael Apple in *The Handbook of Qualitative Research in Education*
(1992). They argue that critically oriented work from the early 1970s to the
present, despite current and previous debates, shares a view of schooling that
is "intimately connected to the patterns of unequal benefits and losses" in
society (p. 508). As they argue:

Education does not stand alone, a neutral instrumentality somehow above the ideological conflicts of the society. Rather, it is deeply implicated in the formation of the
unequal cultural, economic, and political relations that dominate our society. Education has been a major arena in which dominance is reproduced and contested, in
which hegemony is partly formed and partly fractured in the creation of the common
sense of a people. Thus, to think seriously about education, like culture in general, is
also to think just as seriously about power, about the mechanisms through which
certain groups assert their visions, beliefs, and practices. While education is not to-
tally reducible to the political, not to deal with the structural sources of differential
power is not to deal with education as a cultural and social process as well. (p. 509)

This is not to say that schools do nothing but reproduce inequality in society, though they are under "considerable pressure" to do so (p. 509). Rather, Carspecken and Apple suggest that we must acknowledge human struggles with competing social forces within the context of an unequal society (p. 510).

That social inequalities are related to education, or even that social inequalities are unjust and undesirable, may be contested in some quarters. Critical scholars, however, take as a given that society is unequally structured to the detriment of particular populations and to the advantage of others; namely, to the advantage of elites who own the means of production and control the vast majority of wealth. Like other critical scholars, in this critical ethnography my objective is not to challenge the basic tenets of critical scholarship, but to refine and broaden the literature, to make not only an "empirical-descriptive contribution but also a theoretical contribution—deepening our understanding of core social-theoretical concepts" (pp. 511–512). However, I would also argue, drawing on the influence of Paulo Freire's work, that oppression is carried out by human actors, is psychological in nature as well as material, and predates the capitalist system. Capitalism is human greed, expressed in the dehumanization of and exploitation of others, manifest in an ideologically driven economic system.

My methodology in this study is critical ethnography. It is not action research. Nonetheless, I did not experience the problems in my study as distant or simply "academic." The struggles of the young people whom I met affected me on an emotional level. I care about them, as I care about the communities in which they lived. Critical theory and critical ethnography do not aspire only to study subjects; rather, they do so as a vehicle to help individuals and communities to improve their lives and work towards social justice. As Michael Apple has asked, if we can't be angry about the harm done to children, what can we be angry about (1993, p. viii)? As I write these words the economic violence perpetrated against the young people in my study, the racism they experience, as well as the racial profiling and physical abuse that they have reported to me, leave me with a quiet rage.

My research approach is greatly influenced by the work of Paulo Freire. For this reason I refer to it as advocacy ethnography. It is important that I do my best to objectively question my own assumptions and conclusions, but I have no pretence to neutrality. This is methodology *for* the oppressed. The voice, tone, and approach that I take in the writing of this book largely result from my reading of Freire. This book is written in a language that is consistent with its theoretical framework. I call my approach advocacy research because the Freirean scholar attempts to do more than report, but also to struggle with her informants to demand social justice. In writing the book I have attempted, as Paulo Freire (1970/93) urged us, in the dedication of *Pedagogy of the Oppressed*, to "fight at their side." I have also tried to "suffer with them," which has taken the form of my caring about my informants and seeing the good in their hearts, even when they have transgressed against others or society as a whole. I have tried to grow my humanity in this process, so that I can better capture and represent the humanity of my informants to my audience. But the love I have tried to show them is not a blind love. I have attempted to remain critical, open-minded, and to look at the totality of the evidence when constructing explanations for the social phenomena that I discuss. My purpose is not to make excuses for my informants when they have done wrong, but to develop an understanding of them as psychologically motivated, fully human, and sharing in responsibility for their predicaments. This is a critical point. To help the oppressed help themselves, we must be willing to address their role in their own oppression.

My Orientation Towards Sociology

I should discuss briefly my orientation regarding critical ethnography as either the study of culture or as the study of social phenomena. Modern ethnography has developed out of the disciplines of sociology and anthropology (Adler & Adler, 1987; Anderson, 1989; Metz, 2000), but ethnographers do not mete out equal portions of each in their studies. Rather, they gravitate more towards an anthropological orientation or more towards a sociological orientation depending on the nature of the study and research site, as well as their disciplinary training. Critical ethnography, because of its multidisciplinary approach, usually draws upon both orientations. In fact, each tradition supports the other. As Anderson (1989) observed:

Critical ethnography also owes a great debt to interpretive movements in the fields of anthropology and sociology. Influenced by phenomenology, structuralism, semiotics, hermeneutics, and linguistics, interpretive ethnographers in anthropology raised fundamental questions about both the practice of ethnography and the nature of culture. Tracing their lineage to Malinowski's (1922) concern with "the native's point of view," they engaged in discussions of the nature of "local knowledge" and viewed social life as consisting of negotiated meanings (Geertz, 1973, 1983). While interpretivists in anthropology were shifting their attention from the functionalist notions of systems maintenance and equilibrium to what Geertz (1983) called "the analysis of symbol systems" (p. 34), qualitative sociologists were intensifying their epistemological attack on the pervasiveness of positivist assumptions in their field. In sociology the traditions of symbolic interactionism and ethnomethodology provided legitimation for the ethnographic methods. Both interactionists and eth-

nomethodologists were concerned with social interaction as a means of negotiating
meanings in context. (pp. 250–251)

While sociology adopted the methodology of anthropology, its focus has
remained more on understanding patterns, as a social-organism view would
tend to do, than on illuminating cultural meanings.[1] Sociology has developed
an appreciation of the importance of culture, but the tendency in ethnographies with a sociological orientation has been to identify and categorize
subcultures rather than to look for that elusive common cultural glue that
anthropologists tend to view as primary in understanding society. Rather than
treating culture as primary, sociologists tend, as Mary Metz (1992) puts it, to
"emphasize strains, for it is where social systems encounter stress, contradiction, and failure that the influences which shape them are most clearly visible" (p. ix).

In a sociological ethnography there is less of an emphasis on looking for
hidden meanings and implications for culture in the words and actions of
informants. There is, instead, more of an emphasis on summarizing and cate-
gorizing their perspectives, looking for patterns of behaviors that are gov-
erned not so much by culture but by the norms of social interaction and
power dynamics. The glue is not culture, but psychology and socialization.
My thinking is influenced by the traditions in sociology of both social func-
tionalism and conflict theories. My work remains interdisciplinary, but if it
were to be described in the terms of sociology, it would be most closely associated with political socialization and social psychology.

I should also state that the influence of Paulo Freire (whose work was in
large part social psychology even though he was a philosopher) on my thinking results in my having a specific meaning when I speak of forces and systems. Systems are not beings unto themselves. They are made up of
individual human actors who, ultimately, could choose not to participate in
the oppression of others. I view the fundamental (social functionalist) role of
political socialization under late capitalism to be the alienation of the citizenry from this basic realization.[2]

These disciplinary influences explain, in part, my tendency in the book
to summarize and categorize the statements and perspectives of my informants, as I attempt to explain what I take their significance to the study to be.
Getting their perspectives right and conveying their words faithfully is important for both methodological and moral reasons. This is not a book that
simply documents what the young people thought and said, however. It is,
instead, a study of the impact of larger social forces and economic structures
on my participants, forces and structures made up of collections and class
groupings of individuals; individuals who are more powerful, wealthy, and

White privileged than the young people in my study. It is a study of the larger community's participation in the destruction of the young people in my study and the reaction of my participants to their attempted destruction; of their confusion, of their anger, of their psychological coping mechanisms, of their sorrow, of their desperation and despair, but also of their hope, their dignity, their potential, and their joy. I tried to take seriously the role of my informants as colleagues who were helping me to sort out the complex social problems I was addressing. In the end it must be remembered that the conclusions in the book are my own and that I am writing the book not for the sake of an exercise in qualitative methodology, but in an attempt to do what I can to uncover the nature of these problems, and, hopefully, to improve and save lives.

The Constraints Imposed by Human Subjects

The population in my study was considered particularly vulnerable. I was therefore required to gain approval for the research from the full Human Subjects Committee for the school of Education, which was made up of representatives from a range of departments and disciplines. The hearing was held in an auditorium setting. Some of the committee members expressed hostility towards the research, seemed to lack an understanding of qualitative research methodologies, and attempted to delve into areas beyond the scope of their charge. Some members of the committee, for example, challenged my intended use of open-ended questions, revealing their bias against qualitative research.

There was much discussion of what might happen if I were called to court to testify about any participant's alleged illegal activities. I reminded the committee of ethnographic research that has been conducted with participants who were in fact involved in illegal activities, like the work of Terry Williams (1992) with crack dealers, and his refusal to reveal the identities of his informants. I assured the committee that I would not reveal the identities of my informants. Some of the committee members went so far as to discuss the possibility of the university having to pay my legal bills in the hypothetical situation that I should be subpoenaed and refuse to testify, and whether in such an occurrence the committee would get in trouble for having approved my research. The minutes from the meeting are informative in this regard:

> A major concern is that during the time that the researcher is doing interviews or observations, he may become aware of information that could, if revealed, affect the juvenile's sentencing or probation. Even though the researcher has no intention of revealing any such information and will disguise individuals referred to in his re-

search, both by pseudonyms and altered descriptions, we are concerned about potential risks. Committee members determined they would like to get advice from Legal
Services on safeguards for the minors involved in the research, for the researcher,
and also any liability issues for the university.

When the committee sought approval from the university legal counsel, I
was eventually allowed to begin the research, but my research design had
been significantly shaped by the university's human subjects guidelines and
the committee's demands. However well meaning the requirements, I was
forced to use a highly technical consent form in order to gain permission
from guardians to conduct interviews with the young people at the center,
and I was required to have this access before reviewing any records. Undergraduate volunteers at the center had greater access to these records than I
did given the Human Subjects Committee's restrictions.[3] The issue of informed consent was complicated by my multiple roles at the research site as
well as by the restrictions placed on my work by the University Human Subjects Committee. The initial approval by the committee, over the objections
of some of its members, allowed me to engage in conversations with the
young people and staff, but I could not attribute individual personalities to
their quoted statements unless I had obtained specific, signed, informed consent forms from them and their parents. Interviews could not be conducted
without signed consent. The language of these forms, given the scrutiny of
human subjects, was very legalistic and the forms themselves were long.
Only one of the forms was signed over the course of several months.

I had been at the site for well over six months with no formal interviews
when I went back to the smaller body of the Human Subjects Committee that
had finally approved my research protocol. Parents would tell me that I could
talk to their children as much as I wanted, but were not willing to sign anything. I asked that I be allowed to obtain verbal rather than written consent
from guardians. I had read the university guidelines, based on the federal
law, and believed that verbal consent would be, in the case of my research, in
compliance with the guidelines and the law. The committee would not grant
the consent I sought, but agreed to allow me to seek permission from the university's attorney. The attorney agreed with my position, and I was then
granted permission to obtain verbal consent from guardians, documented by
me on a new form. This approach worked. I conducted formal interviews
with 15 young people and two members of the staff towards the end of my
time at the center.

Ultimately, despite the difficulties I experienced gaining access and conducting the study, I was able to successfully interact with a large sample of
young people and staff members over the course of a year and was able to

adequately triangulate my data. Human Subjects continued to limit my research in one way, however. It is customary in ethnographic research to return to the research site with preliminary findings and sections of writing in order to receive feedback from informants. Doing so would have required returning to the Human Subjects Committee for an extension of the amount of time for which I had been approved to conduct research. I decided not to go through that again.

The ways that my research was shaped by the human-subjects review process continued to shape the way that I have presented my work in this book. When I am referring to statements from formal interviews (having gained parental permission) I may identify them as coming from such interviews, and I may refer to an informant by a pseudonym when I think it is particularly important to let his or her personality come through. Most of my data come from conversations with and observations of young people who never granted formal permission (nor did their guardians). In compliance with my agreements with Human Subjects, quotations of statements by participants from whose guardians I did not gain permission to interview are not attributed to pseudonyms. I also took great pains to assure that, even in my notes, the statements could not be traced back to them. In referring to such statements from young people, I have given such descriptive information as seemed important, often including the gender and apparent ethnicity or age of the informant. At times I may have altered facts or physical characteristics to better hide an informant's identity.[4]

The restrictions placed upon my research by human subjects resulted in an unusual style of referring to the statements of the young people at the center. There is a repetition of phrases such as "a Black boy stated," or "most of the young people expressed the view that." Writing in this manner allows me to convey the critical information of what was said, who said it, and how many of my informants held the same view, without attributing quotes to personas. By paraphrasing what groups of young people told me, I was likewise able to convey the important nature of what was said without attributing any direct quotes to individuals. Though I could have created composite personas, as some authors have done quite effectively, I felt that for this project such an approach might obscure subtle differences. I also thought that such an approach could mask over one of the strengths of the study, the sheer number of young people whom I met, observed, and with whom I spoke.

My Style of Quotation

Even when referring to informants from formal interviews, some information may have been changed to better hide their identities. There are only two young people from the study who would be easily identifiable, one to the staff (who were there at the time) and the other to the larger community, given the level of press attention his case attracted. The identities of members of the staff are more easily identified by other members of the staff, particularly when their titles are used. There is no way to provide them with greater protection than I have, by, for example, not naming the state, without undermining the research in general. I have taken the potential impact on my informants and the research site very seriously when weighing both what to reveal and how to describe it. Any attempts to attribute particular statements to individuals at a particular juvenile detention center will not be confirmed on my part. More importantly, such attempts would be misguided. The purpose of this research is not to blame individual actors, especially not hard-working professionals or juveniles who do not pass laws or make policy. The goal of the research is to contribute to theory and policy by giving collective voice to the differing perspectives that one might find in any detention center. This center is special, however, in that it is one of the best. If anyone were to attempt to identify my research site, they should be clear that I evaluate the center very favorably overall.

I should also say something about the use of quotations in this book. Quotations are almost always complete and directly from my notes. Occasionally I might have slightly altered a statement to conform with a general change that I made to better protect the identity of one of my informants, but I have not altered the style or syntax of the statement. I quote my informants as they speak. I do not "clean up" their language for clarity or to conform to mainstream and "proper" vernacular English. There are moments when the way that the young people speak is of obvious importance to understanding what they are trying to communicate. Even when the importance of how they are saying something may be less obvious, and even if the way they are speaking makes them seem inarticulate, I feel that it is not appropriate to change their voice. I make this choice in part because I don't want to mask over subtle meanings in their language, as I cannot assume that I have picked up on everything. There is a growing body of work that examines Black vernacular English (Gee, 1987) and the language of youth culture more broadly. My methodological choice to use direct quotes is not the result of my taking sides in the debate over what language young people should be encouraged to speak. My choice is based on a more fundamental commitment. I will not speak over or for my informants. I present what they said as accurately as I can in an attempt to capture how they said it as well as what I think they were trying to convey. Quotations are either attributed to a given young person when I had parental permission to interview the young person or else they are attributed to no person in particular, but they are verbatim.

Education's Prisoners

The young people in my study are education's prisoners. I mean this literally and figuratively. As Bernadine Dohrn reports, in 1997 there were 180,000 arrests for fights in schools, around 120,000 arrests for theft at school, 110,000 arrests for school vandalism, but fewer than 20,000 violent crimes in schools (violence here being rather broadly defined). Schools are safe places compared to the other places in which many students spend their time, and they have been consistently safe for the past 20 years. In the past, the relatively minor transgressions that today lead to arrest and expulsion would have been handled internally in the school. In fact, students are frequently expelled for behavior that occurs outside of school, while police departments are increasingly allowed unfettered access to student records (2000, p. 162).

The armed camps that many of our nation's schools are becoming illuminate the growing relationship among schooling, the political economy, and the prison industrial complex. Alongside this, even more so than in the past, schools increasingly do not prepare young people from the lower classes, especially young people of color, to contribute to their communities, to develop marketable job skills, or to attend university. Rather, schools actively force these students out of overcrowded classrooms and onto the streets, freeing up room for wealthier and whiter students (Fine, 1991). As one of the young people in my study told me, "I got kicked out of school for not going, 'cause I was locked up at the time." Too often this takes the students down a path to detention and jail cells.

Kathleen Nolan and Jean Anyon (2004) illuminate the parallels between public schooling and jail, reminding us that school practices such as zero-tolerance policies, surveillance, and teachers' views of students of color (pp. 141–142) have essentially merged schools in urban communities with the criminal justice system. Their observations are worth quoting at length:

> "A new school culture … emerges in urban schools with a police presence, high-tech security apparatus, and zero-tolerance policies. Students become used to procedures like hallway sweeps, book-bag and locker searches, 'pat down' and frisks, that treat them like criminals" (McCormick, 2000). Prison metaphors used by teachers,

administrators, and even students characterize a significant portion of the dialogue: "Students are on 'lockdown' " and "That one [referring to a third grade student] has a cell at Rikers with his name on it" (Nolan, unpublished research in progress).

Moreover, ongoing research by Kathleen Nolan indicates that some students, particularly the most marginalized ones who may already have experience in the criminal justice system, typically see little difference between prison and school. They describe both places as hostile environments where students gain nothing and teachers most often misunderstand them. The significant difference between school and prison for these youths are that they are able to leave the school building at 3:00 p.m., whereas in prison it is "24/7." In these ways, in this educational context, urban students are "learning to do time." (pp. 143–144)

For the young people in my study, many of whom will likely end up in prison if current trends continue, their bodies, minds, and spirits have already been chained in the prison that is the mainstream public educational system.

This situation is complicated by the fact that most teachers sincerely desire to see their students learn and succeed in life, though in time their attitudes towards students who do not succeed tend to become embittered. Coldville is an interesting place in which to examine school failure given that the school system is relatively well funded and has clean and structurally sound buildings, available materials, and a myriad of resources often lacking in schools across the country. The police presence and surveillance in schools in Coldville, though weighing heavily on students who are viewed as suspect, are also, usually, more subtle. In fact, students from middle-class families attending the same schools, and to some extent sitting in the same classrooms as the young people in my study, tend to be very successful. Below the surface appearance of equal treatment, however, lie policies, attitudes, and obstacles that assure the failure of large numbers of working-class students of color. It is telling that in a school system that has more resources than most, and a general commitment to discuss and accommodate diversity, that we find unusually high rates of special-education referral, disciplinary actions, suspensions, expulsions, dropouts, arrest and incarceration for students of color (and for students from poor families more generally). I have named the book *Education's Prisoners* to highlight the various ways that schools call to mind the correctional system.

Chapter 2
Historical Context of the Research

The study took place within the context of the boom in incarceration, including the incarceration of minors, that began in the 1980s. In fact, much of the motivation for the focus of the book came from the need to address the consequences of this growth in the numbers of people incarcerated as well as the much greater lengths of sentences. The general climate of punitive sentences and zealous policing has grown despite stable levels of criminal activities and a broad drop off in the number of violent offenses. Fueled by misleading media accounts and the proclamations of policy makers and law enforcement, fear of crime in the citizenry facilitated this situation. The boom in the detention and adjudication of young people was accompanied by the unraveling of protections developed for children, along with the very concept of adolescence, which were established at the turn of the last century. Children, at least some children, had to be redefined as dangerous and adult, to remove notions of compassion and rehabilitation, which stood in the way of the development of the prison industrial complex (see Dohrn, 2000).

In this chapter I will provide a brief examination of the historical development of incarceration in the United States, the rise and fall of juvenile justice, and the current context that emerges from this history. I will look, in particular, at the related educational history. Though the book is not historical in a disciplinary sense, it is appropriate when working within critical theory, an interdisciplinary field of inquiry, to draw on historical analysis. Michael Apple (1990) addressed the uses of history in critical theory as follows:

> First, any subject matter under investigation must be seen in relation to its historical roots – how it evolved, from what conditions it arose, etc. – and its latent contradictions and tendencies in the future. This is the case because in the highly complicated world of critical analysis existing structures are actually in something like continual motion. Contradiction, change, and development are the norm and any institutional structure is 'merely' a stage in process. Thus, institutional reification becomes problematic, as do the patterns of thought that support this lack of institutional change. Second, anything being examined is defined not only by its obvious characteristics, but by its less overt ties to other factors. It is these ties and relationships that make the subject what it is and give it its primary meanings. (p. 132)

My admittedly brief treatment of the historical evidence serves to provide the reader with a context in which to place the study, but fails to provide the thorough treatment of influences and causes that one finds in a historical work. The authors I cite provide such detailed accounts and may be consulted for further review.

The Jails and Schools Grow Together

In his book, *Children in Urban Society* (1971), Joseph Hawes discusses five trends in the development of understandings of juvenile delinquency and the subsequent development of schools and jails. These trends were not rigid stages progressing along a time line, but overlapped. They represented struggle, and traces of earlier trends never completely left us. Ultimately, though, Hawes argues that there was progress, with earlier periods giving way to the development of an understanding of adolescence and delinquency. His notions of progress may be overly optimistic given recent history, but his work provides a sophisticated understanding of the historical context in which my study takes place. I adopt his stages in my review of the relevant history. I include this chapter, albeit a brief chapter, for the reasons identified by Thomas Bernard (1992):

> Our particular laws reflect the philosophical ideas popular in our time and can only be fully understood by studying the process by which they have evolved in response to changing historical conditions. Thus, you cannot really understand law unless you understand both the history and the philosophy behind it. (p. 18)

The Historical Development of Juvenile Delinquency

The Colonial Example (the period of punishment gives way to corrective institutions)

The earliest trend in the New World identified by Hawes was similar to what was happening in England at the time. Common law took precedence over any ordinance, and laws that did exist were of a harsh moralistic nature. The Puritans saw children as miniature adults, and as such play was considered a sin, punishable after the age of five. Crimes such as swearing or not observing the Sabbath could bring harsh punishment, and masters, of servants and apprentices alike, used the courts to enact this punishment. At the time, criminals were not imprisoned but rather were put to death, whipped, fined, or transported.[1] Only persons who had committed some great evil, like treason against the king, sorcery, or debtors, were jailed.[2] Far more debtors died from the conditions in prisons than murderers died through execution. The few prisons that did exist were privately owned. Prisoners were charged for the basic amenities. As Hawes states, "There were cases where men died in prison even though they had been acquitted because they were in debt to the prison keeper" (1971, pp. 21–22).

In 1773 John Howard became sheriff of Bedford, England, and, in an effort to reform prisoners, began to advocate the Amsterdam model of making prisoners work while incarcerated. He published a book entitled *The State of Prisons,* which brought his ideas to the colonies (Hawes, 1971, pp. 22–25; Anderson, 1989). Pennsylvania began to jail prisoners in publicly funded institutions, according to the prisoner's crime and age, which was the method adopted by Howard. Prisoners were kept in almost complete isolation so that they could commune with God. As in modern segregation units and super-max prisons, there were dire consequences for the mental and physical health of the prisoners. Though draconian in application, the penitentiary was built, at least in argument, in response to the concept of rehabilitation (Anderson, 1989, p. 3). New York tried to eliminate solitary confinement in 1823 to avoid the deterioration of health and sanity that had resulted from such captivity. During this period a rift developed between two rival systems in the United States, one that tried to separate the young prisoner from the older inmates, and one that did not, but both systems continued to argue that their purpose was to mete out punishment. Ultimately, neither approach resulted in the reduction of crime or recidivism, their stated goals (Anderson, 1989; Hawes, 1971).

The New York House of Refuge (separating young people from adults)

In 1822 James Gerard and Isaac Collins of the Society for the Prevention of Pauperism began to formulate a report, which they presented in 1823, stating that jails actually hardened juveniles into bigger criminals. They proposed the "house of refuge" as an alternative. In 1825 its doors were opened (Bernard, 1992, p. 62; Hawes, 1971, p. 36), the result a joint effort of private and public entities. Punishments included the ball and chain, handcuffs, leg irons and the barrel. The children were protected from adult inmates, but not from their jailers. As the managers publicly stated, the children "are not to be destroyed [but that] the public must in some measure take the place of those who ought to have been their natural guardians and protectors" (Bernard, 1992, p. 46). This sentiment is an early expression of the tendency to blame parents as solely responsible for the "criminal" behavior of their children. As Thomas Bernard noted, most of the young people held in the House of Refuge had committed no serious crime, but were held for things like vagrancy or stealing, or, in short, for being poor. No conviction was necessary to send them there, and once held they could be kept until they were 21 (boys) or 18 (girls). They were made to work all day making products that were sold by the state (p. 62). The influence of the society resulted in the 1826 Massachusetts law defining juvenile delinquents as those who were beggars, vagabonds, and so forth. A wide net was cast to criminalize poverty, and with little due process (Hawes, 1971). By 1868 there were over 20 houses of refuge in the country, which, over the years, housed as many as 50,000 youth (Bernard, 1992, p. 70).

The bias against poor children and their families went hand in hand with anti-Irish sentiments in the 1840s, during the height of An Gorta Mor (The Great Hunger),[3] a time in which Irish immigrants (many of whom were children who immigrated without their parents) were described as racially inferior (Bernard, 1992, p. 65). The House of Refuge, guided by the belief that the children's home life had corrupted them and that working in nature would inspire them to develop moral character, would soon begin shipping out young people picked up on the streets or taken from their families to serve as forced laborers on farms in various states. As David Nasaw argues in *Schooled to Order* (1984):

> It was presumed — and without need of proof or opportunity for rebuttal — that those who had not the "moral character" to raise themselves out of poverty similarly lacked the qualities needed to rear their children. (p. 10)

The Children's Aid Society later took over this role, under the leadership of Charles Brace, a theology student. He also opened the Newsboys' Lodging House (Hawes, 1971, p. 96). Newsboys exemplified the good moral character, Horatio Alger style, of which these reformers were dreaming. Hawes argues that this effort reflects, "A great faith in the power of education to remedy social evils and to mold American culture" (p. 98). Juvenile delinquency and pauperism meant much the same thing and were treated in the same manner and for the same reasons. Poverty and crime were both viewed as the fault of the youth, and all poor youth were viewed as potential paupers and criminals. The solution that was advocated, or at least the justification for their forced labor, was to change their character.

The criminalization of youth did not occur without struggle. Elija Devoe, for example, a discharged assistant superintendent, wrote a widely read exposé on the cruelty in the House, and a court case in Pennsylvania ordered a boy to be released as he had been convicted on the mere testimony of his father that he was 'idle and disorderly' (Hawes, 1971, pp. 55–58). While there were critics of the excesses of the growing separate prison system, they were unable to stop the growth. What started in New York would spread.

A point that must be emphasized, and which is mostly ignored by Hawes, is that the growth of these juvenile facilities was not the result of the humanitarian impulses of the elite. Rather, these coalitions of powerful and influential people were motivated by their own self interest. In 1828 the "common man" had gained the vote for the first time (Nasaw, 1984, p. 16), without the requirement of property ownership to be eligible, and elected Andrew Jackson, the "Indian Fighter" as President. Elites in the United States were horrified. They assumed that the lack of discipline of working people, which would ultimately lead them to vote for someone like President Jackson, or to agitate for their rights at work, must be the result of an immoral home environment. Thus, it was fear of the working class, particularly the immigrant communities arriving from Europe who were thought to have revolutionary ideals, which motivated the wealthy in society to throw their weight behind the development of juvenile facilities.

State-Supported Institutions
(the separate incarceration of youth becomes government policy)

Reverend Joseph Tuckerman of Boston would spearhead the push for state-funded institutions, but with this push he would put forward a different vision of delinquency. Like the reformers of the House of Refuge period, he saw the problem as a "lack of moral fiber" among the children themselves. If they had been taught good morals, it was reasoned, they would not have strayed. Tuckerman started a farm school in 1832 where boys could be raised in good moral order. The city itself was to be seen as a place of sin (Hawes, 1971, p. 80–81). In 1838 the Massachusetts State Reform School for Boys became the first fully state-funded juvenile institution in the United States (p. 83).

The argument for focusing on juvenile justice and rehabilitation as crime prevention is one we hear often among liberals today (Humes, 1996, p. 128). In 1848, a report issued by the mayor of Boston proclaimed that it "would cost less to school these children than to expand the police, courts, and prisons" (Schultz, 1973, p. 301). Such arguments resonated with reformers and elites alike, so that it became a crime in 1852 for children to be free of "school or factory" (Nasaw, 1984, p. 76). This was, again, tied directly to the fear of poor immigrants. As one reformer stated at the time, "the best police for our cities, the lowest insurance of our houses, the firmest security for our

banks, the most effective means of preventing pauperism, vice, and crime"
(p. 81) was the common school.

It must be noted that the Irish Catholic immigrants who were the targets
of these laws did fight back, but ultimately were only partially successful in
protecting their children (Hawes, 1971, p. 103; Nasaw, 1984). Bill Ayers
(1997) described the situation as follows:

> Large numbers of children, particularly immigrant children, particularly children
> from Catholic countries like Italy and Ireland, found themselves literally swept off
> the streets and ensnared in the legal system, either as delinquents or as paupers,
> forced from their families and shipped away "for their own good." (pp. 25–26)

The father of Mary Ann Crouse petitioned the court for habeus corpus over
the placement of his daughter in the third House of Refuge in Philadelphia.
The Pennsylvania Supreme Court handed down its opinion in 1838:

> The object of the charity is reformation, by training its inmates to industry; by imbu-
> ing their minds with principles of morality and religion; by furnishing them with
> means to earn a living; and, above all, by separating them from the corrupting influ-
> ence of improper associates. To this end, may not the natural parents, when unequal
> to the task of education, or unworthy of it, be superseded by the parens patriae, nor
> common guardian of the community? . . . the infant has been snatched from a course
> which must have ended in confirmed depravity; and not only is the restraint of her
> person lawful, but it would be an act of extreme cruelty to release her from it. (Ber-
> nard, 1992, p. 68)

Despite the coldhearted rulings of judges and state sanction of the theft and
forced labor of children from poor families, these mostly immigrant families
continued to fight for a measure of justice. In Chicago, the parents of Daniel
O'Connell protested the placement of their son, who like Mary Ann Crouse,
had committed no crime. The court ordered him released in 1870, finding,
unlike the Pennsylvannia court, that he was being punished, and therefore
was entitled to due process of law (pp. 71–72). The ruling said that children
must be convicted of a crime before they can be sent to reform schools (p.
73).

The Juvenile Court (to get around the O'Connell ruling)

With the O'Connell ruling, Illinois was faced with the choice of changing its policies towards working people or finding a way to subvert the ruling. As Bernard observed, "Essentially, the juvenile court was invented to
get around the O'Connell ruling. It allowed Illinois once again to send to juvenile institutions poor children who had not committed a criminal offense"

(p. 73). By establishing the juvenile court the appearance of due process could be preserved, though young people could still be removed from their families for non criminal conduct, and could be denied the protections afforded adult defendants such as a jury trial and the standard of proof of guilt beyond a reasonable doubt (pp. 92–93).

Beginning in the mid-1800s adventure books became popular with young boys. These books were soon blamed for juvenile delinquency (in a manner similar to how violence on television is blamed today), in an effort led by William Sumner (Hawes, 1971). Horatio Alger's rags-to-riches books came on the scene in 1870, continuing the arguments about morality and upward mobility from the Tucker period. Soon thereafter Mark Twain's *Tom Sawyer* was published. A socialist, Twain tried to humanize poor youth and understood their poverty as the result of an exploitive economic system. Despite people like Comstock who saw youth in the grips of Satan (pp. 124–125), the ideas of Twain and others began to have some impact on public sentiment, so that around 1870:

> The idea that people freely chose a life of crime or yielded to pauperism because of a lack of moral fiber began to give way to a growing awareness of the operation of social factors in causing such deviant behavior. (p. 143)

The development of the juvenile court was, therefore, the result of the continued desire to control poor children, joined with the emancipatory ideals of the day. In 1899 the juvenile court of Cook County opened (p. 158) and saw 60 to 80 cases each day. The attitude of the court was less punitive than those of courts in the past, with most juveniles getting probation, and with those who were ordered confined receiving indeterminate sentences (p. 146). During the same period the Chicago Women's Club pushed for the enforcement of compulsory education laws and the treatment of children *as* children rather than as adults. These efforts culminated in the passage of the 1899 Juvenile Court Act in Illinois, which affirmed the parental power of the state. Bill Ayers (1997) described the idea that Jane Addams had in mind for the juvenile court, an idea which closely resembled the settlement house philosophy:

> What started in Chicago met the hopes and expectations of the country, and by 1925 special courts and legal proceedings for children existed in all but two states. These reforms were built on the idea of child protection and restoration: judges were expected to act flexibly and informally, and to make their decisions in the best interest of the child. Proceedings were not to be legalistic and punitive, but personal and creative. (p. 26)

John Augustus had become the first probation officer around 1843, and he quickly developed a probation system that was later picked up by these reformers. In 1901 an amendment to the Juvenile Court Act brought parents under scrutiny for the actions of and conditions in which their children lived. This law also broadened the definition of delinquency to include things like association with criminals and idleness. Hawes argues that the juvenile court was a significant development because it signified a change in the manner in which young people were perceived. The earlier juvenile system was a miniature adult system. The new idea was not to determine the guilt or innocence of the child but rather to act on what was in the best interest of the child. As Hawes (1971) puts it:

> The creation of the juvenile court meant that society no longer regarded the juvenile delinquent as a miniature adult who broke the law because he had chosen of his own free will to do so ... Now society could see him as a child. (p. 190)

Criminal Science (punishment more fully gives way to treatment)

A conference on criminal anthropology was held in 1889 (Hawes, 1971, p. 191). The Italian delegation, led by Cesare Lombroso, argued that human skulls and other observable features could indicate a "born criminal" (criminal anthropology). The French delegation, on the other hand, was made up of sociologists, and stressed the social foundations of crime. Lombroso went so far as to argue that the criminal type was a less evolved human being. Herbert Spencer and William Sumner argued in the literature that delinquents were merely inferior and should be left to the devices of natural selection. Lester Frank Ward countered this idea in his book, *Dynamic Sociology*, and argued instead that evolution could be altered by controlling the environment. Stanley Hall, a student of William James, began to argue that adolescence is the age at which people are prone to commit crimes. In the 1890s E.S. Morse argued (in the United States) in a similar vein as Lombardo that crime was hereditary and should be controlled by not allowing criminals to reproduce. Dawson entered the fray with a series of experiments designed to prove the inferiority of the criminal. Enoch Stoddard, a doctor, countered him and called for less punitive treatments of juveniles. These struggles went back and forth, with one camp advocating treatment and the other advocating punishment. In the end, during this period, social science came to see delinquency as a social disease. The notion of adolescence, the development of which was accelerated by the growth of the juvenile court, was solidified by the psychological arguments in the growing field of criminal science.

The juvenile court reflected this change, utilizing the opinions of experts and seeking to treat juveniles rather than to punish them. Judge Ben Lindsey of Denver became a prominent advocate of a national juvenile court (Hawes, 1971, p. 223). By 1915, 46 states had juvenile courts. Jane Addams advocated that the theories of Dr. Healy on mental conflicts be considered in juvenile cases. The courts were beginning to function more as a part of a social services nexus than as the judging body they were when adults went on trial. Though the treatment of young offenders was seemingly more enlightened, notions of what should be considered delinquency came to be more broadly conceived than in earlier periods. As Nasaw informs us, Jane Addams considered junkers (enterprising children who gathered and sold junk) to be delinquents because, she assumed, they would only spend the money on vice (1984, pp. 95–96). Gone was the moral indignation of the period of the first state institutions, but gone also was the potential (at least in theory), in the public mind, for young people to be exceptional. State intervention was considered necessary in the lives of all immigrant children.

The progressive reformers associated with Jane Addams and John Dewey held a sympathetic understanding of the plight of poor people, but their proposed solution, rather than changing the underlying economic structure, was to better socialize and control the poor. The harsh punishments of the past were rejected not because they were viewed as inherently inhumane or unethical, but because they were viewed as less sophisticated and ultimately less effective. This change reflected changes in capitalist production. As Nasaw (1984) states, in the past schools had claimed to train workers to be good entrepreneurs, but now:

> Reformers . . . conceded, such socialization for self-sufficiency had made sense when there were actual possibilities for upward mobility out of wage work. With such possibilities rare, it no longer made sense to socialize workers in this manner. What was now needed was not self-made men and women but team players, individuals ready to sacrifice their personal dreams, hopes, and aspirations for the good of the productive unit. (pp. 102–103)

Understanding the Historical Trends

As Hawes (1971) argues, understandings of delinquency took on several forms at different points in United States history. While he understood the struggles between and overlap of these ideas, he seems to hold a notion of progress as eventually emerging. I would like to challenge this notion. Many of the ideas of earlier periods have re-emerged today, though in modified form, and without necessarily abandoning the science in which Hawes finds such hope. In the colonial example, children were viewed as miniature adults. Today there is increasingly a tendency to see children, not all children but poor children and children of color, as miniature adults (evidence of this can be found in recent trials in which children are increasingly tried as adults). Middle-class children, however, continue to be seen in the enlightened scientific manner advocated by Addams. Though they too can be caught up in the juvenile and criminal justice system [I say system rather than systems intentionally], the system tends to favor leniency towards them (Ayers, 1997, p. 39); with the possible exception of minimum mandatory sentencing in drug-related cases.

In the colonial period, prisons were privately owned, and prisoners were charged for basic needs. These are trends in prisons today. Likewise, prisoners are being returned to chain gangs and are having their labor let out to industry (Microsoft, for example, has been at the forefront of exploiting prison labor in the packaging of its operating systems). There is also a massive return to solitary confinement, in the form of super-max prisons and segregation units (Burton-Rose, 1998). Both the tendency to see children as victims of their environment, as in the House of Refuge and criminal science periods, and the tendency to villainize them, as in the period of the growth of state-supported institutions, continue today. Younger children still receive our sympathy, while older children, though increasingly younger if they are Black, are abandoned to the devil. Education is still held up as the cure for the lack of economic opportunity, and it is still argued that jails are more expensive to build than are children to educate. Today, as in the juvenile court period, entertainment is blamed for juvenile delinquency, though there seems to be a simultaneous return to the idea that criminals choose a life of crime. Perhaps most disturbing is the return of notions of inferiority and genetics as the cause of crime (Breggin & Breggin, 1998), rather than the social-causes arguments in France in the late 1880s (and similar arguments in the 1970s in the United States).

I am not arguing that we have gone back to an earlier period, though at times the parallels are striking. Rather, I am suggesting that all of these perspectives have stayed with us, and different attitudes resurface as dominant theories at different times, given changing conditions. Hanna Tavares (1996), in her article "Classroom Management and Subjectivity," argues that while there has been a historical shift from physical abuse as a way to manage students to psychological control, these two means are simply different metamorphoses of the same impulses. As she states:

> The difference drawn between management in the early nineteenth century and classroom management in the late twentieth century is not merely a difference between the barbaric and the humane or progressive. Rather, it is only a difference in

the mode of operations of power, a shift in which power is increasingly discursive. (p. 196)

In a similar manner, I would like to suggest that the shifts in attitudes regarding delinquency have only been different shades of the same thing, and have always been motivated in the interests of the powerful over the weak. Nasaw (1984) is careful to point out that there were always voices critical of capital and attacks on the poor, but ultimately the powerful defined not only delinquency but also the boundaries of what is considered reasonable debate regarding these matters. It is not so much that we are reliving history as it is that we never really escaped from the historical period that began in the 1700s.

Prisons and Schools in the United States Today

David Anderson (1989) sums up the historical development of incarceration, arguing that during the 19th century prison administrators focused on education, religion, and labor, but with little demonstrable results. In the 20th century psychologists took over where the educators and preachers left off. In 1974 Robert Martinson published a survey that concluded "with few isolated exceptions" nothing had affected recidivism. By the 1980s the idea of rehabilitation had all but been abandoned (pp. 4–5). In this section I will describe the current state of incarceration in the United States (in which my study takes place), and I will suggest how things came to this. The changes that occurred between the mid-1970s and the 1980s, the period in which the idea of rehabilitation was abandoned, have been the focus of a growing body of work. The focus of this section is not primarily on how those changes took root and spread, however, as such an endeavor would require more attention than I can give here and would distract from the trajectory of my arguments. I would argue, in short, that this change was the result of a confluence of factors, primary among them were the supposed war on drugs, the needs of the growing prison industrial complex, and the fear of young people of color drummed up by opportunistic authors, political figures, and the corporate media.

Thomas Bernard argues in his book, *The Cycle of Juvenile Justice* (1992), that a repeating pattern can be documented in which attitudes towards juveniles move from being less to more punitive. I reject the idea of history repeating itself that informs his book, but find the book in other areas to be quite useful. The similarities between the ways in which young people were targeted in earlier historical periods and today are quite striking at times, and can help us to understand the current situation. As Bernard reminds us, juvenile "crime" has always been with us. *Romeo and Juliet* records a youth gang fight (p. 24), the *Code of Hammurabi*, written over 4,000 years ago, indicates that juveniles should be treated more leniently than adults, and the *Talmud* specifies that no corporal punishment be used on those who have not reached puberty (12 for females and 13 for males), and no death penalty be imposed on those under 20 years of age (pp. 28–29). Thus it was in 1954 that *Newsweek* published an article entitled "Our Vicious Young Hoodlums: Is there any hope?" That same year *Time* published an article on the "teenage reign of terror [that] has transformed New York City's public school system into a vast incubator of crime in which wayward and delinquent youngsters receive years of 'protection' while developing into toughened and experienced criminals" (p. 33).

Many of the ideas about and techniques of demonizing and targeting youth have continued into the present time, and the motives of control and economic exploitation have continued as well. The form that these impulses take in the modern era, however, is something new; the past is not merely repeating itself. The needs of late capitalism, the massive power of corporations, the sophistication of the media and other ideological apparatuses, and the scale of the judicial bureaucracy together create a situation that is both unique and daunting. The focus of this section is on the impact that this modern iteration has on young people like those in my study.

That schooling is related to incarceration is well established. As discussed before, historians have documented the connected development of both the educational and penal systems in response to the immigrant "problem"; this documentation focuses largely on Irish immigrant children and the efforts to control them and limit the influence of their parents in shaping their religious and political beliefs (Hawes, 1971; Nasaw, 1984). Today many of the earlier reforms of the penal system begun in the 19th century, especially those involving minors, are being quickly dismantled.

The prison system is the largest growth industry in the United States. Levels of inequality and correlated poverty, violence and human suffering, are quickly approaching those at the beginning of the 20th century. Michael Apple reported in *Education and Power* (1982) that one in seven Americans live in poverty, and that one in five children live in poverty. In 1982 the distribution of wealth and income had not changed since World War II (pp. vi, 7). In 1975 Lester Thurow reported that the top fifth of the population in the United States owned or controlled three quarters of the wealth in the nation, while the remaining four fifths shared the remaining one quarter of the wealth. The bottom fifth of the population owned less than 0.2 percent of the wealth. An article in the *New York Times* in 1995 documents that things have not changed for the better, with the top 1 percent of the population having 40 percent of the wealth, and the top 20 percent having more than 80 percent of the wealth. Income distribution is similarly unequal, with the wealthiest 20 percent of the population stealing 47.9 percent of the total income from the 40 percent of the population who fight over the remaining 15.7 percent (Navarro, 1991). More recent studies reveal that the increase in inequality of wealth and income has not stopped but has only worsened (Fine & Weis, 1998, p. 17).

This is accomplished by the class system that allows for the upward distribution of wealth and income, while maintaining the illusion of relative opportunity. Poverty in the United States is the result of inequality (Connell, 1993), which is a gentler word for class oppression. In the United States, class is a structure that reproduces and increases the material wealth of the minority over the majority. As Vincente Navarro (1991) states, "there are classes in the United States, and how people live, get sick, and die depends not only on their race and gender, but primarily on the class to which they belong" (p. 2). There is, as Connell (1993) reminds us, an "advantage cycle" as well as a "poverty cycle" (p. 27) that reflects the collective efforts of the upper classes to continue to receive the material rewards of exploiting the rest of society. As Michael Apple (1996) states in response to his review of poverty, death rates, and incarceration statistics:

> Based on these numbers, it is clear that the United States seems to have decided to deal with poverty by jailing or allowing to die a large percentage of people of color, many of whose crimes and needs are directly related to the economic and housing conditions and the patterns of racial segregation they experience. This has had a dramatic impact on family structure and on the sense of a future among black youth. (p. 79)

These appalling realities of the incarceration of poor people, who make up the vast majority of the 1,965,495 men and women behind bars in 2001 (Beck et al., 2002), are related to the high levels of educational inequality in this country that scholars such as Michael Apple and Jonathan Kozol have identified.

According to government statistics, reported by Jeffrey Reiman in his book *The Rich Get Richer and the Poor Get Prison* (1990):

> Our prisoners are not a cross-section of America. They are considerably poorer and considerably less likely to be employed than the rest of Americans. Moreover, they are also less educated . . . More than 60 percent were high school dropouts! Compare this with the fact that 78.5 percent of males in the general population have completed at least four years of high school, and 42.5 percent have completed one or more years of college. (p. 134)

Despite the attention of critical scholars such as Reiman, there has been little in-depth systematic and critical study of either the prison system or the relationship of schooling to incarceration, particularly not of the sort that focuses on the lived experience of incarcerated persons. I come to this research topic, therefore, out of a sense of moral urgency along with the belief that the economic and educational inequalities that influence the high levels of incarceration among poor people must be exposed, and out of a desire to portray these people as humans rather than simple statistics.

The Growing Prison Industrial Complex and its Negative Educational Impact

The prison industrial complex has become an integral part of the economy on both the state and federal levels. It is quickly coming to function much as the military industrial complex has historically, providing employment for key constituencies and funding politicians' corporate campaign sponsors with huge government contracts. Bernadine Dohrn (2000) describes the situation as follows:

> Schools have become a major feeder of children into juvenile and adult criminal courts; simultaneously, schools themselves are becoming more prison like. Closed campuses, locker searches, contraband, interrogations and informers, heavily armed tactical police patrols, uniforms... these are elements of public and even private high school life today. It is paradoxical but fundamental that a handful of high-profile school shootings masks a broader and deeper criminalization of school life, accompanied by the policing of schools, which has transformed public schools across America into a principal referral source for juvenile-justice prosecutions. (p. 162)

Such a system of criminal justice, rather than making society safer, tends to further exacerbate the causes of crime by de-funding educational training, as well as psychological and addiction counseling. As social spending is cut to fund prison growth, the most vulnerable segments of society are less able to find meaningful and adequate employment. At the same time that people become most susceptible to despair, there are fewer outlets from which they can find support. These conditions work to increase the likelihood that disenfranchised citizens will turn to crime as a means of survival, to drugs as a way to suppress the pain, or will lash out against the world around them — resulting in higher incarceration rates and more prison expansion. We are in the midst of a downward spiral that can only result in more poverty, more desperation, and more crime. Already, the situation has deteriorated to the point where the need to provide resources to the poorest and most vulnerable segments of society is in conflict with the need of the developing prison industrial economy to maintain a steady supply of inmates.

The rate of incarceration in the United States has grown at an unprecedented rate during the last two decades. There were 1,128,000 prisoners in the United States (in local, state and federal prisons) in 1994, with 1 in every 100 adult males behind bars (Reiman, 1979/90, p. 133). Between 1980 and 1996, the prison population more than tripled from 500,000 to over 1.6 million. The number of persons under some form of correctional supervision (including probation or parole) surpassed 5 million at the end of 1994 (Ambrosio & Schiraldi, 1997, p. 2). The Sentencing Project, a research and advocacy group that advocates alternatives to incarceration, tracked the growth rate of the prison and jail populations to its current level at over 2 million. The rate of incarceration in the United States is already 6 to 10 times higher than that in most industrial nations. These numbers, as dramatic as they are, do not include former inmates now free of correctional supervision.

The most recent statistics show that after a slight lull, prison populations are growing again. As of May 2004 there are almost 2.1 million people in jail or prison, with 1 out of every 75 men currently incarcerated. Approximately 70 percent of the inmates are members of racial or ethnic minorities. Twelve percent of Black men in their 20s are in jail, compared with just 1.6 percent of White men in the same age group (Cass, 2004). Today there are around 6.6 million people either incarcerated, on probation, or on parole in the United States, an increase of 258 percent since 1980 (Nolan & Anyon, 2004, p. 134). There have also been dramatic increases in incarceration rates for both juveniles and women. In a study conducted for the National Council on Crime and Delinquency in 1993, researchers Bloom and Steinhart reported that in 1991 there were 87,000 women incarcerated in the United States. Though women are only 6 percent of prison and 10 percent of the jail population, the rate of increase in incarceration for women is greater than that of males (p. 13).

The incarceration of women has particularly troubling implications for society given their continued role as the primary caregivers for children. Seventy-six percent of female prisoners in the United States were mothers in 1986, according to the Department of Justice's Bureau of Justice Statistics. A study by the American Correctional Association in 1987 had similar findings, reporting that 6 percent of women in prisons and 4 percent in jails were pregnant at the time of their incarceration (p. 14). Using information provided by the Center for the Children of Incarcerated Parents and by the Bureau of Justice Statistics, the association estimates that there are 1.5 million children of incarcerated parents in the United States. In California alone the number exceeded 200,000 (p. 15). A 1992 study by the Center for Children of Incarcerated Parents on the effects of incarceration of parents on a group of children living in South Central Los Angeles County found that the children were more vulnerable as a result of the separation and stress (p. 16). Most of these children live with relatives, usually the maternal grandmother, while only 17 percent stayed with fathers while their mothers were incarcerated. Fifty-four percent of the children had never visited their mothers, and those who did visit did so infrequently (p. 26). Care providers said that 28.8 percent of the children had learning problems and 27.3 percent had behavioral problems (p. 32).

Beyond the obvious emotional cost to these children, there are indications that the incarceration of parents may increase the likelihood of the children later becoming involved in crime. The American Correctional Association survey of female offenders reported that 48 percent of adult female and 64 percent of juvenile female offenders had other family members who had been incarcerated (pp. 16, 70). An interview with a 14-year-old girl, Angela, in a 1978 study is telling and typical. When asked what will happen when her mother, who had been incarcerated for two years for selling drugs, was released the girl stated:

> We'll be together and see how it goes. If it works out fine. If it doesn't, we'll split up... or maybe she'll end up back in jail. Or maybe I'll end up in jail. If she ends up in there again, though, I'm not going to visit her. I've done my time with her... then she can go to hell for all I care. (p. 17)

Perhaps we should not be surprised by this sort of fatalism when we consider that juveniles ages 13 to 17 (who make up 8 percent of the U.S. population) are arrested at a rate twice that of the rest of the population (Bernard, 1992, p. 22).

Violence is a serious problem in the United States, where people face 7 to 10 times the risk of death by homicide than do residents of most European countries and Japan. Californians alone are murdered about 6 times more often than all Canadians, and more Californians are killed with knives alone than Canadians are killed by all means combined. More than three times as many people are killed annually, on average in the United States, than were lost during the height of the Vietnam War (Currie, 1985, p. 6). Los Angeles county has more teen murders than the twelve largest industrial nations (excluding the United States) combined, despite having some of the harshest sentences for adults and juveniles in the country and the largest prison system in the United States (Males & Docuyanan, 1996, pp. 24, 25). The serious crime problem should not scare us away from attempts to understand its causes and to seek lasting solutions. Primary and overarching as an explanation are the inequality and poverty in the United States. As the National Academy of Sciences concluded: "Data from the Centers for Disease Control indicate that the personal and neighborhood income are the strongest predictors of violent crime" (Ayers, 1997, p. 42).

With this information in mind, it might be tempting to view the increase in incarceration as a response to violent crime. In reality, however, only 1 in 10 arrests in the United States is for a violent crime (defined increasingly broadly), while only 3 in 100 arrests are for "violent" crimes that actually result in injury (Ambrosio & Schiraldi, 1997, p. 2). Fully 84 percent of the increase in state and federal prison admissions since 1980 was for nonviolent offences. The boom in incarceration has occurred despite the fact that actual crime rates have been stable over decades (p. 1).

Much of the initial boom in prison expansion was related to the alleged war on drugs. As Anderson (1998) reports, from 1980 to 1989 drug arrests rose 134 percent, while total arrests rose 37 percent (p. 74). In 1980 violent crime accounted for 48.2 percent of new commitments to state prisons, and 6.8 percent for drug crime. By 1992, due to punitive legislation, the drug offenders' rate was up to 30.5 percent, compared to 28.5 percent for violent crime (p. 70). Over 50 percent of arrested persons in cities in the United States test positive for illegal drugs at the time of the arrest, and in some cities the rate is as high as 80 percent. Over 75 percent of inmates report using drugs. Twenty-seven percent say they were under the influence at the time they committed their offense. Two thirds of people in residential drug treatment programs and one third of people in outpatient programs say they committed crimes for money in the year before they began treatment (pp. 69–70). So much of the actual crime in society is driven by the need to feed addictions, but the targeting of drug offenders did nothing to reduce crime rates as measured in victimization studies (p. 11).

An obvious alternative exists for actually reducing drug addiction and related crime. Studies of drug treatment programs and crime have consistently shown that those receiving treatment are no more likely to re-offend than those not receiving treatment, and many programs help people to get off drugs for good. There is a tendency to relapse, but the few studies that have looked at long-term treatment find that drug addicts are more likely to finally kick their addictions after the third round of treatment (pp. 6, 67, 70). As Anderson argues:

> Suppose a 17 year old drug addict commits five burglaries per year. If subjected to the common routine arrest and ineffective probation supervision, he might continue committing his burglaries for, say, three years, until the court finally sends him to

prison. When he comes out a couple of years later, his chances for legitimate employment more blighted than ever, he is likely to resume burglary for several more years, unless arrested again, until he finally "ages out" of his criminality sometime in his late 20s or early 30s. If such a 17 year old were sent instead to a six-month residential drug treatment program, he could well be diverted from committing anymore crimes the rest of his life. (pp. 14–15)

So it can be shown that even a treatment program with a modest success rate adds up to great success and savings overtime.

It costs about $20,000, on average, to incarcerate a person for a year in a cell that costs $50,000 or more to construct. The average annual cost of supervising an offender in the community ranges from $1,000 to $4,000 (p. 5). The boom in incarceration related to drug addiction cannot be viewed as an honest but failed attempt to deal with the problem. The prison-construction industry (p. 10), as well as police and prison guard unions, actually lobbied for stricter sentences. The status quo is also favored by prosecutors who seek to make a name for themselves by pushing the envelope of their power and achieving as many convictions as possible, frequently violating the law themselves to do so (*Win at all costs*, 1998). This mentality carries through to judges, many of whom are former prosecutors, who are hoping to gain appointments to higher courts.[4] Like the first marijuana laws enacted in the South after the Civil War, drug laws directly target poor people of color. The immediate motives of the people who pass these laws and zealously prosecute and sentence Black defendants are their own economic class interests, campaign contributions, career advancement, and power, rather than desires for public service, the actual reduction of crime, or justice. There remains a structural need (though contradicted by other needs) in the capitalist economy to contain surplus labor, but such a motive is not necessarily on the minds of the people in the system who perpetuate this class violence against people below them in the social and economic hierarchy.

The crackdown on nonviolent crime has been accompanied by the media-propelled myth that young people are in the midst of a violent crime explosion, while an actual explosion in the number of abused and neglected children, doubling between 1986 to 1993 to 2.8 million, has been largely ignored (Fuentes, 1998, pp. 20, 21). As William Ayers (1997) reports in his study of the Chicago Juvenile Court, despite the popular assumptions to the contrary, juveniles are responsible for only 13 percent of violent crime. Child murder victims are killed by adults 70 percent of the time, and parents are 6 times more likely to murder their children than the other way around (pp. 74–75).

The war on crime and drugs, according to a study by the Justice Policy Institute, has expanded to the point where spending on incarceration has begun to surpass spending on higher education across the nation, as it already has in California (Ambrosio & Schiraldi, 1997, p. 2). Funding for education is being undermined by the expansion of the prison industrial complex, even though the link between income and educational attainment has been well established (p. 7; Nolan & Anyon, 2004), and despite the fact that unemployment and underemployment have been linked to incarceration (Reiman, 1979/90, pp. 133–34).

This is the current state of education, incarceration and the economy that affects the lives of my informants. The ideas of old, ideas that served at times to justify the oppression directed at the lower classes, mutate but continue to serve the same purposes today. Even the sincere efforts to ameliorate the suffering of the poor, like the development of the juvenile justice system, were perverted by the biases of the wealthy reformers advocating these policies, so that the subjugated status of the poor remained unchanged overall. I would ask the reader to pay attention, as I have attempted to in writing the book, to the assumptions and images that come to mind when reading about the young people in my study. Acknowledge them, but then indulge me by attempting to place oneself in the mindset of my informants.

Chapter 3
Pedagogy at the Center

In this chapter I will discuss the perspectives of my participants regarding their educational experiences. I will also attempt to illuminate aspects of pedagogy as well as school and classroom practices that may contribute to the perspectives, attitudes, and outcomes of my informants, related to the schooling they have received. Because I did not observe the students in the schools that they had attended previously, my analysis is based on the memories of my informants of their previous schooling, as compared with their experiences in the detention center school. In subsequent chapters I will examine the aspirations of the young people as they relate to their views on the economy and the economic benefits of education. In this chapter, however, I will attempt to look more narrowly at teaching and learning.

Most of the young people I spoke with were less than eager to engage in meaningful or in-depth discussions about their educational experiences. This was true over the course of the study, among different young people at the center, in groups and in private, and during both educational and recreational periods. Though the young people were often eager to engage in conversations around a range of difficult issues, and despite their tendency to reveal private aspects of their lives including incriminating statements about their conduct in the community, answers to questions about schooling tended to be guarded, quick, and short.

To compensate for the reluctance to discuss schooling I used a number of strategies. I asked structured questions about their educational backgrounds in interviews. I made a point of explaining that these were questions that I asked of everyone I interviewed, so that students would not feel singled out for scrutiny. Private interviews were especially helpful because students could speak without their peers hearing or seeing them. Another strategy that I used was to pay particular attention to voice inflections, facial expressions, and emotional cues when problems related to schooling were discussed. I also developed the habit of making introductions when first meeting young people at the center by asking them if they had previously been attending school. Depending on the answer and their responsiveness, I would follow up by asking why they were or were not attending school in the community. By making introductions in this manner I was attempting to normalize conversations about school. I was very careful in these introductions to convey a voice inflection and manner that indicated that I was very interested in talking about education, but also that I would not judge them. In general, I looked for opportunities to engage around these issues whenever particular young people seemed receptive or when I was running group discussions.

Given my growing perception of their reluctance to discuss these problems as a symptom of emotional pain related to past educational experiences and resultant lowered self-esteem, I did not force the issue. I tried to make the most of the verbal and nonverbal information that I gained from discussing schooling with my informants while I attempted to avoid alienating them by pushing too hard when I sensed reluctance. Their comments tended to be either negative towards individual teachers or what I would characterize as understanding or forgiving of their teachers, but they seldom conveyed any enthusiasm for the schooling they had received in general. For example, responses to the question "what were your teachers like?" were, "they was straight," "they was good," "they tried," or, "they was mean," "boring," "don't always get along with them," and "they suck." Much of the time responses to my inquiries would not go much further than this.

I would be left to read these choppy statements in the context of my knowledge of them in general and by their overall demeanor when discussing educational topics. I recorded their reluctance to engage as an important finding in itself. I found the difficulty of engaging around educational questions less than ideal, but viewed my informants with sympathy rather than impatience. Eventually I was able to develop an understanding of their perspectives and attitudes related to the schooling they had received, as well as an understanding of what they wanted schooling to be like. This was possible because I listened to silences and nonverbal communications, took advantage of the opportunities for dialogue around these issues that did present themselves, and because I practiced gentle persistence. As one young woman complained, "you always want'a talk about schools."

Assessing Pedagogy and Classroom Environments

The detention center was not the primary focus of my research. The research site gave me access to the population of young people whom I wanted to work with, in an environment that forced them to reflect upon the course of their lives and amidst adult staff who in some cases have worked with similar populations for over 30 years. I did not come to the center to conduct an exposé. I wanted to report the perspectives and stories of the young people. I was not led to believe that research with an explicit focus on the research site would have been disallowed, but given the assurances I had made about the focus of my research, I did not want to bring undue attention, particularly of a negative nature, to the site or its staff. Had I observed abuse I would have felt ethically and legally obligated to report it, but otherwise I was resolved to honor my original objectives.[1]

In the process of spending a year at the research site, however, I have come to believe that there is much at the center that deserves praise and replication. I have also come to realize that it is very difficult to explain the insights and findings that result from my research without explaining, to some extent, what it was like to be at the site from which the data emerged. For those reasons, I will report some of my observations about the daily life of the young people and staff at the center, including classroom pedagogy and practices. I do so to provide context. I do so also to aid the reader in developing an understanding of how I came to view the issues discussed in the book as I have described them. I would like to state very directly that I found the directors, teachers, philosophy, and most of the staff at the center to be exceptional in their commitment to and humane treatment of the young people in their care, despite increasingly hostile attitudes in society towards young people, especially young people of color, and towards juvenile justice.

There were challenges in that the only educational setting I observed my informants in was the center. My informants were capable of describing their educational experiences in public schools, but given their sensitivity to this topic along with the general need in ethnography to triangulate data, it was helpful to also interact with them in the learning process. To make these comparisons I needed to have a reasonable understanding of the extent to which the learning process I observed was particular to schooling at the center and the extent to which it was similar to the education that they received in the public schools. It was also important to keep in mind the situation that the young people were now in, that of being held in detention, and how this might have affected or changed their conduct and attitudes, as compared to when they were in their previous public schools. One strategy that I used to contend with these challenges was to routinely ask the students how school at the center differed from their previous school experiences. My own teaching experiences working with similar populations of students and general knowledge of educational practices in the United States also helped me to make these comparisons. By observing and working with students in the classroom environment at the center and by speaking with them individually and in groups about their educational experiences, I was able to gain insights into the ways that they experience schooling and how classroom learning might be improved.

Curriculum and Pedagogy at the Center

Most of my participants did not report major differences between school at the center and public school in the community, particularly in terms of how teaching occurred. Their observations and perspectives regarding classroom pedagogy and curriculum at the center were consistent with my own. I agreed with them when they told me that this instruction was similar in fundamental ways to the mainstream public education they had received previously. I believe that what I learned from my interactions with the young people at the center school does tell us something about their attitudes towards and perspectives on education in general. What I observed and what they reported related to schooling was not particular to their being in detention, but could help us to understand how they likely functioned in the public schools that they had, at some point, attended previously.

This is not to say that there was nothing distinctive or favorable about the schooling they were receiving at the center as compared to their previous schools. I observed none of the indignities, like, for example, the belittling of students described by Ann Ferguson in *Bad Boys* (2000). Assuming that the conduct she documented is at all common in schools, the center school is far ahead in the humanity and dignity afforded its students. Many of the students reported that things were better at the center because it was easier to focus on their work, with fewer distractions from other students, and because they could receive more individualized attention. As one of the young people stated in a formal interview, comparing school at the center to public schools, instruction was "probably better here than in school, because it's less social and more attention." Other young people in the study commented that the teachers at the center compared to those at their previous schools were "nicer here" or that "they listens here." One young man commented that he prefers schooling at the center because "there's less work here." Only one of my informants reported that the teaching staff at the center were busier and spent less time with her, stating that, "teachers here is less helpful, too busy here." Also, while they described public school teachers ranging from very concerned to lazy or even violent on rare occasions, they spoke with almost universal favor of the center teaching staff for the attention and the respectful treatment showed to the students.

The curriculum at the center consisted primarily of working with reading and math workbooks, crosswords and other handouts, geography map assignments, discussion sessions, occasional educational films, and opportunities to use educational software in the computer room. The school did not use textbooks. Typically, each student would spend part of the day on each of these components. The center teacher would generally run discussion sessions and would supervise computer instruction, while her assistants, including myself, would supervise the other rooms. The underlying pedagogy at the center was mainstream. It was a one-size-fits-all approach, with each student using the same materials and being taught in the same manner, but unlike instruction in most public educational settings, students were able to proceed at their own pace. It was teacher centered and raising questions was not encouraged, but a lecture format was not used. Teaching staff did not stand at the front of the room instructing the class as a whole. There was no blackboard. Rather, the staff came to the students who worked individually around tables. It was not a test-oriented curriculum either, though pre- and post-assessments were conducted to measure gains while at the center school.

My description of the curriculum and pedagogy at the center is based on my participation as a teaching assistant, my observations, and my conversations with the young people about the work they were asked to do. Most of the young people spent much of their time actively trying to avoid doing their work by talking, doodling, writing letters to people in the outside world, or daydreaming. On occasion they would attempt to go to the windows to look outside, something that was not allowed except during breaks. Wearing my teaching assistant hat, I would encourage the students to do their work. Often I was unsuccessful in my attempts, but would receive comments from the young people about their reasons for not wanting to do their work. They would often protest that, "it's boring," or "it's stupid." Given my dual role as a researcher at the center, the students were more likely to volunteer these comments to me than to the other teaching staff. My responsibilities as an educational assistant seldom provided appropriate opportunities to engage in dialogue about what made the assignments boring. I did not want to give the impression of undermining the instruction at the center, even if I secretly disapproved of some aspects of this instruction at times. There was little risk, however, of mistaking the glazed-over look in their eyes for the excitement of learning.

The responses of the teaching staff, which consists of the professional teacher, her assistant, and undergraduate volunteers, to the oppositional behavior of the students varied. At times a given member of the staff would attempt to encourage students to do their work by simply urging them to do so. At times staff might make deals with the students, agreeing to complete one question for the student in exchange for the students completing the next. At other times staff might simply give students the answers. I tended to ask questions or engage in brief conversations related to the topic of a given assignment, in the hope that such context would make the specific assigned

tasks more interesting, before asking them to return to completing the assignment. Students who simply refused to participate in educational activities
could be sent back to their cells for the remainder of the school day and
would also lose privileges that evening. This was a rare occurrence that was
more closely related to stress in the life of a given student, like an upcoming
court date, than to the school environment itself. The professional teacher
seldom became involved in the workbook and worksheet components of instruction. Rather, she focused her efforts on helping students with their computer-based work and group work. Though she did not tell me this, nor did I
ask her, I felt that she may have allowed busywork in the classroom in order
to concentrate her efforts on the group discussions and, especially, on the
computer-based instruction. Even if she had wanted to put more time into
conducting more meaningful assignments, she may not have been allowed to
do so. In my field notes I described the busywork exercises:

> The students are given worksheets where they are to identify the meaning of words
> given example sentences. Some of these words are obscure and difficult for me to
> identify. Other words are more common, but the examples given use obscure secon-
> dary meanings of the words. I try to get the young people at my table to at least at-
> tempt to find the meaning of the words before they ask me for the answers.

The problem with this approach to teaching and learning was not simply
that better worksheets were needed. Rather, this general approach, so common in public schools as well, reduces learning to exercises of underlining,
circling, and filling in blank spaces that have little to do with the useful purposes of reading, writing, and mathematics, much less the real world in
which the young people live. On several occasions different students volunteered to write stories for me rather than complete the worksheets that they
had been assigned. Unfortunately, I did not believe that I could allow them to
undertake these more meaningful projects. I felt that to attempt to do so
would undermine the teaching staff. Through my observations and interactions in this setting I came to believe that many of the young people were
willing to work in school and were interested in learning (even volunteering
to take on larger and more challenging projects), but that the classroom
pedagogy and curriculum were alienating the students from both the subject
matter and learning process.

Working with the students on worksheets and geography maps, I would
typically be as bored as they were,[2] and would look for opportunities to add
context to what we were doing. The geography assignments generally consisted of looking for countries or states on maps and circling them. Understanding geography is an important part of coming to understand one's place

in the world, but the importance of geography was lost on students who cir-
cled random countries, or copied from others at their table, between doodles
or conversations with other students. While working with young people on
their geography maps I would often ask them to show me where in the
United States their families were from and to show me where their ancestors
were from before either migrating to or being taken to the New World (in the
case of most African-Americans) as slaves. Students tended to respond to
this exercise with enthusiasm. On one such occasion an African-American
boy who had been staring blankly at the table began to treat those of us at his
table to a detailed explanation of the history of slavery and the Western Expansion, including the impact of disease on settlers, who, he argued, did not
understand that the water they were drinking was contaminated, but who,
fortunately, would boil water to make coffee, thereby reducing their exposure to bacteria. When I asked him how he knew so much about those historical periods, he stated that his grandmother was a bit of a history buff, and
that everything he ever learned about history he learned from her, "not in
school." The other students at his table listened intently as he spoke. In response to his comments on learning more from his grandmother about history than he had learned in school, one of the young people at the table
replied, laughing, "that's for sure," while other young people at the table
nodded.

This example, like many others from my fieldwork, speaks to me of the
desire among the young people to have a context in which to place the instruction that they were receiving, to have this instruction be free of busywork, and to be able to relate what they were learning to their own lives,
their own histories (see McNeil, 1988, p. 191). Allowed to address the larger
context, these same students who would seem to struggle with simple assignments and who were very reluctant to cooperate in school were suddenly
eager to participate, capable of discussing complex social phenomena at a
high level, and were even able to use their own histories, as in the case of
slavery, as a context for understanding the experiences and histories of White
settlers during the westward expansion.

There are numerous examples of progressive approaches to education
that capture the interest and energy of students, relate instruction to the critical problems facing the populations of young people that my informants represent, and yet successfully teach content (Apple & Beane, 1995; Tewksbury
& Scher, 1998). It is for such an approach to teaching and learning, pedagogy and curriculum, for which the young people, in their own language,
seemed to be longing. Along with the desire for meaningful work related to
their lives, the students also seemed to be looking for culturally relevant cur-

riculum and culturally sensitive instruction that would allow them to better
understand their histories and place in the world. This was particularly so in
the case of the African-American students in my study. My conclusions related to the desire for meaningful and culturally relevant instruction are consistent with the conclusions drawn by Gloria Ladson-Billings (1994) in her
work on culturally relevant instruction, in which she provides examples of
instruction that both engages the interest of students of color and increases
their development of skills.

As I suggested before, the professional teacher at the center was very
fond of a computer-based curriculum that was acquired for the students only
after a great deal of effort on her part to gain approval of and funding for the
expensive system. The system included the computer hardware that they
used as well as an educational software program. This program demonstrated
concepts and then provided students with problems or exercises, sometimes
in the form of educational games. The program then monitored each student's performance and assigned additional problems in remaining areas of
weakness, before expanding upon mastered content with new concepts. Instruction at the center school revolved around the computer component, in a
small room where four students could work before rotating with other students who were waiting for their turn while working in the larger rooms. The
teacher favored the computer instruction because she believed that it captured the interest of students, taught them to use computers in general, and
provided an individualized experience based on constant monitoring by the
computer program of areas of strengths and weaknesses. She cited documented gains as assessed by the computer program itself as proof that the
approach was successful with young people who otherwise were turned off
to learning.

The teaching staff would have liked to view the computer-based instruction as the high point of what they did for students. Unfortunately, the computer-based learning suffered from the same pedagogical inadequacies as did
the regular instruction, in that it was a de-contextualized approach to instruction. My findings related to the use of computer-based instruction are similar
to those of Todd Oppenheimer as expressed in his book *The Flickering Mind*
(2003); Oppenheimer conducted extensive observational research in technol-
ogy-based classrooms, finding little benefit from but many down sides to
these classrooms.

I would not argue that the students learned nothing from the use of the
computers, but I observed the content learning to be no greater than that acquired in the regular classroom. Moreover, the hidden lessons in this instruction,[3] the boredom it inspired, the irrelevance to real life, and the lack of

cultural relevance, were only exacerbated by the isolation of the glowing
screens. The students conveyed their views on this in no uncertain terms
when the teaching staff were not around, stating, for example, that, "this is
boring" or "I hate haven' to be on the computers."[4] They also took every opportunity to avoid the computer lessons, switching to more enjoyable games
or assignments as soon as the teacher left the room. They took these opportunities to interact with each other as well. And yet the students would almost uniformly discipline themselves to the assigned tasks when the center
teacher was in the computer room, in a way that they would not do in the
general classroom, even for her. I did not view this behavior as the result of
their proximity to the teacher, given their failure to respond in the same way
outside of the computer room, nor did I think it was the result of fear of punishment, as she was anything but a strict disciplinarian. Rather, for the reasons just stated, I came to believe that the students understood how dedicated
she was to the use of this technology, that she had acquired it out of caring
for them, and that they did not want to hurt her feelings by criticizing the
program in her presence.

The students did not view instruction at the center as fundamentally different from the instruction they had received in public schools, but there
were some differences in instruction at the center that I found to have an impact on classroom dynamics and learning favorably. Most notably, there
were no exams. There also was no tracking or sorting. Every student who
came to the center school would begin at the same place in his or her workbooks and would progress at his or her own pace. The teacher did not stand
at the front of the room writing on a chalk board or lecturing students. Instruction was individualized, though not in the sense of it being related to
their lives. Students received a great deal of individual attention from the
staff and interns. The ratio of staff to students at the center was often as low
as 1 to 3. The school district in Coldville, by contrast, reports an overall stu-
dent/teacher ratio of 1 to 12, though actual class sizes at the high school level
were obviously much greater than 12 students per teacher. The students reported having been in noisy, large, and disorderly classrooms in the district. I
attributed their willingness to participate in schooling at the center, when
many of them had not been willing to do so in the public schools they had
previously attended, not to coercion but to these differences. Most of the students only tolerated schooling at the center, but this was still an improvement
for many of them, compared to their previous attitudes towards school, and
in doing so they were returning the gesture of respect that the teaching staff
provided them in the classroom. The good efforts of the teaching staff, including their efforts to utilize new and innovative technologies, as well as

their efforts to minimize tracking and formal assessment, however, were undermined by the essentially mainstream approach to instruction at the center.

The limitations of the mainstream instruction that the students at the center received, which was similar to instruction in the public schools they had attended previously, should be qualified by one aspect of instruction at the center. The center teacher would bring the students together each day for a group discussion around critical issues. I considered these sessions to be the most meaningful educational component at the center. They included a range of topics relevant to the lives of the students, including racism, the importance of having an education to compete in the job market, and anger management. Students were eager to participate in these discussions. More than entertainment or a break from monotony for them, the discussions helped them to develop critical thinking skills, helped them to formulate arguments, and exposed them to various perspectives on social problems. They also helped students to confront issues of race, class and gender. The only shortcomings I would identify in this aspect of the curriculum were that the discussions were not, for the most part, tied to content instruction (such as writing assignments), nor were they tied to community projects (to the extent that such projects were possible from inside a juvenile detention setting). In fairness to the center teaching staff, we should acknowledge that the constant turnover of young people at the center would make long-term projects difficult to accomplish. We should also acknowledge that these successful discussion sessions, so obviously needed and desired by the students, are largely missing from our mainstream public schools, except perhaps in gifted classrooms (Sapon-Shevin, 1994). Still, at a minimum, this aspect of the curriculum should be developed and more integrated with the rest of the curriculum at the center, and should be emulated in general public education. When I asked my participants what their favorite thing in public school was, common answers included lunch or hanging out with friends. Occasionally a particular teacher's class or a particular subject was mentioned. When I asked what their favorite part of school in the center was, the answer generally was the group discussions or films.

One discussion session that the center teacher ran is exemplary of the potential of such an approach. The discussion took place on a very busy day at the center. On this particular day the center was so overcrowded that 17 young people had to be transferred temporarily to detention centers in surrounding counties. The young people transferred on these days were almost always those who were held in the center on a longer term basis, so many of the students in the room were new to the teacher and new to each other. We arranged the chairs in the T.V. room into a circle. The teacher and I are both white. The students were a mix of ethnicities; Latino, European-American, and African-American, both boys and girls. There was a nervous energy in the room.

The center teacher began to describe a film that she was planning to show the next day about the track athlete Jesse Owens at the Olympics in Germany just prior to World War II, "when he [Jesse Owens] humiliated Hitler." She asked the group in her usual friendly and patient tone what they could remember about last week's reading on Jesse Owens. Two African-American boys quickly perked up, sitting erect in their chairs, and responded to her question. The following exchange then took place:

> 1st boy: He used to race [against] horses for money.
> 2nd boy: But then he stopped 'cause it made him feel like an animal.
> Teacher: I would have kept doing it if I was him, because the money was so good.
> The two boys then spoke almost at once: I wouldn't!
> 1st boy: It made him feel like an animal. What's important is how you feel.

In my field notes I indicated that I wanted to be sure to recall that I was reminded by this exchange of some of the conflicts between teachers and students that Michelle Fine (1991) has described in her work on the dropout problem, but that this teacher, unlike those in Fine's account, was quite compassionate towards the students in general. Unlike the conflicts described by Fine, or those described by L. Janelle Dance in her book *Tough Fronts* (2002), the difference in the perspectives of the teacher and students in the exchange I just described did not seem to alienate her from the students. The exchange was open and friendly. Yet it was revealing and educational. The young people were learning about the history leading up to World War II as well as the complex and contradictory nature of race relations and racism in the United States at that time. Simultaneously, they were learning to articulate their positions. Both the teacher and students were learning how others view the world differently given their backgrounds and experiences. I thought this was a wonderful educational moment, and there were moments like this in almost every discussion session that the teacher ran.

Student Perspectives on School

Serving as a volunteer assistant to the center teacher, observing students at the center school, and discussing schooling with them helped me to understand the deeper social context in which I could place their statements about schooling. This allowed me not only to hear their statements about their former teachers and educational experiences, but also to judge for myself the extent to which the students would respond to genuine efforts on the part of teachers to help them learn. In this section I will discuss what my informants had to say about classroom pedagogy and curriculum as well as what they said they would do to improve schooling. I will also weigh their statements against my observations of them in the educational setting at the center.

My findings in this section are the result of my observations, conversations, and interviews. I tried to pay attention to voice inflection and body language, as well as to words spoken and silences. I also attempted to pay close attention to the impact my own interactions with my informants may have had on what they were saying and how they were saying it. Some conversations were overheard clandestinely. Working in classrooms I developed the ability to pay attention to several conversations at the same time, an ability that parents will understand. I drew on these skills in the field. Spontaneous conversations about school failure among the young people were not frequent, but they did occur. When overheard, these conversations provided a valuable check on whether they were telling me the same sort of things they were telling each other. I did not find that the overheard conversations, as related to education, were substantially different from those in which I was a participant. I did find, however, that their conversations were both more frank and more clearly articulated in my presence. For example, an overheard exchange from my field notes is as follows: "I can't do no math, know what I mean," to which another student answered, "I feel ya." There was more conveyed in this exchange than the words themselves can reveal; in tone, in cadence, in facial expression, and in body language. Put another way, you had to be there to understand. In this section, and throughout the book, I attempt to convey the information, be it verbal or nonverbal, that brings me to the findings that I am reporting, and to the extent that I can, to convey a sense of what it was like to be there.

Labeling

I did not have access to medical records or to school records from the previous schools that my informants had attended. Given the nature of the class-stratified and racially stratified educational system (Nasaw, 1984; Polakow, 2000), I suspected that many of the young people in my study would have been diagnosed with some sort of learning or behavioral problem, especially that of Attention Deficit Disorder. In fact, approximately one third of the students at the detention center would receive medication on any given day that I was there. Although I saw this as an important issue, I decided not to run the risk of hurting the feelings of my informants, or of alienating them, by asking them about labeling related to disabilities. Despite my not asking, many revealed having been diagnosed and/or medicated. In an interview a 14-year-old White boy he would say only the following about school, though he had been very open in our discussions of various issues, "I don't want to go back. I don't like school. I have ED/LD." A 13-year-old African-American boy described his learning problem this way: "At school they say I get the words backwards." Whether the result of an actual disability or not, it was clearly the case that many of my informants were behind academically from where one would expect them to be for their age. As a Latino boy told me, "Reading is hard for me. Some of the words on this can[5] are hard to read. My teachers didn't teach me to read. They said I had LD, but I just never learned."

The impact of labeling on students in my study almost certainly contributed to their educational difficulties, whatever one thinks of the effectiveness and safety of psychotropic drugs (one young man reported that he "gets the shakes" and has "to take sleeping pills to go to sleep" as a result of being on Ritalin). I also view with great irony the practice of medicating young people when so much of the popular image and self-image of young people of color is defined by the illegal drug trade and perceptions of youth drug use. I am reminded of Michael Apple's (1990) observations regarding the role that labeling plays in the legitimization of the schooling enterprise:

> My point is not to deny that within the existing institutional framework of schooling there are such 'things' as 'slow learners,' 'under-achievers,' or 'poorly motivated students' which we can common-sensically identify, though as I have contended such language hides the more basic issue of inquiring into the conditions under which one group of people consistently labels others as deviant or applies some other taken for granted abstract category on them. Rather, I would like to argue that this linguistic system as it is commonly applied by school people does not serve a psychological or scientific function as much as they would like to suppose. To put it bluntly, it often serves to abase and degrade those individuals and classes of people to whom the designations are so quickly given. (p. 136)

This is an area of weakness in my study that is more glaring given my background working in special education and my continued interest in the area. Given the constraints placed upon my research by human subjects, however, I was unable to access the medical records of participants. And given the vulnerability of my informants I chose not to systematically gather the data by pushing this topic with them, as I feared the emotional ramifications and the impact on my relationship with them had I done so.

The disproportionate impact of labeling on students of color (Breggin & Bregggin, 1998; Coles, 1987), the harm associated with the use of psychotropic drugs such as Prozac or stimulants such as Ritalin (Breggin, 1991), and the function served by labeling in diverting blame for educational failure away from schools and onto less-advantaged students themselves (Skrtic, 1991, 1995), have been well established in the literature. Though I expected to find students who had been labeled and medicated, I came to suspect that the extent could be greater than I had anticipated. The Juvenile Court annual reports do not include the number of students receiving medications or who had been referred to special education in their previous schools. My suspicions were given support by a study released in 2002 that found that Black students were more than twice as likely to be in special education than were White students in the state, despite Blacks representing a minority of residents across the state. The report found that Blacks in Coldville were in special education at more than twice the rate of Whites (with 30 percent of the Black student population being in special education), despite there being a Black population in Coldville of roughly six percent.

School and Student Self-Esteem

Despite the sensitivity of many of my informants to issues related to their educations, I was able to discuss education with them. Their willingness to engage in these conversations depended on a range of factors including their moods, my relationship with them, and the nature of their relationships with the young people near them in a particular area or sitting with them at a table. My informants were more likely to speak freely about their educational backgrounds in formal private interviews, but at times a given young person or group of young people would be very forthcoming. Some of the young people would be more open when I first met them but would be less so after I knew them better (perhaps because they had come to care more about what I thought of them). Most of the young people, however, were more willing to trust me with their educational histories as the days or weeks went by. I also observed that boys were less likely to speak freely about educational difficulties. I say "freely," because they were, for the most part, just as willing as were girls to speak about these difficulties, but boys spoke about them in a more guarded manner. The reluctance or difficulty my informants displayed around educational struggles was made even more apparent by their general eagerness to discuss other matters that I would have expected to be equally sensitive, such as sexuality, drugs, and crime. They were more outspoken regarding their views of the economic viability of education (see chapter 4) than they were about problems more closely related to classroom interactions. I took these findings as additional support for my growing belief that their relative silence on education, especially when it might touch on possible educational difficulties they themselves may have had, was born of psychological pain.

I never asked a young person in my study if he or she felt bad about herself because of problems in school or in life. I was afraid that such a direct question might hurt or alienate my informants. Instead, when appropriate, in informal interviews, conversations, and in formal private interviews, I asked informants questions about their feelings related to school as well as about how they thought other young people at the center felt about school. These questions frequently elicited statements and conversations about the relationship between school failure and self-esteem. When I asked a sixteen-year-old African-American boy in a private interview why young people sell drugs he stated that, "They don't want to look dumb. They can't make it in school. They find their own way." By finding their own way, he meant they dropped out of school. Other statements made by informants in interviews included: "I want to go to school. I don't want to be a dummy. I don't want to sell drugs," and "Reading is hard for me," and "teachers made me feel dumb." None of my informants ever said, "I suffer from a depressed sense of self-worth resulting from my difficulties in school." But as these quotes demonstrate, they expressed some of the same meanings by joining education with being "dumb." My informants who had not yet left school, at least not permanently, hoped that by staying in school, they could redeem themselves from the stigma of being a dropout. Their reasoning was that even if they weren't the best students, at least they were smart enough to stay in school. For my informants who had left, or who were resolved to leave school, attending school at the center was a constant reminder to them that they were "dumb" and was an environment where they felt that their educational inadequacies were constantly on display. Statements like these were sometimes made by my informants in conversations. More often in private. In situations where a young person might feel exposed to peers, however, it was often necessary to read the nonverbal cues, which conveyed the same meanings.

One example of this nonverbal communication of lowered self-esteem in relationship to educational difficulties occurred in a discussion group run by the center teacher, in which she had students read aloud. One African-American boy, larger than the others and somewhat older, who obviously enjoyed respect from his peers at the center, was very reluctant to read. "Tha's ah'right," he repeatedly said while trying to force a smile. Eventually he gave in to the urging of the teacher and attempted to read. He struggled terribly with the basic text. From the look on the face of the teacher I had the impression that she did not realize the extent of his reading difficulties before insisting that he read aloud in the group. She kindly encouraged him to continue to sound out the words while some of the students laughed at him or finished the words for him in an impatient manner. She asked those students to stop and then continued to work patiently with the boy. After several minutes that seemed like an eternity, he finally gave up, saying "Tha's ah'right," slumped slightly down into his chair, trying to maintain a smile, and looked much smaller than before. Having been there for this exchange, I believe that there was no mistaking that he felt bad about himself related to his reading abilities and sought to bolster his self-esteem by receiving "props" from his peers for his street smarts, size, and strength. No other interpretation would be reasonable in my view, though I did not receive confirmation from him that my interpretation was correct.

On another occasion I was working with a young White girl, perhaps 15-years old, with medium length brown hair and round features. She was sent to a separate room at her own table because she had been disrupting the other students and not focusing on her work while in the larger room. I made my way to sit with her at the table, where she was placing random answers to math problems on a worksheet. "How's it going?" I asked her, trying to convey with my voice inflection that I meant the question both academically and personally. "Who are you?" was her response. I told her that I was a student at the university and that I was doing research at the detention center. Just at that time a member of the staff came by and jokingly told me that the girl was "too boy crazy" and distractible to be with the other kids. I wondered if this member of the staff felt the need to justify to me having the girl by herself, a possible indication of feeling scrutinized by my presence, or if she was just trying to be helpful. The girl smiled good-naturedly at the teasing, as she stole another glance at one of the boys in the next room.

As we spoke, in a conversation that was interrupted by frequent pauses as her attention wandered from me to the boys in the next room, she expressed more interest in my being from the university than she did in my role as a researcher or teaching assistant at the center. She asked me about parties and spoke of wanting to meet college boys. While I spoke with her about my university and her schooling, I also attempted to get her to focus more on the math problems on which she was meant to be working. The worksheet consisted of multiplication problems. It began with the multiplication of double-digit numbers by a single-digit number, but then advanced to the multiplication of double-digit numbers by double-digit numbers. I could see that her knowledge of the multiplication tables was very good. When it came to the more difficult problems, however, I soon realized that she did not know how to use a placeholder before multiplying by the second digit of the second number. I showed her how to use a placeholder and correctly add the rows to get the correct answer.

I asked her if she was in school before coming to the detention center. This is a standard question that I typically asked young people when I met them.[6] She told me that she had been banned from school, "til I'm 21." I asked her if she meant that she'd been kicked out of school, to which she replied, "only 'til I'm 21." I responded to this by saying that I thought that meant that she couldn't go back, and that I thought that she might have a right to go back to school. I told her that she could at least take her GED test, because, I said, she would need a degree of some sort in the future. To this she responded with a tone of resignation, "I can't take no test, I can't even do these multiplication tables," as she looked down to avoid my gaze. As she spoke those words I felt the extent of self-deprecation this girl experiences as a result of her difficulties with schoolwork. It was obvious that her teachers had either not taken the time or had been unable to keep her attention long enough, to show her how to use a placeholder in multiplication problems. I suspected that this was the norm for her education thus far. I thought for a moment, then said, "But look, you can do these problems now. It's not your fault that no one showed you how to do this, but now you can do it. You can take that test [the GED] too." She looked me directly in the eye for at least a minute, as if she was trying to decide if she should believe me or not, then she looked away to search for the boy she'd been watching in the next room. From my field notes for this exchange I wrote:

> I wonder what could make a young girl give up on herself like that. If someone had taught her to move the placeholder! She's actually very bright. They gave up on her at school and she gave up on herself.

It was my impression that the school failure this girl has experienced was the cause of her distractibility and not the other way around. In particular, her focus on gaining the attention of boys rather than focusing on her school-work seemed to reveal a need to boost her self-image in what is for her a psychologically painful situation, that of school. That the lessons of math worksheets are isolating and boring did not help either. This girl never told me in so many words that she had a lowered self-esteem related to schooling and therefore sought comfort from the attention of boys, but having been present for our exchange, I am certain that this is the only reasonable inter-pretation.

My findings regarding low self-image as related to schooling are not surprising. They are consistent with the findings of a growing body of re-search going back to the 1960s on school failure and opposition to schools by young people who are not successful in mainstream classrooms (Rist, 1970; Sennett & Cobb, 1972). I was not surprised to find that many of my informants had experienced emotional harm in schools. I was surprised that they would, as a whole, be so reluctant at times to talk about it. It seemed universal that the students in my study who were having trouble in school felt shame related to their difficulties (rather than indignation born of a political critique of limited opportunity via school), whether they also held a critique of the educational system or not.

The lowered self-esteem as related to education that I describe in this chapter is also related to a range of factors, including race, gender, class, and the achievement ideology (MacLeod, 1987/95, p. 112). When the young people at the center are assessing their educational abilities (and self-worth) they are always comparing themselves to notions of what successful and smart students are like. They may know students who fit their notions of a smart student, but often their exposure to such "gifted" students is limited (given differentiated curriculum at the high school level). This notion of the good student may come from parents, peers, the media, or popular culture. Most of the time I expect that it is primarily their teachers who communicate their relative worth to them in spoken, or unspoken, conscious, or even unconscious, ways. The literature on teacher expectations as related to student achievement and self-image has explored the role of teachers in conveying social rank and this literature is consistent with my suspicion (see Levy, 1970; Sennett and Cobb, 1972; Solomon, 1992).

Most of the academic work that has considered student self-esteem, oppositional behavior, and the achievement ideology has documented a similar relationship between school failure and self-esteem. Stacey Lee (1996) in her work on the effects of the model minority stereotype on working-class, Asian-American students describes the impact on their self-esteem as follows:

> I would argue that the intense academic competition at Academic High left many students in the position of being "losers." New wavers like Phum and Ting responded to their situations by refusing to participate in the competition. They felt like losers and believed that they could never win. These students simply resisted any behavior that might have helped them in school. Although their behavior may appear to be self-defeating, their analysis of the situation is not far from the truth. At Academic High, seats in the top tracks were limited and therefore the number of "winners" was limited. (p. 65)

Douglas Foley describes a similar situation in his book *Learning Capitalist Culture* (1990). The following words of a Mexican student measuring himself against his White counterparts are compelling:

I guess I am dumb. I am in the slow classes because I am dumber than the Anglos, I guess. I can't speak English so good, and I can't read very well. I never have done good in school. The teachers go too fast. I wanna be better. My parents want me to go to college. I try real hard, but I can't get it 'cause I must be dumb. (p.91)

Jay MacLeod (1987/95) came to similar conclusions in his study regarding a group of students who actively rejected school:

> The Hallway Hangers may have little of their self-esteem tied up in school, but, as Scully argues, they cannot help but feel "a judgment of academic inferiority cast upon them, be it by teachers, classmates, or their seemingly objective computerized report card." The subculture of the Hallway Hangers must be understood as an attempt by its members to insulate themselves from these negative judgments and to provide a context in which some semblance of self-respect and dignity can be maintained. (p. 117)

The social-psychological process of internalizing economic inequalities as self-blame and self-loathing has been explored by Paulo Freire (1970/93) and Franz Fanon (1963/68).

My finding that self-esteem is closely tied to school failure is consistent with the larger body of literature, as was my finding that perceptions of failure are relative to an idealized norm of the good student, who is also typically whiter and wealthier. These feelings were almost universal among the young people who would cycle through the detention center; however, in other studies these feelings have often been associated with particular sub-groupings of students. I base this conclusion both on a consideration of the reluctance of the young people to speak freely about their education while they were so open about other topics, what I observed, and on what they told me.

Most of the young people at the center had struggled in school and may have been in danger of dropping out in the future. Most of them, however, had not dropped out yet. Most had passed the hurdle of 8th grade when large numbers of students first drop out of school (a phenomenon that is often overlooked by studies of the dropout problem), but had not yet passed the hurdle of 11th grade (see Fine, 1991; Kozol, 1991). Studies in Coldville have found that the White graduation rate is as high as the national average of 87 percent, but that the Black graduation rate is under 50 percent. Hispanics in Coldville have a graduation rate of 65 percent, which is consistent with national averages. The Asian graduation rate, excluding students from South East Asia, is close to 96 percent. In 1998, according to the center's annual report, 98 of 1,035 juveniles referred to the detention center, or roughly 6 percent, reported not being enrolled in school at the time of their detention.

Various studies have shown Coldville to have suspension rates, expulsion rates, and special education referrals for African-American students well above both state and national averages. Given the bias in the Coldville educational system against children of color, and the great likelihood that the young people in my study will drop out of school before graduating, the level of attendance and enrollment reported by my informants is surprising. It is only fair to say that the young people, despite their mixed feelings about schooling, are fighting to stay connected to an educational system that clearly does not favor them. We cannot say that they have simply rejected schooling.

My study suggests that once students begin to feel badly about themselves related to their educational abilities, they are more likely to make choices that will further distance them from opportunities for improvement. This finding is consistent with those of Lee (2001) when she describes students who began skipping classes because their difficulty with the material made them feel bad about themselves, only to fall further behind in a spiral of lowering self-esteem and exacerbated educational failure. This is a complex problem that may require, as an ultimate solution, the elimination of both competitive schools and the competitive capitalist system of which schools are a part (Bowles & Gintis, 1976; Freire, 1970/94).

I will explore the need for change and the implications that my study has for strategies for change in the concluding chapter. In the meantime and on the road towards a more utopian[7] future, there are things that can be done to begin to improve the outcomes and experiences of young people in our public schools. In terms of the self-esteem of students, we could urge teachers to be more sensitive to the impact that their judgments and comparisons have on students. The center teaching staff provide a positive example of how sympathy, patience, and kindness do contribute to improved relationships between students and teachers. More ambitious changes could involve alternative assessment methods, the elimination of grades and tests, and the elimination of the labeling and drugging of disruptive students who are characterized as having a disability. Even if it is not clear how some suggested changes might be practically implemented, I think it is important to name these problems.

The Struggle to Care About School

A recurring theme in what my informants told me was that they struggled to stay in school, to find the motivation to get to school early in the morning, and to stay in classrooms all day. As one African-American boy told me, "I like school when I go. I skip school to go smoke." When I explored with him what might make school more attractive to himself and his friends he suggested that school days be shorter, with shorter weeks, and that the schedule and activities be more varied.

The difficulty that the young people described in sticking with school seemed to result from more than a simple lack of discipline or desire to do well. As one African-American girl told me, "I was reading in school, then I started messing up again. I was getting used to school, then I got in trouble again." For most of my informants, though not all, there was a strong desire to get an education. The young people in my study were conflicted about the usefulness of staying in school (see chapter 4), but most of them were making or had made sincere efforts to stick with school at some point As a 14-year-old African-American girl told me when I asked her how she thought her peers feel about school, she responded, "Mixed. They like it even though they say they don't." A boy told me: "I don't like school. I do and I don't. I like seeing my friends, but not doing the work." Underneath psychological coping mechanisms like hostility and acting disinterested, the young people in my study would like to be successful at staying in school and doing well in school, as many of them described it, to "do the right thing," even as they failed and pretended not to care.

As educators we could, as many educators do, decry the lack of effort on the part of students who do not do well or stay in school. We could also decry the lack of effort on the part of their parents. I have no doubt that students and families often fail in their efforts to function in the educational system and that part of this failure may be the result of lapses in effort. My informants were quick to admit to having made such mistakes. As one Latino boy told me in an interview when I asked him why he got in trouble and failed in school, "I chose to really. I had a chance to do good, but I didn't want to." Another boy, when I asked him why he ended up in detention, put it this way: "If I'd only been thinking," by which he meant that he had not been thinking about his actions.

Despite these admissions, however, my research does not support the notion that there is a simple lack of motivation on the part of these young people and their families. I base this finding on the statements of young people in which they painfully recounted their educational failures. More to the point, even when masking this pain with bravado in front of their peers, their facial expressions, body language, and the look in their eyes would often betray their true feelings. I also base it on the occasional conversations I had with parents. In private interviews my observations would often be confirmed by statements like the one made by a 13-year-old boy who had been born into a gang-involved family: "I want to go to school. I don't want to be a dummy. I don't want to sell drugs." The struggle to find the motivation to do well in school was reflected in the statements of another African-American boy who told me:

> I was skipping in Freshman year, but I was doing better [before I got in trouble]. I like school, but I don't like getting up. My momma makes me go every day. I keep reading. My momma tells me to keep reading and keep praying. I used to skip too much.

Rather than only asking what is wrong with young people and their families when they don't succeed in our school systems, I believe that we should also ask why our cookie-cutter approach to educating students does not work as well for some groups of students as for others. Because my research does not indicate a simple lack of motivation on the part of struggling students and on the part of their teachers, I fear that the common focus on the need for more motivation in failing students is misguided.[8] My research suggests, instead, that we should help students to better channel the motivation that they already bring to their educations.

To Accommodate the Need for Social Interaction

My informants had strong opinions about how to change the educational system so that students like themselves would be more successful. In addition to their words, I also took from the conversations two observations that I thought were very important: 1) they had obviously given a great deal of thought to the question of how to improve schooling prior to having spoken with me about it (they had well-articulated arguments); and 2) taken as a group they were making similar suggestions. I am convinced that we need, at a minimum, to consider what they are telling us about what they need to be comfortable and successful in school, even if their suggestions would require us to make significant changes to classroom practices. Even if their suggestions prove impossible to implement or seem counterproductive, I believe that we must carefully consider what they have to say.

In general, though my informants acknowledged the good intentions of many of their teachers, they reported finding classrooms to be environments lacking in joy that did not relate to their lived experience. Part of this was the natural desire of young people to socialize. As a Latino boy told me, "I love school, meeting girls, b-ball, math, social studies, but we need more field trips." Another boy summed up the need for social interaction when I asked him what his favorite subject in school was and he responded, simply, "lunch." Other students also described lunch as their favorite part of the school day and said that school should have more recess periods. These were high school students who no longer had recess periods. Most of my informants would describe socializing as the aspect of school that they enjoyed the most. If they mentioned any particular academic subjects they were often named as an afterthought, and they would also tend to mention a teacher who they had in earlier grades. When I asked if there were any subjects that they liked most, they would respond in a manner that seemed to indicate that it had not occurred to them that I might be interested in such things. Academics were like an island that floated in the sea of social interactions for my informants.

School should help young people to learn to focus on the task at hand. Teachers cannot and should not allow classrooms to become places where young people socialize to the exclusion of focusing on academics. I do not take what the young people told me to be a demand for playtime in the classroom either. When comparing the classroom at the center to their previous schools many of the young people complained that the classrooms at the public schools they had attended were just such environments where there was too much off-topic socializing and where teachers could not keep the students on task. On the other hand, students complained of the lack of social interaction. In an effort to reconcile these seemingly contradictory arguments, I take my informants to be saying that their teachers had failed to accommodate the need of young people to socialize in their classroom practices.

As Michael Apple has reported, we ask students to sit motionless for long periods of time in uncomfortable and cramped wooden desks without food or water, something that we would find difficult to do even as adults. A 16-year-old African-American girl echoed Apple's concerns when I asked her what she thought would make school better. She responded, "they need to find something for you to do before you can sit there all day." Several young people asked for more hands-on learning projects. When I asked a 16-year-old Mexican-American boy what his teachers were like we had the following exchange:

Student: Some are cool and some are goofy.
Me: What makes them cool and what makes them goofy?
Student: They's cool when they works with you one on one and can take a joke.
Me: Does that disrupt class?
Student: Not really.

This young man then went on to describe how he got in trouble in school when he socialized too much at the end of the last quarter. Another boy told me that schools would be improved if, "the school week was shorter, like three or four days a week, and vary the schedule more." A Latino boy in an interview described a teacher he had in middle school who continued to encourage him over the years. Despite his best efforts to stick with school and please his former teacher, however, he eventually started skipping school. When I asked him why he thought that happened he told me that:

> I got bored doing the same thing every day, doing the same thing in the same room for three hours. I got frustrated. He was a nice teacher. It wasn't him. I don't know man. I was doing dumb stuff.

My informants repeatedly and consistently reported that school is boring. This was reported by boys and girls of various ages and ethnicities. My informants repeatedly criticized the education they had received both in terms of pedagogy and curriculum. They often could not find the words to fully describe what was wrong with the education they had received. Taking the total of my observations, interviews, and conversations with the young people into consideration, I would describe what they are calling for in schools, translated into the academic language of educational theory, as contextualized learning that relates to their actual lives in the community, with teachers who care about them on a personal basis and who can "have a laugh"[9] and "make school fun," experiential and hands-on learning, a classroom environment that includes social interaction such as group work and discussion, as well as a varied routine that includes the opportunity to stretch one's legs.[10]

Reforms of this nature have been advocated by educators going back to John Dewey's laboratory school and can be found today in many alternative school settings. Whether one agrees with them or not, the young people in my study are attempting to make reasonable suggestions about how to improve schools that must be considered by educators, academics, and policy makers. L. Janelle Dance (2002) formed similar conclusions in her study:

> According to the students in my study, the qualities that gave a teacher favorite-teacher status included having a good sense of humor, which makes learning fun yet educational, understanding and encouraging students, being someone whom students can talk and look up to, being concerned about students and having time for them, and believing in students' ability to meet academic requirements. The one characteristic that all favorite teachers have in common is the ability to convince students that they genuinely care. (p. 75)

Put another way, schools need to better account for the energy of youth. But it is more than a matter of youthful energy. If we want students who have struggled with their academics (and who may have numerous difficulties in life that are associated with poverty and racism, who may have depressed self-esteem, and who are not sure if they even believe in the future) to trust us and make better efforts in school, then we need to assure that they are not miserable in the classroom. There are sound pedagogical and even moral reasons for creating the types of learning environments advocated by writers such as Dewey (1916/44), Freire (1970/93), and others. But those approaches to education would also fail, when working with populations of students like my informants, if they were implemented in an idealized manner that did not take into account the physical, emotional, developmental, and intellectual needs of students.

Certainly, no learning can occur if students have the expectation that learning does not require discipline. However, when students are already struggling to find the motivation to exercise this academic discipline, particularly when they are confronted with the range of disadvantages that many of my informants face, I would argue that good teaching must start where students are. We should help them to develop the discipline that they will need, rather than expecting them to come to school ready to function as well as students who, for a variety of reasons (including family support, economic advantages, and prospects for the future) are better able to discipline themselves. By utilizing a more interactive approach to instruction that is also tied to the real-world experiences of the young people it might be possible to kindle the interests of these young people in learning once again. The better aspects of the instruction at the center, such as the discussion sessions, and my interactions with students in which we attempted to place assignments into a more meaningful context, tend to show that by honoring some of the suggestions for educational change my informants have called for, it would be possible to capture their interest more of the time.

Caring Teachers

I have no doubt that there are teachers in the public schools, despite increasing pressure to rank and test, who have meaningful relationships with students, as the center teaching staff have, by virtue of their caring and creativity (Shor, 1980/87). In fact, my informants were quick to mention individual teachers who had encouraged them and cared for them. As one boy told me, despite having been expelled from school, "they [his teachers] helped me and did what they could for me." Caring and attention on the part of teachers are memorable to the population with whom I was working, particularly so because they are not the norms in their experiences. Caring and attention can only go so far towards changing the aspirations and economic prospects of young people from the economic margins of society, but my research seems to indicate that having teachers who are perceived by students as being caring is essential, if not sufficient, for educational improvement. Having caring teachers may also help to counteract the depressed self-esteem of academically struggling students.

When discussing the educational struggles of my informants, it may seem simplistic to suggest that their educational difficulties were even partially the result of teachers not showing them enough compassion or concern. Even when students report having had caring teachers, this has not necessarily prevented them from having difficulties in school or from dropping out. This would seem to indicate that the educational difficulties of my informants are not preventable simply by improving student-teacher interactions. Nonetheless, my informants consistently told me that they considered good teachers and their favorite teachers to be those who took an interest in them on a personal level and attempted to understand their problems. As one 16-year-old girl told me, good teachers "try to understand what kids go through." A boy of the same age described a good teacher as someone who tries to "know you better personally." Speaking of his teachers, a 15-year-old boy commented that, "I don't like 'em. They treated me unfair. Good teachers listen to you." Young people of differing genders, ages, and ethnicities consistently reported this essential characteristic of good teacher as caring. That I heard this so often from young people who were not at the center at the same time was significant.

My research does not suggest that the primary reason that students have educational difficulties is a feeling that their teachers do not care for them on a personal level, nor is it because of conflicts with teachers. It does suggest, however, that the young people in my study, despite having little trust in their teachers in general, still wanted very much for their teachers to be more concerned about them. When they did feel that teachers cared for them and took an interest in them, it made an impact on their lives. The center teacher made such an impression on them, and they spoke of former teachers who cared for them with genuine gratitude. Even when describing teachers whom they perceived as less than compassionate towards them, my informants would often display sympathy towards them. As one boy stated when I asked him what he would change about his teachers if he could, he said he would "make them happy, because they're burned out like a bulb." Underneath the animosity that has so frequently been documented between struggling students and their teachers (Dance, 2002; Fine, 1991), my research suggests that there is an estranged relationship between them, longing for reconciliation.

The young people in my study who expressed such a strong desire to have their teachers care about them might not have repaid the effort on the part of their teachers by being attentive pupils. This was not the case at the center either. I should also state again that I have not observed my informants in their previous schools. From what they described about their classroom experiences and from my observations of them in educational settings at the center, however, I suspect that classroom interactions and learning could be improved if more teachers took the time to deal with students as people first and students second. This is what my informants say that they desire from their teachers. Such improved relations might not have led to improved outcomes for most of these students, but without this quality of interaction it is doubtful that these students will ever respond more favorably to instruction, even if the other obstacles to their educational success were removed.

In his book *Savage Inequalities* (1991), Jonathan Kozol discusses the importance of having caring teachers while cautioning us that caring is not sufficient to effect real changes in student outcomes:

> There are wonderful teachers such as Corla Hawkins almost everywhere in urban schools, and sometimes a number of such teachers in a single school. It is tempting to focus on these teachers and, by doing this, to paint a hopeful portrait of the good things that go on under adverse conditions. There is, indeed, a growing body of such writing; and these books are sometimes very popular, because they are consoling.

> The rationale behind much of this writing is that pedagogic problems in our cities are not chiefly matters of injustice, inequality or segregation, but of insufficient information about teaching strategies: If we could simply learn "what works" in Corla Hawkins' room, we'd then be in a position to repeat this all over Chicago and in every other system.

> But what is unique in Mrs. Hawkins' classroom is not what she does but who she is. Warmth and humor and contagious energy cannot be replicated and cannot be written into any standardized curriculum. (p. 51)

Kozol's findings and analysis are consistent with my own on this point. Though having caring teachers alone cannot make up for structural inequalities, eliminating inequalities alone would not, in and of itself, provide the caring teachers who are needed either.

The expressed desire of my informants to have their teachers care about them may indicate that the defiant or disinterested behavior of young people in classrooms is related to a sense of being insulted or hurt by teachers they perceive as not caring enough about them. Of course, teachers may care about their students and yet their students may not realize it. I have not observed their former teachers in the classroom. It may be that many teachers seem uncaring when they are attempting simply to maintain a professional tone of interaction with their students. With the population of students in my study, however, such a professional stance is probably counterproductive.

Angela Valenzuela (1999) explores in detail the importance of caring in teacher-student relations. Her findings are consistent with my own and the statements of her informants are similar to those made by my informants. Drawing on the work of Noddings and Gilligan, she describes a process in which both students and teachers are actively engaged in caring behaviors towards each other, but with each expressing a different form of caring. Both teachers and students expressed the need to feel cared for by the other. Students wanted to be cared for on a personal basis. Teachers thought they were showing caring by focusing on the academic development of their students. Teachers wanted students to care for them by demonstrating respect and interest in their efforts to teach them. Both teachers and students wanted the respect of their peers. She confirmed the relationship between feelings of not being cared for and student opposition:

> What looks to teachers and administrators like opposition and lack of caring, feels to students like powerlessness and alienation. Some students' clear perception of the weakness of their position politicizes them into deliberately conveying an uncaring attitude as a form of resistance not to education, but to the irrelevant, uncaring, and controlling aspects of schooling. (p. 94)

The desire on the part of students to have teachers relate to them and care about them on a personal basis was also documented by L. Janelle Dance (2002). One of the adult staff at the center who was very good at showing the young people that she cared about them told me in a private interview, "One person caring about them makes the difference in those who survive and those who don't." Teachers are often the most stable adult in the lives of young people from struggling families in struggling communities. Young people need their teachers to believe in and care about them.

In my discussion of the desire on the part of my informants to have teachers who relate to them on a personal basis I do not mean to discount the importance of an academic focus or to ignore the need for teachers to maintain a professional demeanor. For students with more resources in their lives the encouragement of teachers may be less critical when this encouragement is available from parents or other adults. In saying this I do not mean to imply that families of less means do not encourage their children, as a whole.

But for students from neighborhoods and families where there are few examples of academic success, the encouragement of teachers who by definition are academically successful (college educated) carries greater weight. At the same time, young people like those in my study may have serious doubts about their academic abilities as well as about the economic viability of education. They find it very difficult to remain consistently committed to working hard in school because of the promise of some distant future, whereas students from wealthier families are certain of that future. Students like those in my study are more likely to set aside their doubts about the payoff for sticking with school, and to do the harder underlying work of learning to feel better about their own academic potential, if they feel they are returning the favor of their teacher's affection.

The self-esteem struggle of these students reminds me of the work of Paulo Freire teaching peasant farmers literacy in Brazil in the early 1960s. For these people, who had for generations been told by every authority in their lives, from the landlords to the church, that they were intellectually inferior, the greatest obstacle to their learning to read was the internalized belief that they were not capable of intellectual activities in general. To address this emotional struggle, Freire developed a process by which his cultural workers would help the peasants to realize that in various activities, from writing songs to basket weaving, they were already engaged in intellectual activities no less significant than reading. Once the peasants came to this realization they were inspired by their own abilities and learned to read in a very short time frame. Their learning to read so quickly, in as little as 30 hours, was probably assisted by the phonemic nature of the Portuguese language, but it would not have been possible had they not first learned to believe in themselves (Brown, 1974; Freire, 1970a, 1970/94). What I am suggesting is that the first responsibility of a teacher working with students like those in my study is to convince them that they are worthy of care.

Jobs and Education

Reflecting on the statements of my informants in the writing of this section I realize that the desire for and difficulty in finding and keeping employment expressed by many of them speaks to more than their immediate needs and understanding of their economic prospects in the future. When I would ask young people about their struggles in school, they would often raise the issue of employment. At first I found this a bit odd. In time I came to view the close relationship between employment and education, in their way of thinking, as significant. Jobs and education, in their way of thinking, needed to be realized in the present. When I asked one young man if there was anything he'd like to tell my audience, he responded: "stop the violence, get the kids in school, so to find a job." I believe that statements like this do not speak to a future payoff for an education. Such a future is too distant and unknowable. I believe that they were longing for an education that would tie instruction to real work, support them in their efforts to develop the social skills required in the work place, and to provide them with concrete evidence (by way of an employment experience) that they could in fact find a place in the legal job market. They also need the income that work provides.

Where John Dewey taught subject matter around the idea of occupations, the young people in my study would not be satisfied to merely play at or discuss possible future occupations; they wanted instruction tied to real work. One young man in my study spoke of his experience in the past on a work release program, and while he said it was a good thing, it did not provide him with all that he needed. He was simply released into the adult world for part of the day with no guidance. Rather than practicing for the real world of work in an idealized and safe environment, as Dewey conceived of students in school, they wanted and needed to enter the real world of work, but to have their hands held in the process.

Lessons Learned

My informants conveyed, in verbal and nonverbal ways, a great deal of confusion regarding their views on pedagogy and classroom environments. They were quick to admit their failures at focusing on their schoolwork[11] or in attending school regularly, and yet they conveyed their deep desires to be successful in school. At the same time they conveyed the hurt they have experienced from some unkind teachers or teachers they perceived as either not caring about them or not understanding the environments in which they lived. Despite the harm they perceived, my informants were quick to praise teachers whom they believed had attempted to help them. They seemed to have difficulty sorting out the reasons for their own difficulties in school.

The claims that I would make in this chapter are admittedly limited. Classroom practices and educational policies, though worthy of detailed study, are not the focus of this book; my focus is on the relationship between school failure, the political economy, and incarceration. I include this chapter in order to provide some context for the reader about the life of the center and life in the center school. Being the only chapter that sets aside, for the most part, the critical element of the book, this chapter serves as a methodological check on the rest of the book. It is useful in this regard in sorting out the extent to which the problems I might associate with larger structural forces might instead be the result of practical curriculum choices. The strength of my claims in this chapter are also limited by the general reluctance of my informants to discuss their educational difficulties and experiences, and by my unwillingness to push my informants to say more than they felt comfortable saying. Nonetheless, what my informants told me about school practices, along with my attempts to flesh out their tentative statements, deserved to be documented and reported here, if only to provide clues for future inquiries with similar populations that might have a more explicit focus on educational practice and policy.

From the statements of the young people I did identify some suggestions for improving schools. My informants were calling for teachers to know them as individuals, to be more enthusiastic about teaching, to spend time with them individually, to accommodate laughter into classroom discourse, to allow for social interaction in classroom instruction, to use hands-on teaching projects, to have field trips to the outside world, to have their lessons relate to their lives, and to help them sort out the limited choices they perceive for themselves in their futures. Aside from what my informants told me about what would improve education, I observed that most of my informants suffered from some degree of lowered self-esteem related to education. I argued that this lowered self-image must be countered with an approach to teaching that takes as its primary lesson helping young people to come to believe in their own personal and intellectual worth.

I do not know the extent to which such changes in curriculum and pedagogy would have resulted in improved academic outcomes, or in my informants having avoided being in detention. I will argue in the concluding chapter that such changes are essential but not sufficient to improve the lives of young people like those in my study. Conclusions aside, it is useful to examine these educational questions in relative isolation before turning in subsequent chapters to more fully examine the relationship between schooling (both as perceived by informants and in structural terms), the political economy, and the prison industrial complex.

Chapter 4
Perspectives on the Economy
and Hopes for the Future

In this chapter I will discuss the perspectives of my informants on the economy, the importance they attribute to education as it relates to securing employment, both for themselves and their peers, and to their hopes for the future. The impact that their views on education, schooling, and the future have on the choices they make will also be discussed. Finally, the perspectives of my informants, along with my observations and findings, will be compared with those of other ethnographers who have looked at similar questions during this and other historical periods.

The Historical Relationship Between the Economy and Schooling

Few historians would deny that since World War II the importance of having an education in securing employment has increased with each generation. The importance of having a high school diploma in securing employment began to increase during the same period that the first generation of working-class students began attending college with federal financial aid. These were the sons and daughters of World War II veterans who themselves had been the first generation of working-class students to attend college in any significant numbers, given the G.I. Bill. The G.I Bill had been created largely as an unemployment control mechanism to prevent massive unemployment among soldiers returning to an economy that was slowing down from wartime production. The politicians, universities, and social planners had not expected the veterans to be academically successful in college, but most exceeded all expectations, and many were more successful at their studies than the sons and daughters of privilege. For this generation of working-class families who had suffered so much during the Great Depression and the war that followed, the myth of upward mobility and equal opportunity in the United States suddenly seemed a reality as large numbers of working-class men found themselves in professional jobs (Cremin, 1951; Connell, 1993; Nasaw, 1984).

Once the flood of G.I.s had graduated, financial aid was expanded beyond the G.I. Bill in order to accommodate the heightened expectations and demands of working-class families, as well as the enrollment needs of the now larger university system (Presidents Commission on Higher Ed., 1947; Shor, 1980). Higher education was finally within the reach of most academically capable students (though racism restricted the range of institutions available to students of color). Middle- and upper-class professional families found that they had to compete with upstart working-class students for admissions to the same colleges and for the same jobs upon graduation. Working-class students, in no small part in an effort to avoid being drafted to fight in Vietnam, took advantage of financial aid and open enrollment policies. In order to contain this "flood" of the "plain people," who were competing for draft-exempting seats that would otherwise have been taken by middle-class students, admissions requirements to four-year universities and colleges were raised. At the same time a system of community colleges with lower tuition and easier admissions requirements sprung up like mushrooms around the country in a deliberate attempt to divert working-class students away from elite institutions (Kliebard, 1995; Nasaw, 1984; Shor, 1980/87). The high school diploma became the first requirement for admissions to higher education and for receiving federal financial aid. All of this took place in the context of a fairly strong domestic economy, low unemployment, social supports for poor and unemployed families, as well as a largely unionized labor market.

This period of relative economic prosperity, one that did not extend for the most part to poor people of color, was followed by the economic insecurity of the late 1970s (given the instability of capitalist production), the growth of international and then transnational corporations that began to threaten domestically based production jobs, an ever-expanding military budget justified by the Cold War, and finally, by Reaganomics in the 1980s (MacLeod, 1987/95). Working-class families, many of whom now fancied themselves new members of the middle class, saw their American dreams devastated as they found themselves worse off than their parents, unable to buy homes or keep jobs that paid more than a minimal wage. Competition for admissions to college, particularly elite institutions, and for professional employment therefore continued to intensify.

We now find ourselves in a historical period of intense educational competition that reaches down to the earliest grades in school and is accompanied by extreme differences in the quality of educational facilities and instruction available to students given their social class (Kozol, 1991; Polakow, 2000). This intensified competition has contributed to massive dropout rates among working-class students and students of color. Unemployment is relatively low, though deliberately underreported (Miller, 2004; Streitfeld, 2003), but jobs providing a living wage, health benefits, or prospects for advancement are scarce for workers lacking a college degree, and all the more so for those lacking a high school diploma. At the same time the value of the college degree has declined and provides little job security in the new global economy.

In this new global economy the need for a large domestic labor force is declining. Domestic workers, though still needed, are in increasingly lower demand except for service industry jobs, and these jobs are themselves increasingly held by undocumented immigrants who are forced to work sweatshop hours at further reduced wages and jobs that are, to an increasing extent, being replaced by new technologies (McGrew, 2004). Late capitalism, freed from any obligations to the domestic workforce in any given nation-state, holds little opportunity for the lower classes in the United States. Thus, in recent years, the largest growth area in the United States domestic economy has been the prison system and the industries that have developed to support the incarceration of over 2 million persons (Beatty et al., 2000). The new prison economy requires inmates.[1] Resulting from this systemic need (see Parenti, 2000), working-class students, particularly students of color, are more likely to be incarcerated than to attend any institution of higher learning (Justice Policy Institute, 2002).

Educational ethnographies, particularly critical ethnographies, which have attempted to document and interpret the perspectives of working-class students on the economy and their hopes for the future, have done so during the differing historical periods I described. What the students told these ethnographers, as well as their findings and theoretical orientations, were a product of the time in which they were writing. As my informants try to make sense of the economy and the economic benefits of an education, they do so in a historical context that they know little about but which, nonetheless, influences their views and prospects. They have been influenced by the popular notion that an education pays off in terms of employment, at least so far as a college degree is concerned. Teachers, who are among the primary missionaries of the idea of the economic promise of schooling for poor students, often use the promise of economic prosperity or the threat of economic failure in an attempt to discipline students in the classroom (Levy, 1970; MacLeod, 1987/95, p. 97). At the same time, these students have few examples in their own lives of economic mobility resulting from schooling. In evaluating the statements of my participants along with my observations at the research site, I have attempted to keep in mind the historicity that informs both their perspectives and my own.

Reproduction and Resistance

My informants have never heard of reproductive or resistance theories (also referred to, respectively, as social reproduction and cultural production theory). And yet these are the two primary critical theoretical orientations by which social theorists attempt to understand the lives of working-class students. I approached my research assuming that both structural reproduction and resistance would likely be present. I attempted to elicit from my participants their views on these theories and to keep an open mind towards alternative explanations. I thought it likely, given the findings of other studies, that my participants would articulate attitudes of conformity or resistance to schooling in relation to their views of the economic benefits of an education. As will be discussed in this section, however, my conversations with the young people in my study, as well as my review of the literature related to resistance theory, have led me to strictly qualify the extent to which I now view resistance as part of the explanation for the school failure and legal troubles of my informants.

The Historical Development of Reproductive and Productive Theories

Early critical studies of the relationship between the political economy and schooling emphasized the reproductive role of education in maintaining existing class relations. Gerald Levy, in *Ghetto School* (1970), for example, describes in painful detail the process by which teachers in the school where he conducted his fieldwork resorted over time, and despite their good intentions towards their students, to verbal and physical abuse in order to maintain order in the classroom and thereby keep their jobs. Many of these teachers were avoiding the draft by teaching in the school, so the pressure to keep their jobs was greater than normal. He viewed schooling in poor communities of color as training poor students for ghetto life. The most influential of the early reproductive theorists were Samuel Bowles and Herbert Gintis, who published their ideas in *Schooling in Capitalist America* in 1976. They argued that schooling socializes students to their place in the class hierarchy, thereby helping to "defuse and depoliticize the potentially explosive class relations of the production process, and thus serves to perpetuate the social, political, and economic conditions through which a portion of the product of labor is expropriated in the form of profits" (p. 11).

Bowles and Gintis were criticized for being too deterministic in their theory, for viewing the working class in a stereotyped and disrespectful manner, and for failing to consider the intelligence and culture of working-class people in resisting repressive structures and institutions. Apple (1982) makes this point, writing that: "If schools are wholly determined and can do no more than mirror economic relations outside of them, then nothing can be done within the educational sphere" (p. 68). In *Official Knowledge* (1993/2000), Apple expands the argument to account more for the struggles between the right and the left, writing, for instance, that "the powerful are not that powerful. The politics of official knowledge are the politics of accords or compromises" (p. 10).

Schooling in Capitalist America was followed the next year with the publication of *Learning to Labor* (1977/81) by Paul Willis. Willis followed the lives of working-class lads in England. This was a departure from reproductive theories in that it stressed starting with the experiences and perspectives of informants before considering them in the context of economic structures or theories. Willis did not deny the relationship between capitalism and schooling, but stressed that any attempts to impose this reproduction model on working-class students must consider their agency. As he stated, "The difficult thing to explain about how working class kids get working class jobs is why they let themselves. It is much too facile simply to say that they have no choice" (p. 1). He found that it was the opposition of the lads to the view that the wealthier classes held of them that led them to embrace manual labor and to reject intellectual work, thus contributing actively to their own relegation to working-class jobs.[2] The influence of his work contributed greatly to what Raymond Morrow and Carlos Torres described as the shift away from the correspondence principal "beginning in the late 1970s... a move away from the structural link between economic and educational structures" (pp. 44–45).

As the importance of having an education to enter into middle-class professional jobs became more entrenched in society over time, the opposition to education took on new and increasingly complicated forms. Robert Everhart (1983), for instance, found that White working-class boys in the junior-high school where he conducted his research conformed with the expectations of the educational system in order to gain future benefits. That is to say that they played along, but never internalized the ideology of conformity for success as the "ear' oles" had in the study by Willis. Likewise, Weis (1990) found that the working-class boys in her study conformed enough to pass, while rejecting the system to which they were conforming. As she stated: "It is not the flavor of Willis's Lads at all; indeed, even those most negative about school concede the importance of 'credential' " (p. 24). They saw this as the price they had to pay in order to graduate and find skilled jobs that remain associated with the working class and masculinity, such as machinists or mechanics.

A compelling account of the conflicted feelings of working-class folks related to the economic payoff of schooling is provided by Jay MacLeod in his book *Ain't No Makin' It* (1987/95). He found that most of the working-class White youth in his study, the Hallway Hangers, whose parents' expectations had been devastated by the conservative restoration begun under the Reagan presidency, flatly rejected the ideology of upward mobility through education. As he states, "Refusing to risk hope... [they] adjust their occupational goals to the only jobs that they perceive to be available – unskilled manual work" (p. 68). On the other hand, he found that working-class African-American students, the Brothers, had great aspirations towards college and professional employment.[3] In the 1995 edition of the book MacLeod follows up with both groups of students. The Hallway Hangers, who had accepted manual labor as their fate, had been devastated by the shifts in the economy that eliminated many of the jobs that they had thought they could depend on. Now they faced unemployment, low-wage jobs, and jail. The Brothers, who had worked hard in school and believed in the fairness of the new America, had come to feel betrayed by their country or else to blame themselves for their failure. Ultimately, MacLeod argues that structure and agency are inseparable. As he states:

> Super is aware, for example, that the economy's recessionary plunge means fewer legitimate jobs are available and that his high school diploma is far less helpful than he imagined. He also believes that cocaine capitalism proffers more of a career structure than do legitimate jobs in the new postindustrial economy. Pushed from behind and pulled from the front by structural forces, Super's entry into the informal economy is nevertheless his own decision individually taken. Super jumps into the cocaine trade because he wants to... And yet the decision cannot be understood apart from the structural limitation on his options. In the end, perhaps the fairest account is that Super was pushed into jumping. (p. 255)

Additional studies have documented what I and others refer to as the "mixed feelings" (Cho, 1997; Sennett and Cobb, 1972; Connell, 1993) of members of the working class as to the economic viability of a high school or even a college diploma.

A final development in the world of critical theories of education and society has been the influence of poststructural and postmodern theories of power (see Morrow & Torres, 1994), most frequently associated with the work of Michael Foucault and Pierre Bourdieu. There is considerable debate as to whether these theoretical approaches should be considered part of the family of critical studies. I reject this theoretical movement in its most recent forms as being internally inconsistent and out of touch with knowable reality in its denial of the very existence of social class structure. Nonetheless, post-structural theories have brought awareness to subtle, psychological, cultural, "hidden," and even subconscious aspects of power relations. This contribution to our collective knowledge is significant. It is the influence of these theories that leads Philippe Bourgois (2003) to argue that: "This 'street culture of resistance' is not a coherent, conscious universe of political opposition but, rather, a spontaneous set of rebellious practices that in the long term have emerged as an oppositional style" (p. 8).

Resisting Straw Men

I agree that the work of Bowles and Gintis would have been stronger had they done more to include the voices of working-class students. At the same time, I believe the criticism of their work is overstated. They did in fact address the contradictory class-consciousness of human actors and recognized human agency, despite criticism that says otherwise. Consider the following passages from their book:

> Workers are neither machines nor commodities but, rather, human beings who participate in production with the aim of satisfying their personal and social needs. The central problem of the employer is to erect a set of social relationships and organizational forms, both within the enterprise and, if possible, in society at large, that will channel these aims into the production and expropriation of surplus value. Thus as a social process, capitalist production is inherently antagonistic and always potentially explosive. (1976, p. 10)

> ... though the school system has effectively served the interests of profit and political stability, it has hardly been a finely tuned instrument of manipulation in the hands of socially dominant groups... The authoritarian classroom does produce docile workers, but it also produces misfits and rebels. (p. 12)

This is not merely "lip service" to human agency (Weiler, 1988). Rather, they saw the structural needs of reproduction as overwhelming any resistance of the working class, and they saw this as being almost inevitable.[4]

Jeanie Oakes has argued that the work of Bowles and Gintis is not necessarily at odds with that of Willis:

> The existence of student resistance, however, does not contradict Bowles and Gintis's view of the role and function of schools in reproducing the work force. To the contrary, it explains how this happens in a way consistent with what we know

about how many low-achieving students behave. The act of resisting what schools
offer is part of how social and economic reproduction occurs. (1985/2005, p. 120)

A similar argument was made by Rikowski (1997, p. 551). The criticism of
Bowles and Gintis can't be dismissed simply as a failure to read their words
carefully, in my view. I believe they have been treated unfairly. Their own
words contradict the claim that they view the oppressed as "being simply
passive in the face of domination" (Giroux, 1983, p. 108). Rather, as Willis
himself stated in defense of the fact that his study did not address a variety of
important issues, "One chooses a main focus" (1981, p. 62). Bowles and
Gintis chose to take a macroeconomic look at the role of the educational system in capitalism.

The problem that Bowles and Gintis were grappling with is a central
problem that Paulo Friere (1970/93) addressed in most of his work. This is
the problem of working in an educational system that is part of an exploita-
tive economic system, and yet attempting to change the system from within.
Freire provides a sophisticated analysis and strategies for accomplishing this
seemingly contradictory task; a task that Bowles and Gintis argued was impossible. As he wrote:

> Problem-posing education does not and cannot serve the interests of the oppressor.
> No oppressive order could permit the oppressed to begin too question: Why? While
> only a revolutionary society can carry out this education in systematic terms, the
> revolutionary leaders need not take full power before they can employ the method.
> In the revolutionary process, the leaders cannot utilize the banking method as an in-
> terim measure, justified on the grounds of expediency, with the intention of *later*
> behaving in a genuinely revolutionary fashion. They must be revolutionary — that
> is to say, dialogical — from the outset. (p. 86)

The harshest critics of Bowles and Gintis (from the left) would not, I dare
say, criticize Freire in the same manner, and in fact often identify with his
work.[5]

For Freire, education is "an objective structure that reflects dominant interests and values that function to reproduce the contradictions of a given
society within its existing power relations" (Uhl & Tewksbury 1986, p. 81).
Freire was a reproductive theorist. He was also a ruling-class theorist. As he
wrote in *A Pedagogy for Liberation* (Shor & Freire, 1987), "a main task of
the ruling elite, or one of its main tasks proposed by the ruling class for education, or one of its main expectations from schools... is precisely the reproduction of the dominant ideology" (p. 35). He goes on to write that we know
that it's not education that shapes society, but on the contrary, it is society
that shapes education according to the interest of those who have power (pp.

35–36). Driving this point home, in "Twenty Years After Pedagogy of the Oppressed" Freire tells us that:

> A power elite will not enjoy putting in place and practicing a pedagogical form or expression that adds to the social contradictions which reveal the power of the elite classes. It would be naive to think that a power elite would reveal itself for what it is through a pedagogical process that in the end would work against the elite itself. (Torres & Freire, 1994, p. 106)

Criticisms of reproduction theory for what is described as "the reductionist notion of false consciousness" (Giroux, 1983, p. 123) and claims that theories of false consciousness associated with some versions of reproductive theory posit "the ox-like stupidity of the dominated class" (Willis, 1981, p. 54), are a rejection of a central concept in Friere's work (1970/93, p. 74), Marxism, and, more broadly, seem to deny much of the literature in the study of socialization and psychology. Scholars can raise what arguments as they like, but those associated with critical theory undermine the theory with such inconsistencies. The question can be stated rather directly: are there structural forces of reproduction that attempt to maintain existing class positions and roles in the capitalist production process? Whether resistance is occurring, and what we mean by resistance, are separate question that I will address later in this chapter.

While defending Bowles and Gintis against unfair double standards and inconsistency within critical theory, I will mention another area of agreement between them and Friere. They state in *Schooling in Capitalist America* that "the liberal goal of employing the educational system as a corrective device for overcoming the 'inadequacies' of the economic system is vain indeed" (1976, p. 148). This view is reflected in Jean Anyon's recent work:

> Failing public schools in cities are, rather, a logical consequence of the U.S. macroeconomy — and the federal and regional policies and practices that support it. (2005, p. 2)

> As a nation, we have been counting on education to solve the problems of unemployment, joblessness, and poverty for many years... [but] education cannot solve them. An economic system that chases profits and casts people aside (especially people of color) is culpable. (p. 3)

Unlike Anyon, who argues that what is needed is a social movement for economic justice (p. 10) and increased taxation of the wealthy (p. 57), and may view this as sufficient, Bowles and Gintis go beyond this interim stage to argue that what is needed is revolutionary change (p. 246). Freire's examination of oppression and revolution is more sophisticated and multifaceted

(1970/93, p. 128) than the one advanced by Bowles and Gintis. It cannot be reasonably denied, however, that part of his notion of revolution included moving from an economic system of capitalism to a socialist one. Democracy and capitalism are indeed contradictory (Bowles & Gintis, 1986, p. 3). Moreover, capitalism cannot, in the long term, reconcile the drive to maximize profits for the few with the liberal goal of, merely, eliminating poverty among the Proletariat. Here I think I find common ground with Freire, Marx, Bowles and Gintis, and the recent work by McLaren & Scatamburlo-D'Annibale (2004).

At times critics of reproduction theory, especially critics who do not identify with the political left, try to dismiss the entire critical tradition beginning with Marx with their arguments against reproduction theory (Kingston, 1986; Hargreaves, 1982). Arguments that Marxism is vulgar, crass, reductive, deterministic, simplistic, and fails to account for the role of human agency, seem to miss the centrality of struggle in his work. As Michael Apple has noted, "It has been stated that the most significant contribution to the understanding of society made by Marx was his insight that a major source of change and innovation is internal conflict" (1971, p. 35). If Marx had believed that reproduction under capitalism was monolithic and that human actors did not have the potential to exert their agency, he could not have published with Engels, in 1848, those famous words:

> The proletarians have nothing to lose but their chains.   They have the world to
> win. WORKINGMEN OF ALL COUNTRIES, UNITE! (1964, p. 116)

I am not denying that some Marxist scholars have held simplistic reproductive notions, but not Marx himself, and not, as I have argued, Bowles and Gintis. I also am not claiming that Marxism or reproductive theory is perfect, or that I agree with everything written from that perspective. I am claiming that the attacks against reproduction (from scholars associated with critical theory as well as those who are not) have misunderstood the ideas being criticized, have attacked some reproductive theorists while embracing others, and generally have constructed a straw man for their kicking, particularly as related to the work of Bowles and Gintis.

Defining Reproduction, Opposition, and Resistance

This discussion brings us to a significant problem in the critical literature: the lack of clear definitions of what is meant by the use of terms like reproduction, production, opposition, and resistance. Complicating things are authors who do not explicitly identify with reproduction theory, resistance theory, or oppositional culture theory, and yet seem to be working from one of these orientations. Complicating things further are authors who take contradictory positions related to these theoretical orientations, often, it seems, within realizing their self-contradictions or explaining how they might co-exist (see the concluding chapter related to pragmatism). Confusing things is that adherents to resistance/production theory tend to define resistance as conscious/political, unconscious, or some combination of the two. Confounding things is that most of these authors seem to suffer under the illusion that their definition, stated or implicit, is the common and accepted one.

The Need to Name One's Theoretical Orientation

Part of the problem with the lack of an adequate definition for resistance may be the broad use of the word in society and its use by scholars who clearly are not referring to the theory associated with Willis. Howard Zinn for example has stated that for every act of unreported (political) resistance you can assume there are thousands more, leading Stack and Kelly (2006) to argue that there are plural meanings of the word *resistance* (p. 11). Gibson and Ogbu describe defiant behavior, but don't think of it as resistance, using the word *resisted* in a generic manner (1991, p. 182 & 186). Herb Kohl describes politically charged rejections of the false promises of schooling in *I Won't Learn From You* (1994) but does not seem to be articulating resistance theory as such. When we hear *resistance* we think of resistance movements in occupied countries. Waller in *The Sociology of Teaching* uses the word resistance in a generic sense to describe personality struggles between students and teachers (1965, p. 339). We think of the rules of physics. The word carries with it assumptions about intentionality and political motive that Willis may not have intended to convey. If so, it was a bad choice of name. I am not the first author to argue the need for clarity of definitions of resistance (Aggleton & Whitty, 1985; Giroux, 1983; Noguera & Cannella, 2006).

Looking at a pivotal text in the tradition of critical ethnography, *Framing Dropouts* (1991) by Michelle Fine, we see that resistance is not defined, though the word is used, and numerous examples of oppositional behavior are described. The data in the book document the silencing of students by teachers, cultural and interpersonal conflicts between poor students and teachers, and the bureaucratic response to overcrowding. It does not, however, map out a process by which working-class youth reject the false promise of schooling and therefore decide to drop out of school. Though some students possessed a critique of the logic of schooling, or at least some elements of critical consciousness, these were not the reasons young people reported dropping out (p. 116). In *Working Class Without Work* (1990) by Lois Weis, another pivotal text in the field, students, especially girls, accept the logic of schooling, but are not academically prepared for college and do not apply to college. Though reproduction is discussed, resistance is not clearly defined in the book. Stacey Lee (2005) makes arguments using the language of resistance but it is not clear if she means resistance in the way that Willis, Ogbu, or MacLeod would use it.

Is Resistance Unconscious?

Patrick Solomon (1992) seems to have a notion of resistance developing outside of the political consciousness of young people (p. 205), while acknowledging that resistance has been criticized because it "does not distinguish between resistance and other modes of student responses" (p. 12). Michael Apple has described resistance as "almost unconscious" (1980, p. 67). In 1993 McLaren was arguing that resistance can be "unwitting and unconscious" (p. 147). In 1983 Weis argued that resistance was reflected at the cultural level and was unconscious (p. 254–255). Willis himself, of course, has argued that resistance is a matter of "unconscious and collective cultural meanings" (1981, p. 58). There are likely more authors who hold an unconscious notion of resistance than I have identified here.

Is Resistance a Conscious Political Act?

Despite the arguments made by Willis that resistance is not conscious, authors who identify with resistance theory tend to assume that resistance is a conscious act; or else argue that we should call acts that are not political and intentional *opposition* rather than *resistance*. This is ironic in that authors using resistance theory as their orientation do credit Willis for the theory (Gordon, 1984), and, it seems, fail to realize that his notion of resistance is different than their own.

One of the most influential critical ethnographies with a conscious notion of resistance is provided by MacLeod (1987/95). As he stated:

> So the Hallway Hangers are not of the view that success in school is irrelevant but rather that the odds of "making it" are simply too slim to bet on. In what can be likened to a cost-benefit analysis, the Hallway Hangers, much like Willis's lads, conclude that the possibility of upward social mobility is not worth the price of obedience, conformity, and investment of substantial amounts of time, energy, and work in school. (p. 105)

MacLeod engaged in conversations with his informants about the economic viability of an education and his conclusions result from those conversations, so that I have no reason to doubt that the perspectives he presents are accurately those of his informants. I note, however, that he associates his findings with those of Willis, who has a very different notion of what resistance is. Philippe Bourgois (2003) describes the rejection of "legitimate work" in terms that seem to imply a conscious act of resistance. As he states:

> They were usually fired from these jobs, but they treated their return to the world of street dealing as a triumph of free will and resistance on their part. A straightforward refusal to be exploited in the legal labor market pushes them into the crack economy and into substance abuse. (p. 115)

Signithia Fordham (1996) also seems to have a notion of conscious resistance and does not differentiate between resistance and opposition, as she argues that the seeming conformity of Black students to White culture and schooling can also be a form of resistance. Ann Ferguson (2000) describes "active not-learning" as conscious resistance. L. Janelle Dance argues that resistance is a conscious political act when she states that:

> Some students will assume a gansterlike posture as a form of political resistance. These students resist the Euro-assimilationist expectations of mainstream teachers that all students conform to a white, middle-class standard. Student interviews and field observations suggest that mainstream school officials are likely to view boycotting students as troublemakers instead of political activists. (p. 37)

Stacey Lee (2001), working with Hmong students, observed that some students engage in skipping behavior out of a sense of inadequacy related to difficulty in school rather than as a rejection of schooling, while other students resist school "because they do not perceive school to offer real opportunities" (p. 526). In her 2005 book she likewise described conscious politicized resistance among students (p. 31). In her 2004 book Lois Weis now seems to argue that the lads were self-conscious in their rejection of school (p. 197). Additional authors describe and define resistance in a manner that is consistent with it being a conscious act (Abowitz, 2000; Everhart, 1983; Rikowski, 1997; Stack & Kelly, 2006; Valli, 1983; Welsh, 2001).

What's in a Name?

When critical theorists speak of resistance, they may mean different things, while assuming that other critical theorists share their implicit understanding of the meaning of the term. The very name resistance theory implies that what is at issue is resistance to attempts to either reproduce the status of working-class youth or to force upon them the ideology of equal opportunity and mobility. Often what is described as resistance might better be understood as opposition, because it does not stand against the attempts to reproduce class position or force ideology upon the lower classes, but rather describes a complex range of consequences and reactions to these social forces.

I would argue that resistance must be more than defiant behavior. Rather, it must be defiant behavior that constitutes a rejection of the false promise of schooling for equal opportunity and mobility.[6] The Lads in *Learning to Labor* (1977/81) did not deny that white-collar work was preferable to blue-collar work generally, but rather they seemed to think that they were not cut out for it (p. 96). This process might better be described as the internalization of oppression than as resistance.[7] Willis' notions of penetration, in which the Lads seem to have glimpses of reality and question the value of qualifications, could also be viewed as a psychological response to, and lashing out against, the internalized self-loathing that schooling has taught them (p. 78). Oppositional behavior, then, is an attempt to create a sphere of interaction in which the youth could feel good about themselves, as measured against their own standards of worth and not those of the dominant society.

There are many reasons that a young person might engage in oppositional behavior that have nothing to do with rejecting the logic of schooling, such as an attempt to impress a girl in class, an attempt to kill boredom, or a personal dislike of a teacher who is perceived as racist in his attitudes towards students of color. Likewise, it is possible to have a developed and articulated critique of the false promise of education for upward mobility under capitalism, which many young people from the lower classes (and in my study) do possess, without that critique contributing prominently to the motives, choices, or actions of youth. Their critique may be overshadowed, for example, by a sense of fatalism or other immediate concerns. It is my position that to say young people are resisting there must be evidence that the choices they make are largely influenced by their rejection of the false promise of schooling.[8]

A young person in the 1960s who quit school and joined the Black Panther Party in order to learn true history instead of the biased history taught in public schools, for example, was engaged in a political act. A young person who disrupts class for the same reasons, but who remains in school, could also be said to be engaging in a political act. A young person who taunts the teacher in order to be cool and masculine, as opposed to feminine and intellectual, in my view, cannot be said to be engaging in equivalent behavior.

This distinction is critical. In my study I was looking in particular for action born of a critique of schooling and the economy.

In *Reconstructing 'Drop-Out'* (1997), Dei, Zine, Mazucca, and McIsaac follow the observation by Giroux (1983) that resistance must "contain a moment of critique and a potential sensitivity to its own interests, i.e., an interest in radical consciousness raising and collective critical action" (p. 110), but argue, nonetheless, that a range of behaviors may be considered resistance, including "adopting styles of dress which conflict with dominant cultural norms" so long as they are "intended to assert the marginalized perspective and attempt to subvert dominant norms and values" (Dei et al., 1997, p. 25). To the extent that Giroux would agree with their position, I must note that my view of resistance is even more restrictive than his. While symbolic politics and oppositional behavior (see also Giroux, 1981) deserve study and may contribute to collective action,[9] resistance is an act of rejecting an oppressive system and the ideology that supports it, but it is not a transformative act. Liberation is transformative. Collective action and activism are transformative. Students who are engaging in resistance, such as students who drop out of school because they view the promise of schooling as a lie, may be close to developing the critical consciousness described by Freire (1970/93) that can lead to collective action (and here the notion of partial penetrations of reality remains useful, despite the sexist uses of the word in other contexts), but dropping out of school, selling drugs, or joining a gang are not positive activities. They are desperate acts that result from partial penetrations (by individuals rather than by culture), but are not tied to activism, and do not represent the radicalization of the students.

Because "language is also a place of struggle" (hooks, 1989, p. 28), and because of the lack of clarity within critical theory, I am arguing that critical theory should adopt the following definitions:

- that oppositional behavior refer to acting out in ways that are not politically informed as a conscious act,
- that resistance refer to the politically charged rejection of schooling and other false promises in capitalist society, but that take self-destructive directions, and
- that politically informed actions that aim to change oppressive conditions and systems, activism, be known by that name. Activists may suffer for their work, but activism is not a simple lashing out or acting out. The students who fought for the diversity days described by Stacey Lee (2005) were not engaging in resistance. They were engaging in activism.

The Problem with Willis

Looking again at *Learning to Labor* (1977/81), we see that Willis was not describing a rejection of the economic benefits of schooling by his Lads. Rather, he was describing a masculine, working-class counterculture that contributed to their being reproduced into working-class jobs, largely as the result of their own choices and oppositional behavior. Their teachers likewise saw their role towards these boys as attempting to teach them basic reading, writing, and mathematics, while teaching them the more important lessons of punctuality and conformity to authority. He did not ask his Lads if they thought schooling would pay off in terms of employment. Rather, he documented their cultural meanings and culturally informed aspirations. Cultural production refers to the act of creating their shared culture. Opposition refers to the acts of defiance displayed by the Lads. The Lads did not so much reject schooling as they identified with their chums, masculinity, patriarchal family structure, and the inevitability of manual labor. The term resistance is seldom used in the book and is not directly defined. It seems to be used interchangeably with opposition.

Willis (1977/81) describes his notion of production and resistance as follows:

> The counter-school culture is involved in its own way with a relatively subtle, dynamic, and, so to speak, 'opportunity-costed' assessment of the rewards of the conformism and obedience which the school seeks to exact from working class kids. In particular this involves a deep seated skepticism about the value of qualifications in relation to what might be sacrificed to get them: a sacrifice ultimately, not of simple dead time, but of a quality of action, involvement and independence. Immediate gratification is not only immediate, it is a style of life and offers the same thing too in ten years time. To be an 'ear'ole' now and to gain qualifications of dubious value might be to close off for ever the abilities which allow and generate immediate gratifications of any kind at any stage. (p. 126)

In other words, the Lads' culture assesses the likely payoff of getting credentials and determines that the payoff is neither certain nor of sufficient value to merit the extra effort and denial of one's culturally based working-class identity.

There are two problems with this notion of resistance. The first problem is that it is not strongly evidenced in the data chapters of his book. Notions of upward mobility via education are discussed by teachers and conformist students, but not by the Lads or their families (pp. 74–77). The Lads are identifying with their counterculture, not rejecting the false promise of schooling, at least as the reported data seem to indicate. I am not the first author to observe this gap between his data and his overarching theory (Davies, 1995, p. 665; Turner, 1979, p. 337; Walker, 1986, p. 67).

Willis reconciles this gap between his evidence related to culture and his theory regarding resistance (and this is the second problem with his notion of resistance) by describing the culture itself as making penetrations that the members of the culture might not, apparently, be conscious of individually. As he states:

> We must distinguish between the level of the cultural and the level of practical consciousness in our specification of creativity and rationality . . . The argument is not that insights are made consciously in any one mind or even in the same mind or groups of minds over time – although the spoken everyday word might illuminate aspects of it variably and in contradiction with itself or perhaps unconsciously. Direct and explicit consciousness may in some sense be our poorest and least rational guide. It may well reflect only the final stages of cultural processes and the mystified and contradictory forms which basic insights take as they are lived out. (p. 122)

Thus it is the culture of the working-class Lads and not the Lads themselves who are engaged in resistance. This reading of his argument is further supported by statements such as, "the culture makes a kind of assessment of the quality of available work" (p. 127) and:

> The counter-school culture makes a real penetration of what might be called the difference between individual and group logics and the nature of their ideological confusion in modern education. The essence of the cultural penetration concerning the school — made unselfconsciously within the cultural milieu with its own practices and objects but determining all the same an inherently collective perspective — is that the logic of class or group interests is different from the logic of individual interests. (p. 128)

This notion of culture as cognizing for its collective members is one that I find entirely unconvincing. Culture is a collection of related, and even contradictory, shared beliefs, rituals, and assumptions, that may be expressed consciously or may shape individuals in ways that they are not consciously aware of. Culture, therefore, is quite powerful in its impact on individuals and societies. But culture has no mind. It does not assess. It does not think. People do those things.[10]

So that it can't be said that he simply failed to state clearly what he meant, I will quote him at length from different publications over the years. In 2000 he wrote that:

> Penetrations can be imagined as a means of a culture 'thinking' for its members. Cultures are good for many things: good to communicate with, good to find identity through, good for establishing mutuality and reciprocity. They are good for all these,

and more perhaps, because at bottom, they are also good for 'thinking with.' (Willis, 2000, p. 35)

In 2003 he wrote that:

> Only a substantial minority from the working class can hope for mobility, and their cultures and dispositions are adapted accordingly. No one else discusses this, but the lads' culture, despite its disorders and chaos, tells them that no amount of extra qualification will improve the position of the whole class; that would constitute, in fact, the dismantling of the whole class society. (p. 394)

Ignoring for the moment the fact that his own data in *Learning to Labor* demonstrates that his Lads were not so unified in their views on the value of credentials (Turner, 1979, p. 337), I will foreshadow later sections in this chapter by stating that my informants reported confusion and mixed feelings related to the economic benefits of an education, not any uniform view, culturally based or otherwise.

In Quoting from his chapter in the collected work that honors the 25th anniversary of *Learning to Labor*, (1977/81), *Learning to Labor in New Times* (2004), he has held tight to the notion that it is culture itself that is making the cost-benefit analysis for the Lads, as is revealed in the following passages:

> This is the very business of ethnography for me. What sense is this culture making of its situation?

> Through the mediations of the counterschool culture, "the lads" of Learning to Labor, for instance, penetrate the individualism and meritocracy of the school with a group logic that shows that certification and testing will never lift the whole working class, only inflate the currency of qualifications and legitimize middle-class privilege. (p. 173)

> . . .

> The argument about the penetrations of cultural forms is not that they come from fully formed preexisting unified subjects, making individual congnitions directly intended to reveal their conditions of existence. Penetrations come about almost randomly in the profane, corporeal, and un-prefigurable operations of cultural forms as they reconnoiter the land in a de facto kind of way, scraping it in the pursuit of their own fullest development in their own terms and for their own potential and objectives.

> Very often, working-class cultural forms expose aspects of social structure "unconsciously." (p. 177)

. . .

> The immediate objectives of "the lads," for instance, is not to further the class struggle but to pursue fun, diversion, "the laff," and "having a go" at disliked figures or restrictive aspects of the specific and concrete regime of the school as it faces them. They are not trying to be good class warriors; they are trying to be good "lads." In pursuit of that some sort of "lived penetrations" of individualism and meritocracy and the nature of labor, power and laboring under capitalism are accomplished, but these are still only cultural revelations. They are not verbally articulated and have to be analyzed almost as the hidden premises on which cultures depend, unconscious assumptions that their members make about how the world works as far as they are concerned. (pp. 177–178)

Again, I am simply not persuaded that culture can somehow make collective assessments of the economic viability of an education on behalf of its members, while they are busy worrying about their girlfriends and trying to impress their mates. In fact, I think this argument is absurd. That I could find no evidence of authors prior to myself honing in on this particular problem in the resistance theory of Willis surprises me greatly.

Resistance and Reproductive Theories Reconsidered

MacLeod and Lee in their studies, as do I in my own study, solicit directly the perspectives of young people on the economic payoff of education from their own words, rather than making indirect inferences from observed cultural norms among their informants. This is, I believe, what is needed to make claims that would support a theory of resistance. As I will argue below, however, any critique by young people of the economy and schools may not be sufficient to conclude that their negative choices were the result of their analysis. Only if they were motivated to action by their critique (actions such as dropping out, goofing off, skipping school, selling drugs, and so forth) can we say that their behavior is explained by resistance theory. That is to say that, given the reported data in MacLeod's book (1987/95), for example, I cannot determine whether the young people told him in no uncertain words that they quit school to sell drugs because they saw continuing their education as a bad bet, or whether he essentially jumped to that conclusion; given statements against the viability of education, the fact that they were selling drugs rather than attending school, and the expectation in the field that such a link might exist. The importance of this distinction crystallized in my thinking when I had the following exchange with a young person in an informal conversation:

Me: So you were in school before you got arrested?
Student: When I went I was, but I sometimes didn't go. Then I just stopped going.
Me: Do you think you'll go back to school again when you get out?
Student: Nah, I won't go back. School don't help you get a job anyway.
Me: Is that why you skipped school, because it wouldn't help you get a job?
Student: No. I quit going because it was boring. I don't need school anyway 'cause I
    write plays.
Me: Going to college is probably the best way to get to be a writer.
Student: My plays are real good. I can get money when I go to Hollywood.

After this conversation I realized the fundamental importance of the follow-up question "is that why" when discussing the relationship between critiques of the economy and education and the choices and actions of young people.

I did not engage in a direct conversation with my informants about reproductive and resistance theories, so named. I did attempt, however, to elicit from them their perspectives on the promise of education in the economy in such a manner as to illuminate theory. We discussed the same theoretical issues in a less theoretical language. I wanted to explore with them how they understood these questions and whether they were actively resisting capitalist reproduction. In informal small group discussions, group discussions, and private interviews, I explored these questions by discussing their views on whether an education would help them get a good job and whether they would have any trouble finding work if they did not finish high school. While I hoped that they would be able to verbalize their perspectives, I also knew that I would have to watch for nonverbal communications and consider the possibility that their actions could contradict any stated views.

Like MacLeod (1987/95), I found that many of my informants were grappling with complex questions about the relationship between schooling, the political economy, and the prison industrial complex as they tried to weigh their individual and collective opportunities for the future. As MacLeod states, "Like social theorists, both the Brothers and the Hallway Hangers wrestle with the roles of structure, culture, and agency in the reproduction of social inequality" (p. 253). I thought it was important to let them weigh in on the theoretical debates that are used to explain their lives.

My informants relied on their experiences, the messages they received in schools and in the media, and on the conversations within Hip Hop music in their efforts to sort out these issues.[11] While I viewed my informants as grappling with these questions in the manner that MacLeod describes, I also found them to be overwhelmed at times and unable to come to consistent conclusions. This should hardly be surprising when the education that they receive seldom addresses the problems in their lives nor teaches critical thinking skills. Like John Ogbu (1992) I found that, "Many of these young people do not really know why they behave the way they do. Nor do they understand the full consequences of their behaviors" (p. xi).

Typical responses to questions about the economic viability of education were that school is "a waste of time," or "there ain't no job waiting for me after school." While many of my informants expressed doubts that schooling would pay off in terms of employment, further exploration revealed that they actually held contradictory views on the question, or were not sure what ultimately to believe. The same students who would denounce education as a false promise for the future would make statements at another moment like one African-American boy made in a private interview, "You need an education, or you can't get a good job. I'll try to finish and I want to prove to god and mom that I can change." When I asked why they thought they or their peers failed in school or did not attend school, the answers that young people gave never articulated an argument consistent with resistance theory. I found few compelling examples of the articulation of resistance that could confirm the theoretical perspective. That is to say that my informants did not seem to think of themselves as resisting. They might say that schooling holds no economic benefits for them, but would not say that it's hard to stay in school *because* they viewed it as a waste of time. They never said that they "goof off" in class or skip school *because* they actively reject schooling as a false promise.

I did document some statements that approximate a reproductive theoretical perspective in the thinking of my informants. One day I met an African-American boy who was sitting at a table on a break period with another boy. When I asked him if he was in school he smiled and said no. I told him that I thought this wasn't good, that he was thinking short term, and should go back to school. His response to me was, "But I think it's just a waste of time, 'cause the world 'gonna end in 2000 anyways." I asked him if by the world ending he meant the Y2K problem.[12] "No, I don't mean Y2K," he said, "they just 'gonna be lock'n everybody up." Looking to the boy next to him he said, "Know what I mean?" The boy nodded that he did in fact know what he meant. Such fatalistic statements cannot be taken to mean that my informants view questions about schooling and the economy in simple reproductive terms, however, because these statements would often give way to reveal their mixed feelings and inability to be sure of what to believe. In fact, the explanations they gave for school failure or dropping out typically involved the influence of peers, boredom in the classroom, drugs and alcohol, problems with particular teachers, or a failure to listen to their mother or grandmother. As one young man told me, "I didn't listen to my momma and now

I'm in here." Often they expressed an inability to understand their own behavior, "I don't know why... I was messin' up."

The young people in my study, as will be discussed in more detail in
chapter 5, viewed the likelihood of their spending time in jails and prisons in
terms that are consistent with reproductive theory. When examining factors
related to school failure, it is clear that the oppositional behavior of many
young people undermines the realization of their academic potential. The
intelligence of these young people is abundantly obvious, so that it cannot be
said that their oppositional behavior merely masks a lack of potential. Even
students who are behind their peers academically could make great strides if
they applied themselves, and most teachers would make extra efforts to help
a student who was determined to make such an educational recovery. The
cards may be stacked against students from the lower classes, particularly so
in the case of students of color, but their educational failure cannot be understood as simply imposed on them. Likewise, the reality of limited opportunities for upward mobility via education exists for some students (though not
for their class as a whole), at least as things stand today, so that individually
students must participate in the reproduction of their class status by not avail-
ing themselves of the opportunities that do exist. The same cannot be said, in
the view of my informants, when it comes to avoiding the prison system.

The young people in my study believed that they could be arrested,
prosecuted, and jailed without cause. In fact, they saw this as a common occurrence, one that would happen to them "sooner or later," and which many
of them believed they had experienced already. Looking beyond the likelihood of being incarcerated on false charges, they felt it even more likely that
they could be arrested and unfairly prosecuted for illegal activities that are
not prosecuted in the case of wealthier White people. Their perspective on
the racial and economic bias in the criminal justice system is supported by a
growing body of literature, some of which has been cited and discussed in
the proceeding chapters. Likewise, their accusations of false arrest, unfair
prosecutions, and perjured police testimony are supported in the literature
(*Win at all costs*, 1998; Ayers, 1997; Dershowitz, 1998; Mollen Report,
1994).

If what they tell me is true, that the police stop young people of color in
acts of racial profiling, plant evidence, conduct illegal searches, and falsely
testify against them, then it is hard to imagine how these young people could
(by means of oppositional behavior, resistance, cultural production, or conformity) avoid getting caught up in the system. Thus the common expression
among my informants to have "caught a charge," as if they had simply been
exposed to a virus, something beyond their control. This describes a truly

reproductive dynamic, in which some young people will be brought to the criminal justice system (resulting in more educational and economic problems) for reasons completely beyond their control. Even if their perspectives are not consistent with reality (and I believe that they are), we should note nonetheless the impact that their reproductive view of their own life chances has on their behavior. Extending Willis' arguments to the topic of the growth of incarceration in the United States, Nolan and Anyon (2004) argue that:

> Oppositional behavior in school — when enacted by Black urban youth in poverty neighborhoods in the United States — does not lead to the shop floor. Rather, in this postindustrial era of mass incarceration, oppositional behavior by working-class youth of color in educational institutions often leads them directly into the criminal justice system. (p. 133)

School failure, failure that is often accelerated by oppositional behavior, can also accelerate the slide towards incarceration, as Nolan and Anyon describe. The young people in my study, however, are under a different type of double bind. If they were all to work as hard as they could in order to stay out of trouble, graduate, and possibly even attend college, not only would many of them not find the meaningful employment that they would deserve (given the lack of employment opportunity in the economy), but they could also be nabbed under false pretences at any time,[13] making all their efforts for naught. The illicit economy beckons while despair pushes one forward.

The young people who had the most clearly articulated critique of the economy and schooling were also the most likely to be serious, or "hard-core," drug dealers. Ironically, they were also the most likely to dream of having a college education and professional work. This finding was somewhat perplexing at first. Whites, though a minority in my study, were more likely to embrace the view that education contributes to future economic success. The views of the young people of color did not seem to differ by gender, but by their relationship to the drug economy. Even students who had left school to sell drugs did not say that they left school because they saw it as a waste of time, but, instead they cited a variety of more immediate considerations.

Many of my informants had very well-developed critiques of the capitalist economy and racism, which they believed meant that there would not be a sufficient number of good jobs available for them, however well they did in school, and that racism would make it difficult for them to get whatever jobs might be available when competing with Whites. As one African-American boy, who had worked in a fast food restaurant, told me:

> When you go in for a job interview at that company, who do you think they're gonna hire? And even if you do gets the job, what will you do? It was always me who had to clean the bathrooms [at the restaurant].

So here is the triple bind facing the young people in my study. If they survived the minefield of police persecution, and climbed the mountain to graduate from college, they would, in their view, not be able to find employment commensurate with their level of training. Their critique echoes those recorded by Bourgois (2003) and by MacLeod (1987/95). When MacLeod asked different young people about their aspirations for the future they told him:

> I ain't goin' to college. Who wants to go to college? I'd just end up getting a shitty job anyway. (p. 3)

> . . .

> Hard to say. I could be dead tomorrow. Around here, you gotta take life day by day.

> I don't fucking know. Twenty years. I may be fucking dead. I live a day at a time. I'll probably be in the fucking pen.

> Twenty years? I'm gonna be in jail. (p. 62)

It seems that it is the uncertainty of the future that that makes young people like those in my study so vulnerable to despair and self-destructive behavior. The bravado and oppositional behavior displayed by my informants, much like that described by Willis, does not reveal their true feelings. As one young man who had "been robbing people" and selling drugs told me, "I don't feel good about nothing I been doing out there. I don't know what else to do."

While I think that we can confidently say that MacLeod's (1987/95) Brothers or Stacey Lee's (1996) Asian-Identified Students conformed with the expectations of the educational system because they believed that there would be an economic payoff for them in the long term, a belief which is not so different from the conformist students identified by Willis (1977/81), I am not confident that we can say that students who do not conform to the expectations of the system, such as MacLeod's Hallway Hangers or Lee's New Wavers, reject schooling primarily because they reject its economic viability. As far as the young people in my study are concerned, the only thing that we can say they were sure of, speaking of them collectively, was that they were unsure of what to believe (and in my opinion were quite frightened of what the future might bring them).[14]

Not finding reproductive and/or resistance theories to be supported in my study in the forms that I had expected has caused me to examine the issues in this chapter in a different light, as Fordham, (1996, p. 339) was forced to for somewhat different reasons. Though students may resist attempts to be relegated to manual labor and may reject what they view as lies about a future that they do not believe in, and while there may be opportunities for some individual social mobility, the class structure in the United States makes school failure necessary and inevitable for large numbers of working-class youth. Willis described the process by which the oppositional behavior of his informants ultimately contributed to the reproduction of their working-class status. In a similar vein, we could say that the confusion of my informants, their mixed feelings about schooling and whether they should have hopes for a better future, individually, by educational achievement, contributed to the reproduction of their status in the lower class. Their mixed feelings motivated many of my informants to stay in school as they still held out some hope for the promise of graduating, but their doubts about the value of education, joined with other problems in the classroom and in their lives, weakened their motivation to give school their best efforts.

The educational efforts made by the students in my study, though inconsistent, were not inconsequential. The competition in schools and increasingly difficult-to-achieve "standards," however, have left them behind in this rigged race of education. Competing with privileged and successful students, with instruction that favors the culture and language of middle-class White families, they could not afford any moments of doubt, or study nights spent watching siblings, or a lack of concentration from hunger, or a toothache.[15] They fell behind, and eventually many of them resigned themselves to their fate, or embraced the stereotypes with which youth of color are portrayed.

But had they not fallen behind, what would have been different for them, collectively? The structural inequalities in society are not dependent on the theoretical orientations of my informants, and do not change depending on their optimism towards education as a means of upward mobility. Reject school like the Hallway Hangers or embrace it like the Brothers, the distribution of wealth and income in the United States remains perversely biased towards the already wealthy. I believe Michelle Fine (1991) gets at this reality as well as anyone when she states, commenting on her work with dropouts:

> But perhaps most compelling is to consider what would happen, in our present day economy, to these young men and women if they all graduated. Would their em-

ployment and/or poverty prospects improve individually as well as collectively? Would the class, race, and gender differentials be eliminated or even reduced? Or does the absence of a high school diploma only obscure what would otherwise be the obvious conditions of structural unemployment, under employment, and marginal employment. (pp. 4, 7).

The scarcity of jobs, wealth, and income that result from the perverse class-based inequalities in the United States are transmitted through an educational system that cannot increase distribution of credentials in society without simultaneously devaluing them in the economy. The critical questions, then, become whether working-class people understand the structural limits on upward mobility, whether this knowledge, or lack of knowledge, contributes to the choices that they make in life (resisting or accepting their place in society), and ultimately if anything can be done about it.

I continue to believe that the educational system plays a role in reproducing and justifying the class-based inequalities in the United States, as in other capitalist and industrialized nations. In fact, as Freire urged us to do in his book *Pedagogy of Freedom* (1998), it is important to remember that it is precisely the reproductive role of education, its integral connection to the political economy, which allows educational reforms to hold out promise for changes in society as a whole. My study and the studies of other critical ethnographers have gone far in identifying the reproductive role of education and have demonstrated that many young people are quite wise to the nature of the economic system vis-à-vis their future prospects. The opposition of my informants, as well as their critiques of racism and inequality, however, do not rise to the level of what I would characterize as resistance, in part because of a range of conflicted views and immediate needs.

The continued usefulness of reproduction, cultural production and resistance, and oppositional culture theories hinges on the ability of these ideas to help us sort out why young people make the negative choices that they make, in concrete rather than flowery terms. A theory that argues that young people quit school because they do not see its economic viability, for example, might not help us to find ways to prevent their economic failure if the real reasons that young people quit school lie elsewhere. We must listen carefully and be specific. The structural limits on educational and economic success are also concrete realities. The interplay of the subjectivity of individual young people and their collective communities with these realities is important to study, as are their productive cultural expressions. But we must be modest in the reach of our theoretical explanations when they are not firmly supported in what can be observed, measured, and documented. Otherwise we run the risk of creating a new type of black box; one in which culture somehow interacts with structural limits to produce cultural expressions in poor children that ultimately may serve to reproduce their class status. It may be that culture works in the mysterious manner that Willis describes, but how can we be sure if it is invisible and assumed? And ultimately, how does this help us to save lives? How does this help communities and the broader working class to engage in the process of their own liberation?

I did not find resistance (not in the way I have defined it nor in the manner that Willis has described it),[16] but instead I found tentative moves towards resistance that gave way to other impulses; given confusion, worry, and the general uncertainty of youth. I have argued that it is confusion of my informants, as well as a range of struggles and immediate needs, that result in their not taking advantage of what opportunities do exist to obstruct attempts to reproduce their class position (or to outright destroy them). I have also argued that many of them may fall prey to minefields that they cannot resist or avoid, such as racism or bias in the criminal justice system, making theories of resistance not particularly applicable. I see resistance among my informants, and I certainly see oppositional behavior and the significance of cultural production (as I have defined them), but I do not see resistance coming to fruition as an explanation for the negative choices that they ultimately make, not in my study at least. I also see no evidence of activism among my informants.

When my informants tell me that their school failure was the result of emotional problems, drug addiction, and immediate financial needs, I take them at their word. When the young people in my study, like those in the study by MacLeod (1987/95, p. 105), tell me that they need to have education be their job in order to succeed in school, I listen to them with an open mind. Resistance theory does not explain the choices that my informants make that speed them down the road towards school failure and incarceration. My observations, and their observations about themselves, do explain their choices as well as the choices that are sometimes imposed on them (by social agents like judges, police officers, social workers, and others).

I am not the first author to question the validity of resistance theory. It has been suggested that "resistance theorists thus interpret mundane acts of student discontent as having a wider class and ideological significance" (Davies, 1995, p. 665) and that they may have over-generalized from "a small and somewhat unrepresentative sample to the bulk of working-class youth" (p. 681). Several studies have reached conclusions that are contradictory to resistance theory (see McFadden, 1995, p. 296; Robinson, 2007; Ogbu, 1978, p. 4). I may be the first author identified with critical theory, however, to do so. It was my conversations with my informants in the study that first caused me to question my previous assumptions that supported theories of resistance and reproduction. Their perspectives and my review of the literature, and careful re-reading of Willis, cause me to question the idea that resistance theory explains school failure or incarceration, and to question whether it can serve as an organizing theory at all.

If I am correct, then the question that critical theorists must ask ourselves is why we were so willing to embrace the theory despite its problems. How did we miss the illogical claims in *Learning to Labor* related to culture cognizing? Why did we assume that we were all using the same notion of resistance when we were divided over the basic question of whether resistance is conscious? Why have we accepted and repeated the stereotyped criticisms of Bowles and Gintis, and Marx, when a cursory reading of their work undermines the criticisms? Why, as in the example of Weis (1990), have we been so quick to assume that our findings that contradict Willis must not be a refutation of his theory? Why did we fail to realize that in denying that working class students can be passive in the face of oppression we were, in fact, denying their agency (their ability to choose to be passive, even though the choice is not one we would prefer)?

Here I think some of the critics of the left, whatever their agenda, have hit upon something we should have considered seriously. As Kingston argued, Marxists like resistance theory because "they view this resistance within schools as the possible seedbed for a more fundamental challenge to capitalist hegemony" (1986, p. 718). Michael Apple expressed this desire when he described penetrations: "it holds out the possibility of economic and political awareness" (1980, p. 68). Resistance/cultural production theory (as understood by most authors in the field rather than as actually articulated by Willis) was the theory we wanted to find. On the one hand it kept the focus on structural economic inequalities under capitalism. On the other hand it praised poor students for their creativity and intelligence for seeing through and resisting the oppressive order (if in ways that were ultimately self-defeating), and finally it said that students were a stone's throw away from achieving radical political consciousness and storming the Bastille.

Related to the tendency to see what we wanted to see, I think, was an emotional need, surrounded by the evils of capitalist production as we are, to have a hopeful theory. The critical literature is full of talk of cultural production theory being better *because* it is hopeful and optimistic (Apple, 1980, p. 65; McFadden, 1995, p. 295; Willis, 1981, p. 53). I view the desire to see human agency triumphing (as if humans always use their agency to resist injustice) as related to this desire to have a theory with a rosy outlook. We want to believe that where there is oppression, there is resistance; therefore oppressive orders cannot stand for long. Human history shows that while the potential for political resistance is always present, most of the time people conform, or cower, in the face of oppression. Even in Nazi Germany there was resistance, but the resistance came late, was isolated, and tended not to be opposed to the atrocities of the state so much as the difficulties of life during the war (Biddiscombe, 1995; Horn, 1973; Lee, 1939/1999). In the United States the majority of the people were silent or supported the jailing (and usually the death in jail) of those charged under the Sedition Act for merely speaking out against war (Kohn, 1994). They were silent for the relocation of Japanese Americans to internment camps. Reading Howard Zinn's *People's History of the United States* (1999) might be in order. Perhaps millions of Iraqi citizens have died since 1991 as the direct and indirect result of U.S. policies, with relatively little dissent. In the 2008 presidential race "liberal" candidates are refusing to rule out the use of nuclear weapons against Iran with no public outcry. The 4th amendment to the U.S. Constitution is rendered almost useless. Poor victims of hurricane Katrina continue to be victimized by a lack of justice and help from their government, with little public outcry. I could, but won't, go on.

Suffice it to say that we should not choose a theory because it seems optimistic and assumes the presence of human agency. We should choose a theory because it seems to correspond to reality (or helps us to know reality in conjunction with other theoretical perspectives). To reject a theory because it does not seem hopeful, because it is not what we would prefer to have found, reminds me a bit of the three wise monkeys covering their eyes, ears, and mouth. The hope that Freire described in *Pedagogy of Freedom* (1998) comes from the fact that change is always possible. This does not mean that it is likely, much less inevitable. Moreover, the hope he describes comes also from the fact that we can individually and collectively refuse to engage in or suffer oppression willingly; though we may die, acting as fully human, we would be free. We must stare bravely into the mirror. In doing so we must see the need to strictly qualify the use of resistance theory and abandon it as an overarching theory that explains school failure, incarceration, or reproduction.

Trying to Survive and Thinking Long Term

My informants neither completely embraced nor rejected schooling. I found no general view among them on the value of education in the economy. Most of my informants would state, at least some of the time, the belief that getting a college education pays off in terms of employment. Few of the young people in my study, however, expressed any aspirations to attend college or hold professional jobs, and were not preparing themselves to do so.[17] At the same time, most would state that they would have no problem finding well-paying jobs after high school. Some believed that a high school diploma was necessary to find a job. Others believed that they could make a good living (in construction, as rappers, athletes, or actors) without a diploma. These young people would often make mention of personal contacts that they believed would land them good paying jobs. And yet these same young people were not engaged in drama or choir, nor were they involved in organized sports at their schools. There was even less discussion of technical training for jobs like that of an electrician or machinist than there was of gaining a professional job through a college education. To the extent that such technical training was mentioned, it was mostly mentioned by girls who aspired to be nursing assistants or beauticians.

One might be tempted to conclude that most of the young people in my study were optimistic about their hopes for the future even with only a high school diploma (or even without one) and no college education. Such an interpretation could not be substantiated, however, when the surface statements that they made gave way to reveal their insecurities about the future. It was revealing that when I asked students what their plans for the future were, the answers I tended to get were either fanciful or painfully bleak. The young people tended to tell me that they would be famous athletes, musical performers, rappers, or actors, on the one hand, or that they would join the military, had no plans, or that they would probably be in jail, on the other hand. Employment in the illegal trades was often mentioned as a fruitful way to make a living, but not by young people who themselves or whose families were actually actively involved in the drug trade.[18] The same young person who would argue that jobs were plentiful and that high school was unnecessary would, moments later, complain of the lack of jobs, stating, as one young man did, that "I just couldn't find a job."

I ran the group discussion one afternoon on the topic of schooling. This discussion was a typical example of the sorts of exchanges that I would have with my informants about their economic prospects and education. I asked the young people if they liked or did not like school, if an education is necessary, and if it will pay off in the long run in terms of employment. An African-American boy whom I often spoke with, Jermahl, volunteered his position on schooling, "School is a waste of time." Some of the young people disagreed with him. Several, however, felt that they could do just as well without an education. These students, mostly boys, had exaggerated ideas, in my view, of what work they could get without a high school diploma. I asked

Jermahl, "But don't you think that not being in school might have something to do with you getting in trouble?" He grinned coyly, looked towards the group, and said "yah." Another African-American boy in this discussion, Nick, sided with Jermahl, saying that school is a waste of time. In other private conversations, however, he spoke with me of the importance of being goal oriented in life and expressed an interest in going to college, going so far as to ask me for strategies to get in and also about financial aid.

One explanation for this contradiction is that the young people were trying to make themselves feel better about the stark realities that they see for themselves by painting the picture in rosier colors. The interview I had with an Asian-American boy illuminated this possible explanation:

> Boy: It hurt my grades when I got in with a couple of friends and started skipping school. They didn't like school, thought it was boring. Because they're not in school they've got nothing to do. They want to be cool like the people on the streets. They didn't think long term.
>
> Me: How do we get 'em to go to school and think long term?
>
> Boy: Keep 'em up in here (laughs). They think jobs are easy to get without going to school, they'd tell me to bug off when I tried to tell them to go to school. They knew it wasn't true what they were saying. They weren't ashamed but embarrassed that they couldn't get a good job [without an education].

As the group discussion mentioned above continued, a Latino boy who had stated that a high school diploma is unnecessary to find a good-paying job began to describe his efforts to find a job. "I really wanted a job," he said, "but no one would give me a chance. When I filled out the application the manager said he'd call me if they had anything for me. I told him that I saw how it is and left."

For many of my informants the contradiction between their belief in economic opportunities in general and their pessimism about the opportunities available to them as individuals (despite their public face of bravado) is reconciled by the belief that it is racism that prevents them from attaining the opportunities that they see as available to White people, rather than economic structure. Racism is real and discrimination is still common.[19] Certainly, discrimination greatly contributes to the struggles of people of color to find employment. The analysis of my informants who held fast to this explanation, however, fails to account for the poverty of White people in the community or structural unemployment. A smaller number of my informants held a critique of economic opportunity that was almost Marxist in its flavor. These young people also tended to be those from drug-involved families.

A White boy in the group discussion took issue with the explanations of economic and educational failure being expressed by many of the youth of color. He stated that, "kids that don't want to be there [in school] shouldn't be there," and that if they didn't care enough to attend classes that they should be expelled. Jermahl and Nick reacted simultaneously to this. "It's better to keep them in school in detention than to suspend or expel them," otherwise, they argued, we create a situation where they are on the street and never in class. The White boy was thinking in terms of just rewards and meritocracy. The youth of color were looking at a wider range of dynamics and consequences, and thinking practically about ways to keep kids, like themselves, in school.

I came to realize that most of my informants were not thinking primarily in terms of their long-term economic prospects via education when they made choices about whether to attend school, turn to crime, or have hope for the future. They did think about these prospects, but their thoughts were much more focused on their immediate needs. When they spoke to me about the relationship between schooling and employment, they didn't just mean in the future, they meant now. As MacLeod (1987/95) observed, "believing they have missed out on the indulgences of American consumerism, they are starved for immediate financial success" (p. 106). What my informants described was more than a desire for materialist consumption. They were also motivated by real and immediate survival needs, as well as the self-esteem boost that they experienced by having the material things that wealthier kids have.

The lack of hope for the future that many of the young people in my study expressed revealed a lack of belief in *any* future. Where only a few years ago ethnographers reported that their working-class participants were debating whether they would have the opportunity to have professional jobs or must accept manual labor (MacLeod, 1987/95), the young people in my study did not really believe (beneath a layer of bravado and interspersed with hopeful moments) that they had any future other than prison. For many of these young people the future seems very far off and remote. When I asked them about the future I imagined them at 30 years of age. It took me a while to realize that my question led them to imagine themselves at 18 or maybe 21 years of age. That was the future.[20]

This distinction was brought home to me one evening as I sat with an African-American boy with whom I was conducting an interview. He was visibly shaken. The next day he would be taken to juvenile prison where he would remain until he was old enough to be transferred to adult prison. He had been facing juvenile charges, but after he became upset with a staff member and threw an orange at her,[21] the district attorney waived him to adult court. When I asked him about school he stated:

I'll never be in high school again. I'm going to jail. I've been waived. I'm facing 50 years. I threw an orange at a staff so they waived me.

"How can you be so calm," I asked him. He replied simply, "I can't do nothing about it." I couldn't stand to leave him when he needed so much to talk with someone, and the staff were sympathetic towards him, so they allowed us to speak for a long period of time. He told me the story of his life, in gangs, and dealing in drugs:

My daddy got killed in front of me when I was five. He got shot in his eye. Most of my family is in federal prison. My lawyer tried to tell the judge what I've been through but Higs just said he's been through the same thing.

Despite his situation, this young man only seemed to regret that he wouldn't be able to attend the senior prom at his high school. As he stated, "My mom and I used to sit around and think of senior prom. Seeing people got to the prom and thinking about my senior prom." For this young man the future *was* the senior prom. Attending the prom really was his greatest aspiration in life. I asked him why he committed his crime. "I needed the money to buy food and take care of my little cousin," he told me. "What money she do get she gotta pay rent with that." I asked him if there was anything he wanted to add that I might not have asked him about. "I won't be asked why or what," he told me, "I'll just be asked what's my plea."

Conversations about the economic benefit of schooling were some of the most difficult in which I engaged. When speaking with young people who have had so many problems in their short lives, I could not bring myself to tell them that I agreed with much of their analysis of the economic system. I did not want to tell them that everything I knew about the political economy meant that, while there might be limited individual mobility available for some of them if they worked very hard at their schooling, there was little hope for collective class mobility or racial equity. I did not tell them that I held out little hope for most of them having joyful lives; in the absence of revolutionary change born of collective action (see the concluding chapter). Instead, I told them to think more about the long term, that without at least a GED life would be very difficult, and that it was never too late to apply themselves educationally in order to learn a trade or even attend college. I told them that I really hoped and wanted for them to have happy and materially comfortable lives. Based on my interactions with them, I think they understood that my encouragement to "stay in school" was well meaning. What else was I to do? I would have liked to have taught them the tools of social activism, but my competing roles at the center prevented me from doing so.

Drug Trade Dreams and Drug Trade Realities

The White participants in my study, when they claimed to be able to make a good living without a high school diploma, tended to name a number of traditional working-class jobs, such as construction jobs (off the books). They seemed to have little concern for the perils of such work, the lack of retirement or health benefits, and so forth. My informants with rare exceptions did not mention technical training for jobs such as machinist or electrician or talk about these as likely future jobs for them, whatever their race. Many of my informants, especially but not only African-American males, expressed the belief that they could always fall back on drug dealing as a way to make a living.

Young people whose families or who themselves were not involved in the drug trade tended to have romantic notions of selling drugs and exaggerated notions of the amount of money they could make. Young people who were closer to the drug trade had few illusions about what it meant and did not feel good about what they had done. Even these participants in the drug trade viewed it as one of their only options in life. The relationship between the drug culture, illegal drug trade, and popular notions about Black culture and the drug trade (which are frequently internalized by young people), and the perspectives of my informants on schooling and on their economic prospects, are intertwined in the way they think about the world. For most of the young people in my study these were the choices that they saw for themselves: stay in school in hopes of getting some distant middle-class job, join the military, or sell drugs. There were exceptions. One boy I interviewed, for example, expressed the desire to go to college and be an engineer (though he also reported skipping school). Even these bleak choices, from the point of view of my informants, became less of a choice given economic necessities in their lives. It took me a while to realize that when I asked what I thought was an open and non-leading question like, "what sort of work do you think you'll do in the future?" many of the young people in my study took me to be asking them if they would sell drugs.

To sell drugs was mostly a male aspiration. The annual reports from the Juvenile Court back this up, with very few girls being charged with intent to deliver.[22] Girls would discuss job prospects in private interviews and in group discussions with other girls, but they would tend to say little when job prospects were being discussed in the presence of boys. Many of the girls in my study seemed to have patriarchal fantasies about staying home to raise families, supported by their husbands if possible.[23] The jobs they mentioned tended to be stereotypical "women's employment," such as beautician. There

were exceptions. Two girls, for example, stated that they would pursue professional careers (a lawyer and an architect, though they were not doing well
in school). Another girl said she might join the Marines. I never had the experience of any of the young women in my study telling me that marriage
was not for them, or that they would put off having a family until their careers were established (as Weis documented in 1990).

My findings related to the job aspirations of my informants, particularly
related to the traditionalist aspirations of many of the girls, are somewhat
surprising. The lowered aspirations of the young people, both White and
Black, are consistent with the findings in the updated edition of MacLeod's
study (1987/95). They are not consistent with the findings of Weis (1990)
and Luttrell (1997), who reported that the working-class women in their
studies aspired to find professional employment and to break with traditional
and patriarchal notions of motherhood and marriage. Weis, whose findings
were a departure from earlier studies that documented the patriarchal domestic aspirations of most working-class girls (consistent with those expressed
by my informants), attributed the career aspirations of the girls in her study
to changes in the deindustrialization of the economy (which reduced the
number of high-paying, male-centered, working-class jobs), hard-won open-
ings for women in the job market, and lessons taught to daughters by mothers not to rely on a man for financial support or relegate themselves to the
home. My findings are more consistent with the earlier studies that she described, such as those by McRobbie or Gaskell.

I do not know if the seeming reversal in my findings from those of Weis
are because the changing attitudes among the women she worked with never
emerged in the population in my study (poor Black women from northern
urban centers) or if the disproportionate effects of current economic trends
on African-Americans, such as much higher rates of unemployment (Leondar-Wright, 2004), have forced the young women in my study to put on hold
the sort of aspirations she describes. It is also possible that at least some of
the young women in my study would have revealed far more of themselves
to a woman researcher. Given how open and frank the girls in my study
tended to be with me, however, I don't believe that most of them were pull-
ing my leg when it came to their traditional notions of family and work. The
girls in my study aspired to marry and raise families. They were not career
driven, but neither did they express subservient attitudes towards the men in
their lives.

Nancy Lopez in her book *Hopeful Girls, Troubled Boys* (2003) explored
the race, gender, and class dynamics that result in more young women of
color graduating from high school and attending college than boys, despite

the continuation of patriarchy. As in my study, she found that the young women in her study, mostly from Latino families, defined themselves in relationship to the family, accepted, for the most part, the cultural notion that they be the primary care givers and home makers, and desired both husbands and children. So my findings are partially consistent with hers. Unlike my study, however, she found that the gendered way in which the young women in her study were viewed allowed them to have better relationships with school personnel and to have better job prospects after graduating. The women in her study also defined themselves by and desired careers, having a "dual frame of reference" that the men in her study lacked (p. 140). I find her account to be thoughtful and rather convincing, and note also that her fieldwork occurred at the same time as my own. I cannot account for the differences in our findings. I trust her findings, however, just as I trust my own. The explanation may lie in the geographical and racial differences between her population and mine. Another possible explanation could be that her population was made up largely of young women who had done well in school and were attending or aspiring to attend college, while my population, on the other hand, consisted of the least educationally successful young people in the community in which I was working.

Given the bleak economic prospects for the young people in my study, we could conclude that the young women were making a more rational assessment of their options. Again, boys and girls expressed the belief that there was great opportunity in the economy in general, that a college degree was valuable for getting a good job, and that they could find jobs that would pay well without having to compete with Whites in the formal job market. As I have argued, I took much of this to be bravado, face-saving, and defense mechanisms. I note that it was the boys in my study, almost exclusively, who insisted that they would be race car drivers, actors, rappers, and so forth. These lofty goals were the stuff of day dreams. These day dreams were a necessary psychological coping mechanism for some of the young men who did not want to think about their bleak prospects for the future. The girls were much more sober in their answers. They were more likely to simply tell me that they "don't know" what they will do in the future or "have no plans" for the future.

When I asked the young people with whom I conducted formal interviews what their parents did for a living, they described low-paying factory work, work as nursing assistants in elder care, work at low-paying mechanical jobs, work in unlicensed day care or housecleaning, or they informed me that they were not working, or that one or more of their parents were either dead or in prison. One parent was said to be a truck driver and another an accountant. These two fathers were not very involved in their children's lives, however. The most common answers, by far, were that their parents worked in factories, were unemployed, or in jail.

My study was conducted in Wisconsin as the welfare changes initiated by Governor Thompson were taking effect, and the like-minded changes out of the Clinton administration were beginning. Mothers who had been receiving living assistance for themselves and their families were now being forced to work in exchange for their benefits, were being forced off the rolls, and were being transitioned to low-paying employment. Nationally, as a result of these changes, the mothers who found employment were worse off economically, receiving poverty wages. They generally lacked health insurance or child care, with around 40 percent of the families forced off support while having no source of legal income (Albelda, 1999). I never asked a single young person in my study if his or her family was on welfare or if his or her parent's employment was assigned by welfare. These sorts of questions were simply too potentially painful for them. But these were questions that did not have to be asked; the answers being obvious.

The young people in my study, both male and female, did not aspire to attend college, or even trade schools, and were at great risk of dropping out of school. They dreamed of lucrative careers as athletes, actors, or rappers. When challenged about the odds of making it in those careers, they would either cling stubbornly to the dreams or would insist that they could find working-class jobs through personal contacts, jobs that would be hard work, but would pay well. African-American boys were more likely, compared to White boys, to describe drug dealing as a lucrative career choice of last resort. In private moments, however, the young people in my study would admit to seeing bleak futures for themselves. The boys in my study seemed to be more depressed about the future. Many of the girls took some comfort in the idea that they could have children, and thereby have love in their lives if not material things. Many of the boys romanticized gangster fantasies as future employment. The young people who actually were involved in the drug trade, however, saw themselves as dead or in prison.

Drug-Involved Families

Tynicia was a quiet and muscular African-American girl who was about 16-years old. Even though she didn't say much, the young people around her seemed to give her respect. They did not seem to fear her, as far as I could tell, but when she did speak they listened to her. I assumed they knew her or knew of her on the outside. She often looked suspiciously at my interactions with the young people in the center. So I was a bit surprised, but very pleased, when she asked me if I would interview her. She was in the detention center on a charge of serious battery. She had seriously injured another girl in a fight while she was drunk. As she explained her case:

> I hardly talk to people at school cause you get a lot of friends that's when the trouble starts. She accused me of stealing. I was drunk and stoned. She hit me. I snapped. I couldn't believe I did that. Judge said I'm a danger to the community, but if I wasn't drunk or high I wouldn't have done that.

She admitted freely to having a drinking problem:

> My mom asks me why I'm always drunk. I don't know. I guess cause I don't have nothing else to do. The weed makes me lazy though and forgetful. I don't go outside too much. I stay in the house. I get paranoid.

Later in the interview she made reference to some life experiences that might tend to explain her violence and substance abuse as being more than the result of simple boredom, "My uncle was killed," she said, "and since then I've been violent."

Tynicia's uncle was a mid level drug dealer. It's a family business, and she claims they are gang affiliated. "My cousins sold dope and went to jail for lack of jobs," she told me, "but it's a waste of time cause you kill your race and others race. I looked up to them cause they always gave us money, but now I wish they hadn't done it." One of her cousins had also been killed by a rival drug dealer. I asked her why young people sell drugs. She said that they do it for the money and popularity. Despite this explanation she volunteered that her family never made a great deal of money from the drug trade, "I've only known two dealers whose made much money... drug dealing is a hard, long hour job."

Ironically, Tynicia's family had moved to Coldville from Chicago in order to "have a better life" and access to better schools. Though they sold drugs themselves, the adults in her family hoped that she, her brothers, and her cousins would focus on school instead. Things didn't work out that way, however, when the bread winners in the family died or went to prison. The younger boys then took over the family drug-dealing business. "School wasn't nothin' to my brothers. I respect my one brother 'cause he only got locked up once. His girl kept him out of jail. My other brother got locked up for child support." She assured me that no one in her family wanted to continue in the drug trade, but that they could not see another way to make ends meet. The money did not go far, she explained, because every drug dealer was helping to support a number of family members. I asked her if making school more appealing or having better paying jobs would keep young people out of the drug trade. "Even with more jobs," she said, "some folks would still want the fast life."

Stories like hers were repeated time and again by young people who were involved in gangs and the drug trade. When I asked a 16-year-old African-American boy why people rob and sell drugs, he told me that it was for the money. "I'm in the gang to get money. What they got I got, and they got my back." He had been arrested for attacking some White boys in order to steal some marijuana that they had. The marijuana was not mentioned at trial, he said. When I asked him why he did it he told me that, "I did it cause I didn't have no money to buy." Then he went on to say that, "I don't even care if I die. You live to die." A 13-year-old gang member told me that, "I make money in gang. I don't know anybody who's not in a gang that has money," but, he added, "I'm trying to change my way myself." He was brought to detention because, "I beat up and robbed people." When I asked him if there was anything he'd like to say that hadn't been covered in the interview he stated that, "I hate snitches. Someone told on me when I robbed their car." He shared with me some of his fondest memories spending time with his father, counting the money from his father's drug trade, "I love counting money, cause it reminds me of my pops."

I view with some irony the fact that the informants in my study who are actually involved in the drug trade and gang-affiliated are the most likely to reject arguments for the drug trade as a viable way to make a living, especially in the long term. But these same young people feel pushed and pulled into the very activities that they reject. Tyrone, a 16-year-old African-American boy, assured me that "if I get out today I'll never come back [to detention], I want to change." From my notes I recorded the following exchange:

> Me: Is there anything I should put in my notes that we haven't covered yet?
> Tyrone: Just cause kids do things that doesn't mean they're all bad. And kids can change.
> Me: Why do people think that you can't change?
> Tyrone: They don't understand. They don't come up like us. When you don't have much you look to find your own.
> Me: Why do people sell drugs?
> Tyrone: They don't want to look dumb. They find their own way.
> Me: Should we put people in jail for drugs?
> Tyrone: It's too harsh, especially in Wisconsin.

As Tyrone was attempting to convey, young people like himself are not drawn into gangs and drug dealing because they view this as a positive career move. Rather, they fall back into criminal activities when they fail at their attempts to focus on schooling as a means of upward mobility, when they are desperate for money to support their families, and when they seek the emotional support that gangs provide. As the director of the center stated in our interview, "Why do gangs attract kids? They have no steady connections. There's no evil motive." This life of crime is functional for some of the young people in my study, at the same time that it has dysfunctional aspects to it.[24] The gang- and drug-trade-affiliated young people in my study were very clear about these distinctions. They saw gang involvement as having positive aspects for themselves and their communities, even while they understood the dangers and harm caused by violence and drugs. One boy described the contradictory nature of gangs, "Gangs is good cause they was formed to help the community to survive, but gangs are bad, cause you can mess around and get hurt."

There is a growing body of work that associates violence with hypermasculinity and a desire to feel powerful. Gilligan (1996) reports this phenomenon as follows:

> Some people think armed robbers commit their crimes in order to get money. And of course, sometimes, that is the way they rationalize their behavior. But when you sit down and talk with people who repeatedly commit such crimes, what you hear is, "I never got so much respect before in my life as I did when I first pointed a gun at somebody," or, "you wouldn't believe how much respect you get when you have a gun pointed at some dude's face." For men who have lived a lifetime on a diet of contempt and disdain, the temptation to gain instant respect in this way can be worth far more than the cost of going to prison, or even dying. (p. 109)

My study does find some support for what Gilligan is describing. When I asked one White boy in an interview if there was anything he would like to say that I had not covered in the questions, he said, "tell them we're more capable than people think. I could take their car, their money." Often my informants listed pent-up anger as a primary reason that young people have the problems that they have. While sitting at a table with a White boy of about 15 and a couple of White girls, the boy recounted his tale of getting in a verbal conflict with another boy, going to get an ink pen, and returning to stab the other boy. "I was surprised it felt so good," he told me smiling, "I didn't expect it to feel so good." Before viewing this boy as a monster or superpredator, your view should be complicated by the fact that he was generally considerate and kind when I observed him. One of the adult counselors described this sort of emotional response among young people this way: "It can feel good to lash out given their pain, even though it damages them, for that moment it feels good."

While I found some support for the notion that young people often feel powerless and that acts of violence can provide them with a temporary feeling of power or release of anger, my study does not support the notion that young people rob or commit acts of violence primarily in order to have this experience of being powerful. The vast majority of the young people in my study reported that they engaged in illegal activities in order to make money, or to get drugs to numb the emotional pain in their lives, and that their violent actions were seldom calculated acts, but rather were uncontrolled outbursts, often fueled by alcohol or drugs. When acts of violence were planned they were related to gang initiations, stealing, or to save public face when challenged. It is, largely, about the need for money, and the need to have a tough front in a violent street environment. For young people in some neighborhoods violence is a practical but regrettable choice. As a young Asian boy told me in an interview:

> Gangs are bad. They just want to be cool and be protected when they get in fights. Once in a gang you have to fight. But if you're not in a gang, then people jump you. Happens all the times. And gangs backstab their new members, especially if they say they're scared.

The statements documented by Gilligan related to the motivation to commit crimes are important, but I suspect that the causal connection between the desire to feel powerful and stealing may be overstated. Most of the young people in my study who reported engaging in robberies (far more than were arrested for these acts) told me that they did it out of desperation or anger, or were under the influence, and that they did not enjoy or feel good about what they had done.

Wannabes and Making Money

I spent a great deal of time addressing the issue of gangs in Coldville with my informants. Most of them would report that there are in fact a large number of gangs in the area and that they are in fact real gangs. A smaller set of informants told me that the real number of gang members is much less. When I asked Tynicia if there are real gangs in Coldville she responded as follows: "Yes and no. Anyone can say they're in gangs. I don't want to be known by the police for being a gang member 'cause the police think all gang members are doing crimes." After a while I was able to sort out the young people who I believed to be involved in the drug trade and gang affiliated, and those who they referred to as "false flaggers," "pancakes," "fags," and "wannabes." As one young man, who was a third-generation gang member, told me, "gangs in Coldville aren't legitimate. Only those who moved here [from larger cities] are legit." I suppose that I could have it wrong about who was and was not actually involved in organized gang activity. The larger group of young people who claimed to be in gangs, and whom I came to view as wannabes, tended to exaggerate the amount of money which could be made selling drugs, however, while the group that I believed were actually involved in the drug trade told me things about the money that could be made that were more consistent with what I knew about the drug trade. All my instincts, their tone of voice, body language, and facial expressions also led me to believe them. I do not say that the larger group that claimed gang affiliation were lying. Rather, I think they mistook their small crew for an actual nationally affiliated gang. Lee (2004) has also found that the level of gang involvement among youth of color, in the community where she conducted her research, is greatly exaggerated in public perception.[25]

The question of the profitability of drug dealing is crucial to understand the motivations of the wannabe drug dealers. I call them this because the actual drug-affiliated young people called them this. Selling drugs is, in my view, more of a fantasy than a real option for them. They did not have the connections to take over the established drug spots in the community, and would not have been able to take over the established territory if they had wanted to. After all, a neighborhood can only support a limited number of street corner dealers.[26] These are gangster fantasies, like kids in the 1970s imagining that they could be like the characters in *The Godfather*, but they are fantasies with real consequences for the choices that these young people make. They are fantasies because they are not realistic options for these young people, unlike those young people who actually have the connections, but they are dangerous because, unlike the bravado discussed earlier, many of these young people actually seemed to believe in the fantasy, and the decisions that they make could be influenced by this imagined future.

The young people who had unrealistic and romanticized notions about the drug trade would insist that they could sell drugs any time they wanted and that they would make easily $100 or more an hour. A group of boys in a group discussion claimed to be able to make $2000 a week working a couple of hours each day. When an African-American staff member and I challenged them on their numbers, they admitted that they might have to work longer hours, but insisted that they could make thousands of dollars each week as low-level drug dealers. I challenged them some more, telling them that I had met young people in the detention center who were arrested for selling drugs and that I had been to the homes of some of their parents, but that they did not have any material things, not even a nice TV or expensive sneakers. Unfazed by this evidence, they responded that the kids I met might be stashing the money and keeping a low profile, even though it meant having a public defender rather than a private attorney of their choosing. They held on to the notion that they could make great money selling drugs like blind faith, though most of them did not claim to have actually sold drugs themselves.

Some well-meaning researchers have dutifully reported similar claims and accepted them as accurate. As Vorrasi and Garbarino (2000) report:

> Economically impoverished children and youth often turn to drug dealing as a way to make money – lots of money. Adolescent males living in the poorest housing developments of New York City report earning potentials from $100 to $800 per day. This has two important implications for the poverty-violence equation. First, many of these teen entrepreneurs use their street earnings to supplement their family's income. It is not uncommon for parents in poor communities to fail to meet the day-to-day physical needs of their families, and in many cases, drug dealing sons or close relatives help offset the cost of such things as food, shelter, and clothing. Second, money gives poor individuals a feeling of power and adequacy, even if only on a superficial level. Dealing drugs for just a few hours a day has the ability to make "haves" out of "have-nots" like no other profession or pseudo-profession. (p. 73)

I would take issue with the notion that most low-level drug dealers are entrepreneurs. They are low-level commissioned workers, like ice cream truck drivers. Nonetheless, there is much value in the observations of Vorrasi and Garbarino as to why some young people sell drugs, consistent with my own observations (though I question the amount of money reported). Certainly there are exceptions. Midlevel and upper-level drug dealers make significantly more money. Insiders in drug families share in the family wealth. Drug spots with lots of traffic by White clients from the suburbs make a volume business that can add up quickly. But a poor kid on a street corner in the freezing rain for 12 hours is not making the sort of money reported, even in larger cities like New York. Bourgois (2003) does a great job of sorting this out:

> Street dealers tend to brag to outsiders and to themselves about how much money they make each night. In fact, their income is almost never as consistently high as they report it to be. Most street sellers, like Primo, are paid on a piece-rate commission basis. In other words, their take home pay is a function of how much they sell. When converted into an hourly wage, this is often a relatively paltry sum. According to my calculations, Ray's workers, for example, averaged slightly less than double the legal minimum wage — between seven and eight dollars an hour. There were plenty of exceptional nights, however, when they made up to ten times minimum wage — and these are the nights they remember when they reminisce ... It took me several years to realize how inconsistent and meager crack income can be. (pp. 91–92)

The drug economy in Coldville, in terms of street-level crack sales, is not providing a middle-class income for any of the dealers standing on the corner, and even if it were, it would not be able to support the hundreds of young people in my study who told me that their back-up strategy was to sell drugs if they couldn't find a better job.[27]

The fact that so many of my informants mentioned dealing drugs as a viable career choice should give us pause. The young people who actually had sold drugs or whose families were involved in the drug trade had few illusions about what such a life means. They would like to do something else, but were not educationally successful, lacked job skills, had trouble adjusting to workplace norms, and felt demeaned by the types of jobs that they could find. Bourgois (2003) has a good chapter dealing with these cultural conflicts. Many of my informants who were from drug-involved families were simply too young to find legal work, leaving them to work in the drug trade (as spotters or holders). For the young people who held to the gangster fantasy, like the fantasy of playing professional basketball (that of getting discovered at the neighborhood park if they dropped out of school and thus were not playing on a organized team), it might have contributed to decisions to not focus on their schooling, to skip school, or to drop out.

Seeing is Believing

Critical ethnographies, and critical theory more broadly, when examining the role of education in society, have attempted to sort out the reasons that students from wealthier families tend to be so much more successful educationally and in their adult job prospects. The reasons are, of course, numerous and complex, and require the knowledge provided by scholarship outside of critical theory as well. As a small part of the larger explanation that is needed, this chapter has attempted to sort out how my informants, during the time of the Clinton presidency, viewed their prospects for the future, the nature of the economy, and the economic benefits of an education in securing their futures. In order to address these questions I began by placing my study in the current historical context and then used the theories of cultural production and reproduction to sort out what I had asked, heard, and observed. Ultimately, I came to believe that resistance was only one aspect of what was happening with my informants, and could not explain their negative choices.

Most of my informants were not motivated to work hard in school in order to get into a good college, like so many of the middle-class students with whom they have sat in classrooms.[28] Though young people come to the detention center for a variety of reasons (from running away, to petty ordinance violations, to drug violations or serious acts of violence) the young people who were most likely to be represented in my study were those who were actually held at the center for longer periods of time. These tended to be young people facing more serious charges or with less stable home environments.

While I met the range of young people who cycled through the center over the course of a year, my study most accurately reflects the perspectives and life histories of poor students and students of color. My study's focus, therefore, is on young people who are most likely to experience educational failure, to drop out of school, and to be incarcerated both as juveniles and as adults. Perhaps there is a tendency to make too much out of the issue of young people of color from poor families not knowing what they will do for a living when they grow up, given that middle-class White youth are uncertain of their future careers as well. What is different is that middle-class youth believe they will have *some* positive future.

The young people in my study live lives where they are constantly trying to find hope for a future that their intelligence and experience tells them does not exist. This struggle is always related to their ideas about schooling. They fluctuate between thinking that school is a waste of time, to realizing that their chances of economic success and even survival are better if they stay in school, to thinking that there is no point in working hard in school when they can be arrested at any time, convicted on false testimony, and incarcerated. When I ask young people about schooling, they talk about economic deprivation, the lack of jobs for young people, police misconduct and perjury. I read this as an indication that for them, from their perspective, the realities of racism and economic violence are not separate from the educational system. To them the educational system seems, at times, to be a part of the same system that they see as oppressing them, even as they also often see education as their only, albeit remote, hope for a better life. The immediate struggles in their lives are not compartmentalized, in their thought processes, from their educational and economic aspirations.

The young people whom I met at the detention center did not truly think that there were many opportunities for them to have good jobs in the future. In fact, to them the future extended for only a few years. They hoped to survive in the meantime. At times, of course, they would think of the future and would weigh their chances via education for a better life, but the unlikely nature of this future would prove too painful to contemplate for long, so they would suppress such thoughts. In my interview with him, the director of the center made a similar observation stating that: "Kids were the same 20 years ago. They think the world acts on them and they have no control over it. They don't believe in future positive outcomes."

In sum, regarding the perspectives of the majority of my informants (poor people of color) on the economy, the importance they attribute to education as it relates to securing employment both for themselves and their peers, and their hopes for the future, I did find that the young people think about these questions in relation to their lives and the choices they make about whether to work hard or even stay in school. However, for the young people in my study these questions were not primary in their decision-making processes. They are unable, for the most part, to come to firm conclusions on the issue of whether school (high school or college) pays off in terms of employment, so such questions become remote given the immediacy of the pressures and problems in their lives. They do not have goals for the future. They have daydreams and fears. Some see futures of selling drugs leading to death or incarceration. This is especially true of young people from families that have been involved in the drug trade. Other young people romanticize and fantasize about selling drugs, playing sports, or being entertainers, but they try not to think about the future most of the time. Instead, they seek distractions and moments of comfort or happiness.

I believe that the perspectives of my informants and my findings that differ from earlier studies that also looked at the economic benefits of schooling for working-class youth do so, in part, because of the new historical situation in which we live in. For young men of color in particular, discussions of future job prospects via education seem remote and hypothetical. The Latino boy I mentioned earlier had not been prepared to successfully negotiate job interviews, but he had been prepared for life in jail. As he told me, "My uncle taught me to not think about outside, just to stay out of trouble and to think about the day-to-day." For the young people in my study from the lower classes, especially those of color, the promise and hope that were present for earlier generations seem all but gone, outsourced and replaced like the jobs that their grandfathers worked.

Chapter 5
Corruption and Racism in the Legal System

In this chapter I will discuss the perspectives of my informants on crime and how they came to be held at the detention center. I will also address their attitudes towards drug use, the growing prison industrial complex, racial profiling, the historical context that led to the current state of affairs, and the relationship between the criminalization of youth and educational failure. Finally, I will document the abuse, and I would say torture, of some of the young people in my study while they were temporarily held in a neighboring county detention center, due to overcrowding at the research site.

What's Wrong with Gettin' High?

The young people in my study, regardless of ethnicity, race, or gender, reported high levels of at least occasional use of marijuana and alcohol. Though crack cocaine is the drug that African-American dealers are most likely to sell on the street, the young people in my research denied that they had ever tried crack. In fact, one of the worst insults that they had was to call someone a crack head or to accuse someone of "being on crack." My findings that even dealers of crack hold negative views of crack use are consistent with the findings of Terry Williams (1992), who has studied crack use and dealing culture extensively. The use of marijuana was routine with many of the young people, and its use seemed perfectly normal to them.

In a group discussion one evening an African-American male member of the staff and I discussed the use of drugs with some of the young people. The views of one Black girl were representative of the views of most of her peers:

Girl: What's wrong with weed?
Staff member: There are some harmful effects that are possible with marijuana use.
Girl: But it's not like crack, it's just weed. What's weed gonna' hurt? Weed never hurt nobody.
Staff member: I'm not saying that it's as harmful as alcohol or other drugs, or that it should be illegal, but it's not harmless.
Girl: I can't see how weed ever hurt anyone.

Me: Marijuana smoking can hurt your lungs, can cause you to crash your car, can
     make you lazy, or can cause you to make bad decisions.
Girl: It's just marijuana!

Jermahl backed up the girl's arguments by stating that marijuana is about "as bad for you as air." The African-American man quickly responded by asking him, in a tone of voice that seemed both perplexed and stern, "Jermahl, let me ask you, all the times you got in trouble, were you high?" Jermahl grinned, diverted his eyes towards the ground, and responded, "yeah." The man went on, "would you have done those things if you weren't high at the time?" "No," Jermahl answered, "I don't think I would."

Drug offenses accounted for only about 10 percent of the young people referred to the Juvenile Court (Annual Report). Although the majority of incarcerated adults nationally, in recent years, were convicted of drug possession or distribution, with marijuana-related prosecutions on the rise relative to other drugs, prosecutors in Coldville did not seem to have the same emphasis on charging juveniles for possession as they did in the case of adults. My research seems to indicate, however, that marijuana use among the young people in my study is higher than use by adults. Research that has looked at arrest rates of youth and adults in Coldville has confirmed that the rate of arrest for possession is lower than in many other localities, though Black youth are arrested about three times as often for these offenses. Nationally, drug offenses account for about 10 percent of juvenile and adult arrests, while in Coldville they account for about 6 percent of adult and 4 percent of juvenile arrests. Self-report data also seem to support my findings, with around 25 percent of all youth in Coldville reporting that they have used marijuana and around 50 percent reporting that they have used alcohol. While the arrests for marijuana, among juveniles, are at a relatively low rate, and while they tend to be prosecuted as juveniles for these acts (with adults in Coldville arrested in possession of marijuana being just as likely to be charged with crimes as with municipal violations),[1] we must remember that these arrests fall disproportionately on the young people in my study. Of the 4 percent arrested for marijuana (10 percent for some drug-related charge), the majority of the young people captured by these numbers were poor, Black, and living in one of five ghettoized and heavily policed neighborhoods.[2]

One does not have to support the criminalization of the use of marijuana and alcohol to be concerned by the high levels of use among young people. For most young people in the community the use of alcohol and marijuana is occasional and social. The harmful effects of this usage could be reduced by adult supervision if the law allowed it. For some young people, and disproportionately so for the children of color in my study, the use of alcohol (especially among Whites) and marijuana (especially among Blacks) was not recreational but a means for managing emotional pain and despair. The exaggerations that young people hear related to the dangers of marijuana and alcohol may actually contribute to their abuse of these substances, because they are less likely to believe legitimate warnings about use and abuse. The use of these drugs can quickly become addictive (in the case of alcohol) and a desperately desired crutch.

The use of both marijuana and alcohol contributes to the difficulties in school experienced by my informants (who can not study when they are high), contributes to bad decision making (which can land them in trouble), and is often the motivation for property crimes in order to afford these substances. As one boy stated, "weed makes me lazy and forgetful, but alcohol makes me violent." Another boy reported that, "I stole that weed cause I didn't have money to buy any." A Latino boy summed up his views on alcohol and marijuana this way, "Society should be more orderly, marijuana should be legal, but alcohol should be illegal, cause it makes some people violent." Honesty regarding these substances, advice on how to drink or smoke responsibly, the availability of drug counseling, adult supervision when using, and a de-emphasis on the criminalization of marijuana could potentially help the young people in my study to stay out of trouble. As things stand now, many of the young people in my study are hiding their use of alcohol and marijuana, though they are using frequently.[3] Their dependency on these substances, coupled with a lack of money or opportunity to purchase alcohol, are contributing to illegal activities and bad choices.

The Criminalization of Youth and Racism
in the Criminal Justice System

As I mentioned in the last chapter, Coldville is a community with a large politically liberal population. Wisconsin, the state that broke the Fugitive Slave Act when its citizens engaged in their right of jury nullification and refused to convict runaway slaves, is not a place where it is socially acceptable in most circles to express openly racist views. It is a community where White people want to think of themselves as not being racist. As a White person I often heard views expressed that I found racist in their implications, but these comments were usually carefully qualified with statements like, "not all Black people, of course, but just these people from Chicago." Most White people whom you would meet in Coldville would profess their willingness to judge each person on his or her own merits, with no consideration of the race of the person. The self-image of Whites in Coldville, however, is not consistent with my observations of the community nor with statistical evidence of police stops, arrests, convictions, and sentences that are, quite literally, some of the most racially biased in the country. These indicators of racial bias are so profound that they can only be accounted for by racism in the system and on the part of individual actors in the system; including officers, district attorneys, judges, and jury members.

In Coldville I witnessed White passengers moving to the front of the bus when Black youth sat down in the back of the bus. I noticed that two or three police cars would routinely arrive when I saw a Black driver pulled over. Having volunteered in some of the low-income neighborhoods in Coldville, I have seen police officers randomly stop young African-Americans. One afternoon, when I went to a local mall, I noticed several adults, one after the next, (who happened to all be middle-aged White women) stop before they entered the mall, and look at something that I could not see because the cars in the lot were blocking my view. A group of White teenagers were leaning up against the glass and were laughing at something. When I came close enough to see what had caught their attention I realized that they were all looking at an African-American child around the age of two. He could walk, but could not talk. He was crying and wandering around the parking lot. He was in grave danger of being struck by a car. All of these White people chose to leave that child to his fate rather than get involved. I ran up to the boy, took his hand, and went inside to look for his mother. I have told this story many times. Most of the Whites in Coldville whom I described this event to not only denied that it was evidence of latent racism in Coldville, but also denied that it was evidence of racism among the particular White people who did not help the child. Who can believe, however, that they would not have helped a two-year-old White child in danger of being struck by a car? So I entered the research process knowing that things were not ideal in the community, so far as race relations were concerned. But they were worse than I had expected.

Racial Profiling and Racial Bias in the System

Wisconsin, despite the great historical contributions of its citizens to the freeing of enslaved Africans in the United States, has one of the highest per capita rates of incarceration of Blacks of any state in the union (Beck et al., 2002). Nationally, Black incarceration rates, in 2001, were six times higher than those of Whites, while in Wisconsin the rate was 10 to one. These national statistics are also supported by the findings of sociologist Pam Oliver who has conducted federally funded research in Wisconsin related to bias in arrests and incarceration. Research that focuses on racial biases in Coldville, for both juveniles and adults, has found that Coldville has some of highest rates of arrest and incarceration per capita for Blacks in Wisconsin. In per capita arrest and incarceration numbers, Coldville is one of the most racially biased communities in the nation.

Additional evidence specific to Coldville makes the point: while the overall arrest and imprisonment rate in Coldville is relatively low, the tiny African-American population has extremely high rates of arrest and incarceration. Despite being only 4 percent of the population, more Blacks are sent to prison from Coldville, in raw numbers, than are Whites. The imprisonment rate for men of color between the ages of 20 and 29 was at a ratio of 36 to every 1 White man imprisoned. For African-American women in the same age group the ratio was 42 to 1. Young Blacks from Coldville are sent to prison at even higher rates than Whites in the same age group. In one year the rate (per 100,000) of 18- and 19-year-old Blacks sent to prison from Coldville was over 9,600, while the rate for Whites was around 300. As in the rest of the country, and despite the lower arrest levels for drugs in Coldville, around 40 percent of new prison sentences for Blacks are for drug offenses, versus 13 percent for Whites. When looking at younger age groups, the disparity is even more glaring. Arrests of Whites in Coldville are only 80 percent of those in Milwaukee County, but Blacks are 150 percent more likely to be arrested in Coldville than in Milwaukee County.

Most arrests are not for serious crimes. In fact, the percentage of arrests for serious crimes is even lower in Coldville than in much of the nation. Arrests for "public order" offenses, however, are 14 percent higher for adults and 10 percent higher for juveniles in Coldville than they are nationally. Property crimes account for about 11 percent of adult arrests nationally and 7 percent in Coldville, but 20 percent of juveniles in Coldville are arrested for property crimes, compared to a national figure of 7 percent.

The patterns of arrest, detention, and incarceration of youth of color in Coldville (who make up most of the young people in my study) are of the same nature as those in the rest of the country, except that they are far worse in Coldville. A report by the Office of Juvenile Justice and Delinquency Prevention in December 1999 reviewed juvenile arrest records, looked at disparities in the records by race and gender, and compared these to self-reported data. The report found that minorities, especially Blacks, engaged in criminal behavior no more than their White counterparts (with the possible exception of a slightly elevated level of violent crimes as reported by victims' data), and yet were more likely to be arrested and held in detention,[4] were more likely to be held in detention for longer periods of time, were more likely to receive harsher sentences and to be tried as adults, and were more likely to go to either juvenile or adult prison than were White offenders. The report made no claims that these numbers were the result of discrimination, though the numbers themselves strongly imply this, and concluded that, "questions regarding the causes of observed disparity and overrepresentation remain unanswered."

Statements like this assume a needed level of evidence which would not be required regarding any other issue; a level of evidence than can never be had. A racially biased system is made up of people who make racially biased decisions and who implement racially biased policies. This chapter, for example, contains the verbal evidence presented by victims of racial profiling and is the same sort of evidence gathered by human rights monitoring organizations (such as the Red Cross and Human Rights Watch), but this testimony is often dismissed; despite the fact that the claims are repeated so often by different young people who do not know each other. The tendency to ignore their claims is, in my view, another example of the same racist bias that I am attempting to reveal. When their claims are bolstered by statistical evidence, the numbers are accepted, but it is argued (not for any logical or methodological reason, but more on faith) that the numbers must be explained by some elusive cause rather than by racism among individual police officers and in the system as a whole. No amount of evidence will suffice, it seems, to get most White people to face their racism and the racism in the system. Even when systemic racism and bias are acknowledged, for example in media reports, one is hard pressed to find an individual occurrence that will be characterized as a biased act. It is as if systems are not made up of people.

Around the time that I was conducting my fieldwork in Coldville a report was released that documented the growing bias in stops and arrests of African-Americans in Coldville. Many Black drivers came forward to describe instances of racial profiling. White employers of Black drivers came forward to confirm their accounts. This caused enough of an outcry that the city formed a committee to look into the allegations and submit recommendations. The committee reported that the claimed instances of racial profiling seemed to be the result of actual, and not merely perceived, bias on the part of police officers. The committee recommended that officers hand out business cards identifying themselves to every motorist they stopped and that careful records be kept and monitored explaining the motivations for and results of every stop, including the apparent race or ethnicity of the people in the vehicle.

The powers that be in the community balked at this. They felt that the committee simply could not have gotten it right. A larger task force was convened, loaded up with prominent citizens, and carefully balanced with conservative and liberal members. The task force listened to testimony for a long period of time. Then, when most people in the community had forgotten why the task force was formed in the first place (and they were not reminded by the local media), the task force announced its recommendations: there should be a series of talking circles around issues of race in the community so that Whites and people of color could better understand one another and there should be publicly funded interracial swimming pools, so White kids and Black kids could grow up liking one another. There has yet to be an investigation of the misconduct of these officers. No convictions have been reconsidered. The police have been forced, however, to gather stop data, which continue to show racial bias.

Officers have learned, it would seem, to make up excuses for their racially motivated stops. The district attorney declined to prosecute a motorist for petty possession of marijuana when his car was stopped on the excuse that he had an air freshener hanging from his rear view mirror. The police claimed that he gave permission for the search. The media account made no mention of whether the standard issue police video camera was recording this alleged granting of permission to search. There are not, it is suggested, individual acts of bias, only evidence of systemic bias, the causes of which, it is alleged, cannot be identified.

When I spoke with the young people in my study I explained that I was trying to understand why young people get in trouble and what they thought about education and the economy, and I was trying to give them an opportunity to let the larger society hear them on the issues affecting their lives. I promised to do my best to accurately represent what they told me, even if I did not necessarily agree with what they told me. What they told me about racial profiling in their neighborhoods, and to some extent in their public schools, I believed. I believed them because they had been, for the most part, very forthright on other matters, because I heard the same sorts of stories in different settings (private interviews, group discussion, and so forth) over time from different young people who could not have coordinated their accounts, and because what they said was consistent with other evidence available to me regarding national, state, and local patterns of racial profiling and racism in the justice system.

One afternoon in a group discussion with a large number of young people, some of the participants raised the issue of racial profiling. I asked for a show of hands in response to their comments, "How many of you have been stopped and searched for no reason by the police." All of the hands in the room went up. I clarified what I was asking, that I did not mean something that resulted from or led to an arrest. All of the hands went up again. Taken aback, I asked if the police had asked them for permission before searching them. One White girl's hand went up and one Black boy raised his index finger and said, "one time they did." I responded by asking, "one time?" as the meaning of what they were telling me sank in. Then I asked the group, "How many of you have been stopped and searched without permission and for no reason, and then released without being arrested, more than five times?" All the hands went up. Then one of the Black girls began to speak, "there's one community police officer in North Beach who stops kids out of uniform and searches them, what's his name — I think it's Pat McCroy, and he says he won't stop 'til he gets us all."[5]

After this discussion, the prevalence of racial profiling became a central issue in all of my private interviews and in the research as a whole. Of the young people whom I interviewed, two informed me that they had not been searched by the police, two told me that they had not been harassed by the police, and nine told me that the police had searched them on the street. Of those who reported being searched by the police, only one reported that the police asked permission first. All nine told me that they had been harassed by the police. This was consistent with what other young people told me over the course of the year, in private and in front of anyone who would listen. They described being subject to frequent searches as they came home from school or went about on foot in their neighborhoods, and they described the constant threat of being searched that they felt due to the regular presence of police officers and police cars in their neighborhoods. The implications of this police behavior were that all Blacks were criminals, or potential criminals, and that the police had no respect for their rights.

An African-American boy of 16 told me in an interview that he had moved to Coldville from Chicago with his family. He said that the police are different in Coldville, giving out tickets for curfew and marijuana possession, while in Chicago the police were looking for guns and let marijuana slide. As he stated about the police in Coldville:

> Boy: Most of the time the cops stop you for no reason. One day I'm coming from school or just outside with the wrong people. They search you for no reason. Where you been? Let me search you. I say you search me I'm not doing anything wrong.
> Me: Did you say no?
> Boy: Sometimes. They search you anyway. Some cops are racist, but not all. But if you live in the wrong neighborhood they consider you a drug dealer.

A Latino boy of 18 echoed these sentiments in a private interview:

> The police stop people for no reason. Police search 'em anyway if they say no. Sometimes I think people think "these are just juveniles, there's no hope for them, they'll always be in trouble."

In an interview, an Asian-American boy described what became a consistent theme when speaking with the young people about this issue:

> Boy: The police didn't ask to search me. I had to remind them to ask. I said sure 'cause I've got nothing on me. It made me feel bad.
> Me: What would happen if you'd said no?
> Boy: I thought they'd hassle me all the time they saw me and search me anyway.

Another Black boy described the actions of the police in Coldville as follows:

> Walking down the street cops stopped me. Put us on the wall and said, "all Black people sell drugs so I have to search you." I just go along with it like in Chicago.

Even when young people are targeted by the police and volunteer to be searched, they do so because they feel that they have no choice. Experience has taught them not to get on the bad side of the police who will remember them, target them for harassment, or even make up charges against them. Even though the police may be within the letter of the law, as currently defined by a conservative Supreme Court, the consequences in terms of the lives of these young people are profound. They are targeted because they are Black and then coerced into allowing an invasive and degrading body search.

Most of the young people I spoke with reported that the police either did not ask to search them, or searched them anyway if they refused. As one 14-year-old Cuban-American boy told me:

> Cops don't have shit to do but bother us here. Cops stop us, "what you doing, you got any drugs?" I told the cop he couldn't search me. I said 4th amendment. I had some green. He kept asking me. Then he looked in my mouth.

This boy reported that the police harassed him on one occasion in his own front yard. "My mom told them to let go of me," he told me, "and the police called me nigger."

Reports of police misconduct went beyond racial profiling and illegal or coerced searches. One White boy told me the following, which his mother confirmed in a phone conversation:

They cops beat me up. I was out of hand. Squirming. Wrist restraints. They didn't
handle it well. They threatened to arrest my brother for staring at them.

An African-American boy recounted a similar encounter with the
police in Coldville:

On Halloween we was throwing eggs at houses. The police came. I said he couldn't
search us without permission. He whispered in my ear, "you better shut up before I
take you someplace and beat you." Once in an apartment the police came and
search us all. They just said get on the wall.

A Black girl reported that the local police threatened to kill her brothers
when they stopped them for walking around with White girls. A Latino boy
recounted to me how the police told him he would "be in jail like your bitch
ass dad."

One afternoon I noticed a boy sitting by himself, not goofing around
with the other young people. An African-American, he had a short hair cut
and stood about 5'10". He introduced himself, and here I'll call him Raymond. He asked me who I was and why I was there, so I explained my research to him. He began to tell me about the charges he was facing. He had
been the passenger in a car that was stopped by the police. He was searched
and a quantity of crack cocaine was found on his person. He was holding it
for an older boy who was driving the car. He was part of a sophisticated
criminal enterprise, whose members knew to move drugs on juveniles, and to
hide them on the body of a juvenile passenger who could not (under the law
at that time) be searched without consent.

I asked him: Why did the police pull your car over and search you?
Raymond: The light was supposedly out, but they had no probable cause to search
    us.
Me: No one said they could?
Raymond: No.
Me: Did you tell this to your lawyer?
Raymond: I had to get my own lawyer.
Me: That costs money.
Raymond: I know, but a public defender wouldn't fight for me.

The police report is in his intake file.[6] The police mention the headlight
being out as an excuse for the stop, and that the driver was a "known drug
dealer." The report makes no mention of asking or receiving consent to
search, but notes that the drugs were removed by medical personnel. Two
months later I sat at his table discussing his case and the cases of some other
boys. He told me that the police lied to justify the search. He told me that the

judge already ruled against him, but was waiting to sentence him. "She called me a menace to society," he told me, "just like the name of that movie." I asked him how they beat him at trial. He told me that several officers came to testify that he gave them permission to search him. He leaned forward and said in a quiet voice, so only I could hear him, "I've got 22 grams of crack hidden in my ass so the police can't feel it, now how'm I gonna say they can search me?!"

Another Black boy participating in the conversation told me that he was searched without permission and that the police found a small quantity of marijuana on him. I asked them if the judges in their cases really believe the police, or choose to believe them. They told me that they think the prosecutor and the judges are all in it together, and that afterwards "they have a drink and a cigarette and laugh about it." Nick said, "no one believes us and no one will listen." I promised to repeat what they told me when I wrote up my research. I asked them if they think people will be more likely to believe that the police lie when I report it than when they do themselves. Raymond responded for the table, "Some will, some won't, but they'll want to believe the cops." Raymond was ordered to a shelter setting by his judge and was lucky not to have been prosecuted as an adult, but angered by what he considered unfair treatment in a system that allowed police perjury, he ran away from the placement.[7]

Later that night I listened as a young girl conversed with a female staff member, a woman who managed the young people with patience and love. The girl was back in detention because she hit her teacher with a chair after, she says, he slapped her. "Why didn't you go to the principal?" the staff member asked her. "He's not going to believe me, a shelter girl." "Next time you come to me and I'll go with you," the woman told her. To this the girl continued, "If you were in my place what would you have done?" When the young people had all gone to bed I asked this staff member if she believed the things that the young people told us, about misconduct by the police and by their teachers. She told me that most of the time she does believe them.

Of course, patterns of police misconduct and racial profiling have been well documented nationally, ranging from fabricated traffic citations, illegal searches, physical abuse, to the recurring Serpico-like scandals (Maas, 2005). Policeabuse.com is a web site that publishes videotaped evidence of police misconduct and abuse of people of color and is run by a former officer. Policecrimes.com is a web based discussion forum where individuals discuss and document instances of police brutality. Indymedia.org has documented numerous examples of police repression of political expression. Even a casual use of internet search engines and news media databases reveals thousands of examples of documented police misconduct. In a 1999 report, the American Civil Liberties Union in *Driving While Black* documented widespread racial profiling in the United States. Human Rights Watch documented the scope of police misconduct and lack of accountability in *Shielded from Justice*. The October Twenty-Second Coalition has documented thousands of cases of deaths resulting from wrongful shootings, brutality, neglect, and negligence by law enforcement officers and by other employees in the criminal justice system. The volume of documentation available would take up all the pages in this book and bibliography. The frequency with which officers lie on the stand is well understood among insiders in the criminal justice system and those who study it. They call it "testilying" or going to the liars' club. Yet the popular notion that the police should be believed is continuously reinforced by police unions, prosecutors, the media, and juries. No amount of evidence seems sufficient to overcome the word of the police. So perhaps the word of the police against the police will convince. The following is a quote from a former police officer, who wrote a letter to the *Los Angeles Times* on February 11, 1996, breaking the "blue line" of silence among officers:

> Not many people took defense attorney Alan M. Dershowitz seriously when he charged that Los Angeles cops are taught to lie at the birth of their careers at the Police Academy. But as someone who spent 35 years wearing a police uniform, I've come to believe that hundreds of thousands of law-enforcement officers commit felony perjury every year testifying about drug arrests... [they] swear under oath that the drugs were in plain view or that the defendant gave consent to a search. This may happen occasionally but it defies belief that so many drug users are careless enough to leave illegal drugs where the police can see them or so dumb as to give cops consent to search them when they posses drugs. But without this kind of police testimony the evidence would be excluded.

Former police officers have exposed the cultural expectations within law enforcement that urge them to lie to get convictions and keep silent about misconduct by other officers (Quinn, 2004; *Minneapolis Star Tribune*, October 28, 2004; Juarez, 2004; Stamper, 2005). Cops never lie, the myth tells us, unless they claim that there is a culture of perjury by police officers, in which case, they are lying.

Another example from my fieldwork is revealing. During a break period the young people are allowed to sit at tables, four to a table. They play cards, board games like chess and checkers, or write letters. I joined a table of four African-American boys who were discussing one of their cases. I asked a boy to explain his situation to me. He said that he was outside in the neighborhood and witnessed some other boys commit an armed robbery. The judge and the social worker, he told me, confronted him asking, "How could you watch someone get brutalized like that and not do anything about it." He paused for a moment then his voice rose to a pitch as he related the following in one breath:

> I see people get brutalized on TV all the time. It's hard to not be around people in the neighborhood. I wasn't really with them, but I was charged with being a party to the crime. Everyone is just outside together. What, I'm gonna get myself shot over someone trying to buy drugs in our neighborhood?

I told him that I understood what he meant, that I thought robbery was a big problem and dangerous, but that I understood that he was not really involved. In my notes, I questioned how likely the judge and social worker, much less the average person, would be to intervene in a robbery. I have, myself, almost been attacked for trying to protect a younger Mexican boy from some older Puerto Rican boys on a subway in New York City, while several adults in business attire pretended not to notice, much less go for help. It occurred to me that these court officials were holding this boy to a standard to which they would not hold the average person, especially a White person, and that they failed to consider the dangers of informing in this boy's world.

I wanted to explore their thoughts on this difference of perspective, so I asked them if they would rather have a woman or a man judge. To my surprise they all agreed that a male judge is better. Then the boy facing the party to the crime charge volunteered, "We need to get some young judges in there, because these old judges don't understand what's going on in the streets." I responded by saying that it might not help if the judges still came from a different and privileged background. From my field notes:

> They seem to think the judges just don't understand the reality of what they must deal with. This is a very generous attitude for him to have. He is being targeted for being poor, Black, and for simply being outside.

I am familiar with the neighborhood in which this boy lived. Like the other neighborhoods of concentrated poverty in Coldville (the result of housing policies actively lobbied for by a powerful apartment owners' association) his neighborhood occupies a small geographic area. In this particular case the neighborhood consists of several blocks of apartments on the same straight street. Unlike the boys who actually committed the robbery, this young man was guilty only of being outside in his own neighborhood, where anyone can easily see any illegal activities from any location on the street. I am still struck by how generous these particular boys were towards the judge, even as the judge was far from generous towards this young man. The

young people in my study are from poor families and are disproportionately
African-American. Native Americans, Latinos and South East Asians are
also disproportionately represented in my study, though not nearly to the extent that Blacks are. The young people in my study are arrested more often
than their White counterparts. Even though self-reporting data show that
White youth violate the law at comparable levels, Blacks are held in detention more often and for longer periods of time, receive harsher sentences, are
more likely to be tried as adults, and are more likely to be sent to juvenile
prison (by judges) or adult prison (by mostly White juries). Their explanation
for their overrepresentation in the juvenile justice system is disproportionate
targeting by the police, who target them because of their race and the
neighborhoods they live in, and violate their fourth amendment rights.

Their explanation seems reasonable, is consistent with statistical evidence, is repeated by large numbers of young people over time in a variety of
settings, and is consistent with the reports of human rights organizations and
with the findings of other ethnographers.[8] The only remaining explanations
are either discredited or unreasonable. Discredited are the ideas that Black
youth commit crimes at higher rates than Whites (which is contradicted by
self-reporting studies) or that the illegal activities of Black youth are simply
more visible (which cannot account for the decision to focus on their
neighborhoods in the first place, rather than on house-based dealing in White
neighborhoods, which have a constant coming and going of cars). Unreasonable ideas include the suggestion that some systemic problem at all levels of
the juvenile justice system creates the racial disparities free of any human
bias. Unless every interaction between the police and the citizenry is mandated to be videotaped or audiotaped (something which I would support but
the police oppose), we will never have more compelling evidence than what
exists today.

But even mandated recordings of all interactions with the police (when
the police refuse to routinely record interrogations and alleged confessions in
most jurisdictions) would not protect young people of color, nor the adults in
their neighborhoods, from the decision to scrutinize their communities in the
first place. It is the initial decision to target people of color, in hopes of finding something incriminating, that *is* racial profiling. Subsequent searches,
whether forced or coerced, add insult to injury. At some point I realized, and
this is one of the major findings of my study, that the targeting of youth of
color for surveillance and scrutiny by the police is actually pushing young
people to drop out of school and engage in illegal activities.

The director of the detention center was a strong advocate of restorative
justice because it teaches young people to face the consequences of the harm

they have done, allows for healing between themselves and their victims (and the community), and because it is an easier political sell in this conservative climate. As he stated:

> Economic arguments don't resonate with people who just want to feel safe. Restorative justice can bring people together from different political perspectives, even the right. It is not a victim or villain dialectic. You can't go to people and tell them how tough a life a kid has had. Child advocates get pitted against community safety that way.

Restorative justice is a wonderful approach to take with young people who have real victims, where perpetrators are confronted by their victims and must make amends. It is an approach that can and should be widely implemented. But it will not do anything to stop the juggernaut that is the prosecution of young people for behavior that should not be criminalized

Consider again the unsolicited comments that often accompanied their answers when I asked them if they had been harassed or searched by the police. All of these interactions remind them of how the police and society views them. For a young man who is trying to maintain hope for a future via success in an educational system in which he is already struggling (and which has been shown to be biased against him), who is poor, needs money, and does not know if there is any future to look forward to, and who is already being treated as if he were a drug dealer (the harassment by the police), might easily come to the conclusion that he might as well sell drugs. He is already paying the price, as he perceives it, for selling drugs. The price is the stopping and searching by the police, but is also, more importantly, the viewing of him as a criminal by the police; with none of the material benefits of selling drugs, which he so desperately needs[9] given our unjust social and economic order.

The humiliation and feelings of powerlessness that are instilled in the young people by these police officers, officers who themselves may be feeding a psychological desire to feel powerful and superior, festers in the soul. Some of these young people may give in to feelings of self-loathing, and thereby engage in negative and self-destructive behaviors. Others may attempt to bolster their self-image by being good at something — drug dealing — when they believe that they have failed as students or in finding gainful legal employment. Still others may declare war on their tormentors, and the larger society, but lacking examples of community organizing and liberation struggle like those in the 1960s and early 1970s, take as the means of their resistance (instead of engaging in activism) the very trade that has funded death squads in Central America as it destroyed countless lives in the United

States. The police (aided by prosecutors, judges, politicians, reporters, and juries) create the criminals that their livelihoods, ambitions, and self-image require.

The Criminalization of Youth

When I had my interview with the director of the juvenile detention center, he commented on the popular image of youth crime perpetuated by the media and politicians:

> Are kids different today? Typical question I get. People want to believe the super-predator stuff. I typically say that, no, kids aren't different now. They're still kids, they're still changeable. They're in survival mode. That's just how you get by. They don't feel good about it or bad about it.

This man, and his detention center, were, at least when I was there, exceptional. They continued to believe in the concept of adolescence and to provide young people with a second chance when they landed in trouble. They did so, however, in the midst of a tornado. Young people were coming into the juvenile justice system in increasing numbers, and for increasingly minor offenses. Politicians and prosecutors were pushing to incarcerate younger and younger children as adults in a constant war against juvenile justice and the very concept of adolescence[10] (in so far as poor children are concerned). Prosecutors hope to become judges by being as tough as possible on crime. Judges hope to advance to higher courts. The public, wanting to feel safe, has accepted the notion that young people are the greatest threat to their safety.

Super-Predators or Super-Scapegoats?

Barry Feld wrote in his book, *Bad Kids* (1999), in response to the image of young Black males as super-predators at the forefront of a tidal wave of crime (an image perpetuated by John Dilulio and James Fox): "The political demonization of young black males as morally impoverished 'super-predators' and the depiction of delinquents as responsible offenders have eroded the Progressives' social construction of 'childhood' innocence and vulnerability." These intellectual darlings of the Right, Dilulio and Fox, were embraced by the mainstream media. Together they worked to convince the public of the wave of dangerous youth; the image of whom was always dark skinned, even when they were not explicitly described as such.

These scholars built their careers on these claims while media outlets sold products and scared their audiences. The super-predator arguments were lies, which thoughtful scholars exposed as such. The voices of reason were ignored until the promised explosion of youth violence failed to present itself. As Zimring (1998) demonstrates in his review of crime statistics and media coverage, from 1980 to 1997 arrests for rape and robbery showed no upward trend, the increase in arrest rates for assault was due to changes in the way the police tracked and classified these arrests (defining assault ever more broadly), and the homicide rate for juveniles had been in sharp decline since 1992. In a report in 1998 Amnesty International condemned the violation of rights of juveniles and documented patterns of mistreatment and abuse of juveniles while in detention. The report documents that from 1986 to 1995 the number of children confined before their cases were heard or following convictions grew by more than 30 percent, even though the children were being held for increasingly minor conduct. In fact, in 1995, fewer than half of the cases that juvenile court judges transferred to adult court involved violence against people (p. 15). This increasingly harsh treatment, they argued, was in response to the media reports of "super predators flooding the nations streets" and "teenage time bombs" (p. 5).

The most horrifying form of this attack on young people, especially young people of color, was the Violence Initiative, funded with federal dollars, and pushed by Frederick Goodman of the National Institute of Mental Health. This initiative sought to identify inner-city children who were presumed to have a biological or genetic predisposition towards violent behavior, and to mandate that they be administered experimental (and almost certainly dangerous) medications, purchased from the same drug companies that brought us drugs like Ritalin and Prozac, and all to be paid for with tax dollars (Breggin & Breggin, 1998).

Fistfights or Assault?

If we look at why young people come to the detention center in the first place, we see that assault or battery was the majority charge for young men, with disorderly conduct a close second. Disorderly conduct was first for young women with assault or battery a close second. The next large category was made up of crimes against property, which includes joy riding, vandalism (including graffiti art), and theft. These numbers do not include all the behaviors that can land a kid in a police car, like being out after curfew or drinking alcohol, which would not result in the seizure of an adult. When a young person is charged with a scary-sounding offense like battery it is easy for the public to assume (an assumption that is seldom challenged by the news media) that the offending child has gone after someone with a knife or baseball bat. The majority of battery charges, however, are simple fistfights. The prevalence of fist fighting is no greater than in earlier generations, but what were once dismissed as youthful mistakes are increasingly criminalized. Zero-tolerance policies in schools result in the suspension, expulsion, and arrest of young people who engage in fighting behavior. Perhaps fighting is not something that is in the memories of wealthy policy makers or upper-middle class intellectuals, but as a product of a working-class community I can attest to the fact that a willingness to fight to defend oneself was essential in order to avoid being targeted as weak and thereafter being harassed on a regular basis. The phrase, "Never start a fight, but always finish them," is parental advice that most working-class people will remember.

The young people in my study were quite perplexed by the criminalization of fighting. As one young African-American girl who was in for battery, specifically for a fistfight with another girl, told me, "I come from a family of scrappers, and if one of my family gets in a fight the rest are expected to enter the fight too." When I asked young people why they or their peers engaged in fighting behavior, they told me that half the time it was because young people "have a lot of anger in 'em" or need anger management training. The rest of the time, however, they insisted that there was often no choice but to defend themselves against attacks. There is little allowance for the right of self-defense in this new criminalization of youth. As a young person told me:

> People like to fight. When I fight my whole family fights. Fight to be safe and just do it. Dad says so. People shouldn't get in trouble for fighting.[11]

When young people are arrested and charged for fist fighting, especially working-class youth, it is, in their way of looking at things, about as reasonable as arresting them for cussing (something which can and has occurred). As distasteful as fighting is (and I am all for helping young people find alternatives to violence as a means of resolving conflicts), when it is criminalized it is done so to deliberately cast a wide net aimed at catching working-class youth, especially those of color. It is a racially and class-biased policy, given the cultural norms of the working class and the realities of life on the streets of these communities. One staff member put a different spin on this theme:

> Why do they get in trouble? You have a violent society raised on Westerns. Westerns are like gangs, calling someone coward, and having to fight.

My findings regarding the role that fighting plays in the lives of working-class youth, and the realities of street life that make it very difficult, if not impossible, for these youth to avoid fighting, are consistent with those reported by Noguera (2000). As his informants stated:

> If you tell a teacher that somebody wants to fight with you it's not like they're gonna walk you home. The most they can do is get the person sent to the office, but if the fight didn't happen yet, the person ain't even gonna get in trouble (p. 145).

> When someone wants to fight you, they usually don't give you a chance to do any talking. That stuff (conflict resolution) only works if the principal or somebody is around. If it's just you and the other person, you got to let your fists do the talking otherwise you could get hurt. I usually try to get the first punch in. That usually works better than trying to talk about it (p. 146).

Though fighting is common among the working class, especially among boys, the rituals built around fighting and the context in which it occurs vary by geography, race, and ethnicity. I'm reminded of my move to New York City, where I befriended an African-American man who was about my age at the time and from a struggling neighborhood. He instructed me on how to walk around in the tougher areas:

> First, when you pass another man, you look him in the eyes so he knows you're not afraid, otherwise he might think you're weak and jump you. Then, you look away, otherwise he'll think you're staring at him and will either take offense, or else he'll think you're about to jump him, so he'll swing on you first.

By criminalizing the fighting behavior of youth of color and working-class youth in general, without providing them with meaningful alternatives that account for the realities of life in their communities, society is simply casting a net from which these youth cannot escape.

After conducting my interview with the girl who identified herself as a "scrapper," the girl and I joined the rest of the young people who were watching a Disney film. It was the story of a young White boy who wanted a hunting dog. He worked and saved the money to order his dog. When the shipment of the puppy was delayed in a distant town, he ran away to retrieve his pet. With his new dog he became a successful hunter, rivaling a neighbor boy. They engaged in a hunting contest in which our hero won. The neighbor boy became enraged and attacked him. The boy took our hero's hatchet and attempted to kill his dog. Our hero tripped the boy, who fell on the hatchet and died. Later at the funeral, the hero's father stated that this was an accident and nobody's fault. The character was not arrested for running away nor for the death of his rival. The irony of this film being shown to these young people in detention, and the messages it conveyed about fighting, did not escape me. Today if the boy in the film lived in Coldville, Wisconsin, and especially if he had dark skin, he would likely have been charged as an adult with first-degree intentional homicide.

Get 'em While They're Young

One afternoon a senior staff member stopped me to explain that the current district attorney liked to threaten to charge juveniles as adults in order to get them to plead guilty as juveniles. This member of the staff had little to say to me over the course of my research, but clearly wanted this observation documented and exposed in the community. In Wisconsin, juveniles as young as 15 may be waived to adult court on motion of the prosecutor, a decision made by a solitary judge. Some offenses fall within the adult court jurisdiction automatically. In the years of 1998 and 1999 the district attorney petitioned to have well over 200 juveniles transferred to adult court. In the end, only about a third of these juveniles were actually waived to adult court, either because they gave in to her blackmail and pled guilty as a juvenile, or because a judge refused to go along with the ambitions of the prosecutor (who has since been rewarded with an appointment to the appeals court by the former governor). With high-profile cases, the district attorney, like other prosecutors across the country,[12] sought to prosecute (or threatened to prosecute) very young people as adults.

There are two dramatic examples captured in my research of this attempt to make a reputation by prosecuting very young offenders. The first was related to some young African-American boys who had been arrested for sexual assault after rubbing up against a young girl in a sexually suggestive manner. There was no nudity involved, and certainly no penetration. While not wanting to minimize their hurtful behavior in any way, these boys were 11 and 12 years of age. It simply was not rape. Not in the sense that such charges are typically understood.

The second example involved a Black boy, who at the age of 12, accidentally shot a girl with whom he was friends, at point blank range in the face.[13] He was with a group of young people that had found the guns behind the counter of a local shop where they stopped from time to time to speak with the owner. The gun was not secured and was loaded. They stole it. He was charged with first-degree murder, of executing her, and was threatened with being charged as an adult. Eventually, he took a deal to plead guilty as a juvenile, and is now in prison. His case had a profound impact on the research site, and illuminated issues of race and the ambitions of the district attorney.

When I first met Scott he was 13 years old, small, and timid. He was visibly scared, shaking. As I came to know him better and observe him around other young people and adults, it was obvious that he was one of these children in great need of attention, approval, and affection. He wanted to please adults and be liked by his peers. He was almost always smiling. Nothing in his behavior was aggressive or threatening. Though only 12 at the time, his photo had been published on the front of a major newspaper and his name (which as a juvenile should be kept confidential) had been widely published. The photo on the front of the paper was taken from such an angle (from a kneeling position looking up) as to make it appear that Scott was a large, menacing, Black man. The story that went with the photo, found deep in the paper (disembodied from the photo), commented on how he was taller than his attorney, again in an apparent effort to enhance the perception that he was large and menacing. In reality, Scott was the smallest boy in the detention center.

He could best be described as immature for his age. He was a child, not a cold-blooded killer. In time Scott began to come out of his timid shell. In many ways I think that being in the detention center was good for him. He was safe and was cared for by the staff. The extent of his immaturity became more evident as he became more comfortable. He was impulsive and had a great deal of nervous energy. Apart from the immaturity of a 13-year-old boy, Scott displayed real intellectual curiosity at times. On one occasion he engaged me in a lengthy conversation about the meaning of the term "culture." Despite his obvious intelligence, he seemed to have no understanding of his situation. He knew that it was an accident. He expected to go home soon.

Accidental Shooting or Murder?

Scott insisted that he had thought that the gun was not loaded and that the shooting was an accident. There was much discussion of the fact that Scott was originally from Chicago and had fled back there after the shooting. The district attorney and press also made much of the reports of other friends who were with Scott and said that Scott had stated that he was going to shoot someone — which might merely be childish fantasy talk from an immature child who got hold of a revolver rather than proof of premeditation. Only after he had been sent to juvenile prison were many of the court records released to the public by the district attorney's office. The facts of the case, like the fact that he had been joking with the girl only moments before the shooting, all seemed to indicate that this had been an accident. At his sentencing, the local judge made pronouncements about the need to protect the public from Scott, and gave him an unusual sentence for a juvenile that will hold him under supervision until the age of 25.

The allegation that the district attorney may have acted in bad faith, threatening to prosecute as an adult and prosecuting a child who was most likely innocent, may seem extreme to readers who are unfamiliar with the conduct of prosecutors. The evidence of prosecutorial misconduct goes far beyond the racial bias reflected in prosecution statistics. Prosecutors have gained convictions against defendants who they knew were likely innocent and have intentionally withheld exculpatory evidence. They have charged Blacks with crimes they knew were committed by Whites, and visa versa. Prosecutorial misconduct is widespread and national in scope, occurring on both the federal and state levels. Prosecutors generally receive almost complete immunity for anything that they do in an official capacity. Even in the highly publicized cases of exoneration based on DNA evidence, numerous prosecutors have fought tooth and nail to keep innocent people in jail, even arguing in some cases, in court, that actual innocence is irrelevant once procedural time limits have elapsed. This misconduct was carefully documented in two newspaper series, *Win at all Costs,* one in the *Pittsburg Post-Gazette* and the other in the *Chicago Tribune.*

Even the editorials of a weekly news magazine in Coldville which had advocated for the view that Scott did not intentionally shoot the girl, stated that he was clearly a dangerous person for stealing the guns and causing the death of his friend. However, the condemnation of Scott did not extend the other children who were with him at the time, nor to other children in Wisconsin who had accidentally shot someone when adults had carelessly left guns within their reach. Perhaps they were not charged because they were not Black boys from Chicago who had shot a White girl. The *Wisconsin State Journal* reported on May 9, 1999, shortly after the sentencing of Scott, that a 12-year-old Wisconsin boy was shot by a friend who thought that the bullets were out of the gun. The paper described the children, the same age that Scott had been, as "playing with" the gun. The Coldville District Attorney who charged Scott with murder declined to bring charges in November of 1999 against a White boy who had accidentally shot and killed a White girl with whom he was friends. A study by the Children's Defense Fund found that between 1979 and 1999, more than 10,000 children and teenagers died from accidental shootings across the United States. In Wisconsin alone, from 1997 to 1999, 12 young people were killed in accidental shootings, and more than 70 committed suicide by guns (press release of Wisconsin Governor Doyle, October 27, 2003). Scott's friend, however, was not counted among these 12.

A study by the Violence Policy Center found that there were at least 222 accidental shootings of young people in 40 states during a nine-month period in 1996. The Center for Disease Control reported that the rate of accidental shootings resulting in death in the United States was at a rate 9 times higher than those in 26 countries studied. In a 2004 report the Children's Defense Fund puts the rate at 12 times higher in the United States. The National Safe Kids Campaign reported in 1999 that an estimated 1,500 children under age 14 are treated in hospital emergency rooms for unintentional firearm-related injuries annually, and that in 1997 alone, over 10,000 children were treated for non-powder-gun-related injuries (from pellet guns, for example). Children are injured on a routine basis by guns, and in the absence of adult supervision and training, these injuries often take the form of accidental shootings that frequently result in death.[14] When these shootings occur, it is assumed that the shootings are accidents. The fact that the kids were friends and were playing with the guns together is considered in most cases. In Scott's case, however, the opposite assumption — that he meticulously executed his friend for the fun of it — was made and accepted by the public and the media in Coldville. Scott was Black, from Chicago, and his victim was a White girl.

Torture

Towards the end of my year in the Juvenile Court some young people confided in me that while they were held in a neighboring county detention center, having been shipped there because of overcrowding, they were abused by the guards. The facilities at this location stressed control and technology rather than close adult guidance as in the facility in Coldville. The physical plant was set up more like a maximum-security prison than a juvenile holding facility. The guards, reportedly, thought of themselves more as prison guards than as influential adults in the lives of struggling young people. The young people told me that, because of some power struggles over petty matters, several of them had been pepper sprayed. What was worse, they told me, was that they had been pepper sprayed while restrained, by handcuffing them to chairs or beds, unable even to shield their eyes from the direct blasts. They had brought to my attention felony assault (and I would call it torture), on minors by their caregivers in a detention facility.

I encouraged them to tell their parents about what had happened to them. All of the young people involved expressed the view that their parents could not do anything about it, that it was business as usual, and that no one would believe them anyway. This was an ethical dilemma. If the young people would not blow the whistle on their abuse, then I had to consider the very real possibility that the abuse would continue to happen to other young people sent to this detention facility. I had an obligation to report abuse. On the other hand, I feared that reporting what I had learned might jeopardize my access to the research site. I decided to document their statements over the period of a couple of weeks while I waited to have my scheduled interview with the director.

Six of the young people who told me they had been sent to this detention center during this time period told me that they had been pepper sprayed. As different young people described their abuse as follows:

> I got sprayed. I got locked down for sharing my food. Then I was talking so they sprayed me. They use it every day all day for anything that happens.

> They didn't have to spray anybody. It was completely unnecessary.

> They shackle your arms and legs for doing anything bad, like cussing. Beating on the wall. They sprayed me with the pepper spray while I was shackled cause I cussed at the guard.

One boy was skeptical of the claims that pepper spray had been used, though he claimed to have been abused in other ways in the neighboring detention center:

> I've been to [the detention center] I got beat up by staff there. I never saw that there. Hell no, they're lying. They do have pepper spray, but I've never seen it used.

When I interviewed the director of the detention center in Coldville, I explained that if I had seen any abuse I would have been obligated to report it, but that I had never seen any behavior on the part of his staff that came close to being abusive, to which he responded, "good." I then went on to say that, "Some of the young people tell me that when they were shipped out to [the other county], that they were pepper sprayed, even while they were shackled." He quickly responded, stating that, "They stopped using pepper spray." "So it's true what they were telling me?" I asked. "Yes, but we put an end to it. It won't happen again."

I believed the director when he told me that he had put an end to the abusive behavior in the neighboring county. Because no young people were in immediate danger of being pepper sprayed and because I believed that they would be monitoring what went on at the neighboring center, I decided that I could continue my research and could wait to release my findings when the book was published.

Blame it on the Goths

On April 20, 1999, two heavily armed boys committed a massacre in their high school, Columbine, killing 23 of their fellow students and teachers before taking their own lives. Over 25 students and faculty were injured in the attack (*Chicago Tribune*, April 23, 1999). The attackers methodically hunted their victims among the trapped student body, at times firing randomly, but often seeking out students who they felt had belittled them, or were associated with groups that had belittled them; such as student athletes. In the rush to find some explanation for this tragic event, the media quickly latched onto the fact that the young people dressed in a style associated with alternative music. Marilyn Manson, a musician they were said to listen to, was widely blamed for the shootings because of the angry lyrics in some of his songs. Though Marilyn Manson's music is not gothic, and the young people were not actually associated with the gothic subculture, the media assured us that gothic music was to blame.

A social worker at the detention center stopped me shortly after the shootings as I was coming in one afternoon to tell me about the Goths whom she had met in her work and whom she viewed as walking time bombs. Everyone was scared. Goths seemed alien to most people, dressing strangely, and listening to music that they did not (as far as they knew) listen to themselves. Wearing black became a sign of delinquency and dangerousness.

I was in a unique position to judge the claims made in the media and repeated in the Juvenile Court about the gothic subculture. As an undergraduate I had promoted dance nights that featured Gothic and New Wave music in New York City. For years I had dressed in the style of this subculture, and had worn a backwards Mohawk haircut. Gothic music and culture grew out of Punk Rock and New Wave, and was influenced by Rock acts such as Stevie Nicks and The Velvet Underground. Some examples of gothic bands are far more mainstream than many people realize, including such well-known acts as The Cure, Joy Division, and Peter Murphy. What is so ironic about the branding of the gothic subculture as dangerous is that gothic music developed in part as a move away from the violence in Punk Rock. The Gothic subculture is politically liberal, gay friendly, antiracist, and has almost no violence associated with concerts and other public events, unlike most Rock, Country, and Hip Hop music scenes.

Fear of a Young Planet

Following the massacre in Colorado, a number of threats were made by alienated young people in schools around the country to repeat what had happened in Littleton (*Chicago Tribune*, April 28, 1999). The trend towards zero tolerance in schools was joined by a healthy dose of paranoia. Young people began to be arrested and expelled for any behavior that hinted of violent intentions. There were serious discussions about arming teachers to keep schools safe (*Isthmus*, September 3, 1999). A student in Texas who was given an assignment to write a scary story wrote about violence in school and was arrested (*Wisconsin State Journal*, November 11, 1999). A high school student in Virginia was arrested for writing a similar tale in a creative writing test (*Wisconsin State Journal*, May 24, 1999). The Wisconsin legislature assigned $10 million in grant money to identify potentially violent students (*Wisconsin State Journal*, May 22, 1999). The Wisconsin Safe School Task Force took this as an opportunity to push for having the police in every high school in the state (*Simpson Street Free Press*, December 1999).

There were, reportedly, some plots to carry out Columbine-like attacks that were prevented (though the seriousness with which these attacks were being planned is questionable). It was certainly very reasonable for school and community officials to be alert and reach out to young people who might be in need of help or harboring ambitions towards violence. What happened, however, was something much more punitive and hysterical. Senator Orrin Hatch, a Republican from Utah, took this as an opportunity to try to give prosecutors blanket authority to move juveniles into adult court. Opposed by the American Civil Liberties Union, his effort was narrowly defeated (ACLU press release, March 10, 1999). These efforts to further criminalize young people in the wake of Columbine were occurring despite the government's own findings that serious violent crime among young people was rare and compared to that among adults, on the decline (Heaviside et al., 1998; Kaufman, Chandler, & Rand, 1998), and that students were safer, on average, while in school than at any other time of their day (*Annual Report on School Safety*, 1998). In the wave of hysteria and opportunism on the part of those who would destroy juvenile justice and the very concept of adolescence, calmer voices again tried to find access to the public through the media, but were largely ignored. The Justice Policy Institute and the Children and Family Justice Center, for example, published a wonderful collection of success stories of prominent citizens who were given a second chance by the juvenile justice system (1999).

The definition of what behavior was to be considered dangerous was broadened dramatically, much as the definition of assault had been broadened. A girl in Wisconsin received a sentence of a year of probation for making a hit list of people she did not like (*Capital Times*, December 1, 1999). Any angry outburst, any dark humor, was evidence of a crime, or at least delinquency. These measures were necessary, we were assured, because young people today are more violent and more dangerous than in any other historical period. This claim, of course, was false. In 1866 in Wisconsin a teacher attempted to punish a boy by beating him with switches. The boy struggled with his teacher, eventually striking the teacher with a stick of wood, resulting in the teacher's death. The boy was charged with murder (*Wisconsin Journal of Education*). Moreover, there have always been children who have had a morbid sense of humor when it comes to schooling. I remembered a childhood song that reflected this and asked my students at the university if they could share any with me that they remembered. There were several variations of the song I remembered, which has evolved but survived over the years:

> Glory Glory hallelujah
> Teacher hit me with a ruler
> Got my 44, blew her out the door
> She ain't my teacher no more

Other songs went like this:

> From the Halls of (fill in the school name)
> To the Shores of bubble gum bay
> We will fight our teachers' battles with spitballs, gum, and clay
> First we fight for rights and freedoms
> Next to keep our desks a mess
> We are proud to claim the title of the teacher's number one pest.

> Row, Row, Row your boat
> Gently Down the Stream
> Throw your teacher over board
> And listen to her scream

It is no exaggeration to say that singing these songs in the current climate could easily result in arrest and expulsion. This is not the first time in the history of the United States that young people were singled out as targets for our fears, as the first part of this chapter shows. We have always had trouble "right here in River City."

This Is No Accident

The young people whom I spent time with in the Juvenile Court, especially those who were held for longer periods of time, were not always entirely blameless. Some of them had engaged in truly horrible acts. Others had demonstrated a need for intervention in their lives by responsible adults if not by the state. Most of the young people, however, were being held in detention because of the political winds and economic trends of the historical period in which they were coming of age. They did the sort of reckless and thoughtless things that young people have always done, like stealing or getting into fights. Some of them were caught, after humiliating and racially motivated searches, with small quantities of a mood-altering drug that is safer than Tylenol. Even the young people who have committed terrible acts and must be held responsible for them are not sole actors in their crimes. They had with them a coconspirator in the form of racism, self-loathing, and poverty.

The tremendous resources that went into their capture and captivity, which could have been spent on after-school programs or greater financial aid to their families, were instead allocated to a punitive approach to juvenile justice. The reasons for this choice in terms of how to allocate resources are complex. There are, however, three motivations that are primary: 1) it moves our nation towards a form of neo-fascism, a police state, which is the clear aspiration of the far right (and of some liberals too); 2) it is profitable for the shareholders, professions, and industries that benefit from the boom in prison building and incarceration; and 3) it minimizes employment competition between working-class Whites and Blacks in an economy that is shrinking its domestic labor needs (through outsourcing and technology) in favor of Whites; that is, Whites get jobs guarding Black prisoners.

The situation that the young people in my study were in was predictable, given changes in the political economy. The exact forms that their alienation would take could have varied, but the stark inequalities in our society dictate that the social order must either distribute resources more fairly, prevent the growing masses of disenfranchised citizens from taking collective action, or reduce their numbers in the population. So far, the first option has been violently resisted by the powerful in our society, who favor, instead, more inequality backed up by an ever-expanding police apparatus.

Though the massive growth in incarceration of adults and juveniles in the United States is functional to the needs of late capitalism, this does not mean that these outcomes were the result of distant economic forces beyond the control of humans. I named this chapter "corruption and racism" because the violence (economic, legal, psychological, and bodily) perpetuated against these young people and their communities is carried out by people. The ruling elites in our society are the most responsible for this violence, as are the overseers whom they hire to patrol the plantation, but we are all guilty. We are guilty first and foremost for allowing genocidal attacks on poor people of color to occur in our silence and even with our complicity. We need not take up arms, at least not initially, to demand true justice for our brothers and sisters. The White and the relatively comfortable in our society have not (in any numbers) bothered to vote our consciences, to call our media, or to use any of the skills and resources that we bring to bear on chain stores that try to move into our neighborhoods, to help these youth. Go to any court in our nation. Look at the faces of those facing criminal charges, civil citations, or delinquency complaints alike. They are disproportionately young, poor, and dark skinned. As this chapter has demonstrated, they are there not by accident, and their actions, even when they are "guilty," do not explain the absence of Whites in these courtroom, who are equally "guilty," but have not been targeted (by the police, prosecutors, and judges) to the same extent or in the same manner as has the population in my study.

Chapter 6
Race, Class, and Gender

In this chapter I will discuss how racism, class bias, and gendered expectations of masculinity contributed to the attitudes, behaviors, and choices of my participants.

The Racist Gaze

One aspect of racism, as it functions psychologically, is that well-meaning White people can engage in racist behavior without realizing it. Even more importantly, the way they view people of color can be influenced by the climate of racism without their realizing it. As such, it is difficult to guard against the resulting harm that can occur to children of color, much less to engage in dialogue around these issues with Whites who simply can not or will not consider the implications of the ways in which they construct people of color, however well meaning they may be. The forms that this unintended racism takes vary. It can take the form of the imposition of school dress codes that favor the norms of middle-class Whites or it can take the form of an unspoken fear, a heightened alertness, when Black boys pass by (whether communicated by the clutching of a purse or the crossing of the street). It can also take the form White people being more likely to believe that young people of color are more predator than foolish, more dangerous than immature. Too often Black youth in particular are viewed very differently than White youth.

The discussion around Scott's case (the boy who shot his friend), as an example, at the detention center, told me as much about individual staff members as it did about Scott's case. Opinions as to whether the shooting was intentional varied, of course, and tended to break down along racial lines. None of the African-American staff believed that Scott had intended to shoot his friend. Only one White staff member, a person with much empathy for the kids, doubted his guilt. I do not know how the director felt about his case.

On a rainy morning, a special visitor came to the center in a visit arranged by the directors. This woman had been shot by two boys who found her at home as they were in the process of robbing her home. They shot her with the intent of killing her. She survived, but is mostly blind and partially paralyzed. She speaks to groups about her experience and is in mediation with her attackers. Rather than simply condemn her attackers or sink into obsessions with revenge, she has sought to forgive them and to help young people learn from her situation to make better choices; informed by an understanding of the impact that such violence can have. We organized a circle of chairs and she stood in the middle.

On this morning a member of the staff was there who has a tendency to yell at the young people and in general had a negative view of them (the same woman whose complaint resulted in the boy being charged as an adult after he threw an orange at her, egged on by her authoritarian behavior). I intentionally sat next to Scott on this morning because I was afraid this talk would cause him to act out. I wanted to be able to calm him before this staff member could set him off, setting him up (intentionally or not) for punishment; getting in trouble in detention could have serious consequences for his eventual sentence. As the visitor told her story, Scott looked visibly shaken. He hid his face by looking at the ground and slumped in his seat. The staff member interpreted the looking away by the young people while the woman told graphic details of her attack as a sign of disrespect. She insisted that they sit up straight and still, and that they look at the woman the entire time she was talking.

After the visitor finished her story this staff member began making the young people state why they were in the detention center. As they would admit their offenses, the visitor would challenge them on their conduct and ask them to change their ways. I found this very troubling, as she was compelling the young people to say things that could potentially be used against them in a juvenile proceeding or criminal trial.[1] In my notes I wrote:

> I have mixed feelings about this speaker. There's the implication that these kids are
> all potential killers. Some of them are just runaways. I saw Scott struggle, and he's
> already very fragile emotionally.

After the talk a White female intern asked me if I thought the kids benefited from the talk. I said I thought so, but that I thought this was a very disturbing experience for Scott. She said that she did not notice him reacting at all, and that his lack of an emotional response, she thought, demonstrated once again that he was not remorseful. My eyes and her eyes saw two different people. I saw a young Black boy who was physically shaking, averting his eyes in a desperate attempt to avoid crying in public. She saw a cold-blooded killer, and described him as such. She argued that he had to be guilty, that he stole the gun, that he said he wanted to shoot someone that day, and that he fled back to Chicago after the shooting. I argued that young people accidentally shoot each other all the time; they point the gun at someone, pull the trigger as they say "bang," and then watch in disbelief as a bullet comes out of the gun they thought was unloaded.

But this intern was not a racist, though she may have been influenced by the racism all around us. She was known for working with students at the center around racial conflicts. In other situations I had observed her to be very compassionate towards young people of color. Later she would tell me that I was right, that Scott had told her, "why'd you have to have that lady talk? She made me cry." Her eyes had seen the same emotional response in Scott that I had, but her gaze, the way her mind had been conditioned to view youth of color as violent, prevented her from accurately recognizing what she saw. His remorseful words were able to reach her, however. Most White people would not be as willing as Stephanie was to reconsider her initial conclusions.

A year later this visitor would return. On the second occasion the woman staff member who had forced the young people to confess was no longer working at the detention center. I thought the talk was much more beneficial to the young people the second time. This time they were not defensive as the young people had been on the first visit, because they were no longer being accused of being killers or potential killers. On this visit their questions expressed interest in how the visitor could forgive her attackers and enter mediation with them, after the horrible things they had done to her.

The Meaning of, and Boredom with, Racism

I met Sam on the day of his placement hearing. He had been in trouble all day long and was eventually sent to his room for repeatedly swearing. The intern who sent him to his room was very concerned about him and told me that he had been severely abused by his father in Chicago. "He hates White people," she told me. Later she went to Sam's status hearing with him. This is unusual, especially for an intern, but she wanted to be there to support him and put in a word about his better potential if asked. Sam, however, lost his temper at the hearing, swearing at the judge, and assumed that the intern had come to the meeting to get him in trouble.

I tried to speak with him later that day. I tried to assure him that this intern, of all the people at the center, was on his side. I told him that I had no doubt that he had experienced racism in his life, but that sometimes his anger prevented him from seeing that some White people like him. I explained to him that the intern would have spoken for him at the hearing, if given the chance.

A few days later I was asked to run group in the evening. We discussed violence on the street and how to avoid fights. The boys told stories of experiences with violence, and I told similar stories. Some White girls complained that the topic was boring. A boy responded to the girls complaints of boredom, stating that, "You're bored because it doesn't happen to you, but it happens to us all the time."

Sam joined the group, back from his time-out in his room. At first he refused to sit in the group with a White boy, the only White youth in the room, because, he claimed, the boy had made racist remarks towards him, which had resulted in his being sent to his room. The boy responded that he "just said it to get at Sam" who is always accusing him of being racist simply because he is White. I calmed them down before another fight could erupt.

Two male staff members, one African-American and the other Latino, joined the conversation. They confronted Sam about his racist paranoia. Sam responded by saying that the Black staff member was racist for sending him to his room earlier when he got in the fight. Sam then called him an "Uncle Tom." I spoke to the students about Malcolm X and how some of his ideas about White people changed after he visited Mecca. The students seemed very interested in this.

Later in the week I came back in the evening. Eager to continue where the conversation had left off, I had arranged to show the Spike Lee film *4 Little Girls*. I was surprised to find that many of the students of color were very bored with the film. "Why's the staff maken' us do all this race stuff," one boy asked. An African-American girl meekly stated that she thought it was interesting. When footage of an African-American civil rights leader being beaten was shown on the film, some of the boys laughed at him. The girl snapped at them, stating that, "it's not funny." After the film, I tried to explain to the students, who were continuing to complain about my choice of film, why I showed it. I told them that I wanted to give them an opportunity to discuss the issues it addresses. One of the boys said that, "people don't know their history."

I asked the young people what topic they would prefer to discuss in group. One of the boys said, "Freedom." I told him that was a good topic. I asked them what freedom meant to them. At first they were reluctant to speak. One of the girls seemed to take pity on me for the silence and volunteered, "being out of here." Others agreed saying things like, "being able to do what you want, when you want." I asked the girl who had come to my rescue if she could really do anything she wanted at anytime on the outside. She looked at me in a puzzled way, so I elaborated:

> I know being in here that you think about being able to do what you want, and that staff have to control things to keep you safe in here. But there's more to freedom than that, and thinking you can always do what you want can get you in trouble.

I asked again what they thought of when they thought of freedom. One of the boys responded that he thought of Martin Luther King. "So you think of the civil rights movement?" I asked him. "No," he replied, "I just think of the name Martin Luther King." Another boy interrupted us. "I think of free will," he said. I said that this is a good example, that free will is an old concept that means not only freedom but also refers to the responsibility that goes with freedom. The young people acknowledged my point, but were tired of being spoken to about responsibility. The conversation faded, so I asked for other topics they wanted to discuss...

The young people in my study experienced racism in their lives. In fact, many of the young people of color identified racism as a primary reason for their being in detention. Though they were acutely sensitive to acts of racism, and sometimes interpreted events as racist that were not (and certainly were not intended as such), they also seemed to lack any analysis of racism. Many of them could articulate clear and powerful critiques of the inequalities in society, tied to the efforts of the wealthy to remain wealthy at their expense. Yet the racism that they identified and complained of was something that just happened, it seemed, because White people did not like them. They articulated little analysis of why White people had racism in their hearts, or why even well-meaning Whites might behave in a racist manner at times. Despite the courageous efforts of the parents and grandparents of this generation of young people to secure racial justice in the United States, both through the civil rights movement and liberation struggles, these young people were disconnected from a community of activism and even seemed bored with the subject. Perhaps this is because they live in a time when the civil rights movement is not as visible and active, or perhaps it is because their communities have become road weary from the ongoing struggle for justice. There are, of course, courageous community members and leaders in Coldville who struggle every day for racial and social justice. But the promise of collective action does not reach or excite most of these young people. In fact, the young people who did understand and care about the continuation of struggles for justice expressed their disgust and impatience with their peers for their seeming apathy.

On Being a Father

On a summer afternoon the center was thick with nervous energy. The teacher was on summer break and the summer substitute teacher had not been hired yet, so staff and two female interns were running the school. The class was working on a crossword puzzle in groups at each table. A story that was to accompany the crossword puzzle was missing, so a cheat sheet circulated the room. I sat at a table with two African-American boys and an African-American girl. I held the cheat sheet. I tried to get the students to at least try to find the meaning of the words before they asked me for the answers. I was not very successful at this, though. As one of the boys copied from a girl's paper I teased him for cheating. He smiled and told me, "copying's not cheating!"

I asked the girl why she was in detention. She said, "nothing," that she had done nothing. I joked with her that she probably robbed a bank. She answered, in a matter-of-fact tone, that she did nothing, she just didn't keep a court date. The two boys broke out laughing at this. She shouted back at them that she "never keeps court dates." Curious about this contradiction between knowing the consequences of not keeping court dates and still not keeping them, I asked her why she got in trouble in the first place. She said that she was in for battery, for a fistfight with another girl.

One of the interns came over at that time to ask if I would run group for them on that day, as she was less experienced at it. I told her that I would. The other intern, who I had not met, suggested that we talk about teenage pregnancy and the responsibility of both parents taking care of the child. She asked the group why fathers sometimes do not do their part. A little nervous about the tone of this accusation, and knowing the strong reaction that could result might be more than she expected, I said that I knew that this does not happen all the time, but when it does happen, "sometimes," I asked them, "why does it." The boys were silent. One of the African-American girls responded that, "Some kids is just irresponsible." A girl interjected that everyone in Coldville has slept with everyone else, "and that babies just pop up just like AIDS is going to be popping up." Two of the boys gathered the strength to respond at this point. "Some does" take care of their kids, the first boy stated, "my brother does." The second boy agreed, "I would if I had a kid." The other boys in the group all agree that they would take care of their kids "if they could." A girl interrupted them. She pointed to some of the boys saying, "he would," but pointed to others saying, "he wouldn't take care of his kids." She was playful and they were all laughing, but I think she also meant what she was saying.

I asked if they knew anyone who has failed to take care of his kids. I clarified that I did not just mean this in terms of money, but in other ways too. The intern who brought up the topic commented at this point that her friend had been abandoned by the father of her child. I could see the boys in the group growing visibly irritated by her comments, so I interjected:

> I know that it's a stereotype that Black men don't take care of their kids, as some of you have been pointing out, but why does that stereotype exist? And these men and boys who don't take care of their kids, why do you think that is? I've heard from some of you that sometimes drug dealers are trying to get money to help their kids. I don't mean it's ok to sell drugs, but at least they try to take care of their kids.

One of the boys stated that, "almost every drug dealer I know has kids." The intern responded to him by saying, "there's more to being a father than buying things, like helping with child care." A girl, to the intern, shot back, in defense of the boys, "I think it's just racism," by which she meant that she thought the things the intern was saying were racist.

The young people of color in this discussion, male and female, insisted that most fathers in their community would take care of their children if they could. Moreover, they insisted that it was the drug dealers in the community who were most likely to take care of their children even though what they were doing in the community was harmful. They argued that most drug dealers were selling drugs in order to support their children or extended families (this perspective was conveyed by my informants over time, in different settings). The White intern had certain perceptions of men, and of Black men in particular, and she seemed to assume that the girls would back her up when she confronted the boys. She seemed to want to force the boys to take a hard look at their behavior and to be more responsible fathers, currently or in the future. It was the girls of color who challenged the intern, in the end dismissing her arguments as racist.

This sort of conflict in which White people assume that their perspective is correct related to issues of race or gender has been documented in other studies. Kathleen Weiler (1988), for example, described a conflict between a class of women, their feminist teacher, and a Black boy, John. The teacher was using a passage from Malcolm X's autobiography in which Malcom X's teacher tells him that he could not be a lawyer because he was a "nigger." The teacher intended to use the passage "to discuss the way that people build a self-image from the way their identity is reflected in the opinions and attitudes of others" (p.140):

Teacher: What was Mr. Ostrowski telling him?
Black girl: He knew you couldn't have Black lawyers back then.

John: (interrupts) He's indirectly telling him to change his goals. Because he's a nigger.

Teacher: He's being told to be realistic . . .

John: Negative.

White boy: His character was such that he saw it as a challenge.

Teacher: We do not have to accept the image other people give us.

John: Mr. Ostrowski was threatened by the Black guy's motivation, that the Black guy's aiming high.

Teacher: Okay, we're not talking about Mr. Ostrowski right now . . . (p.140).

John dropped the class the next day and the teacher was relieved because she considered him a discipline problem. Becoming more sensitive to these conflicts can allow for a broader view of oppression.

Weiler describes a feminist studies class where the teacher avoided a potential conflict that began as follows:

White boy: What is Herstory?

White girl: His Story

Teacher: Who writes the history?

White girl: Men.

Black girl: White men (p.142).

Rather than favor one understanding of the historical lack of representation, the teacher included the exclusion of "Blacks, Indians and others who don't have a voice" along with the exclusion of women in the discussion. In this class it was possible to directly examine the commonalities and conflicts between sexism and racism. Girls from the lower-classes often have a different understanding of gender than their middle-class teachers. The girls' defense of the Black boys in the group discussion does not mean that they are passive young woman or that they do not have a critique of patriarchy, but their understanding of the lived reality of the men in their community allowed them to see the complex interplay of poverty and psychology that contributes to some fathers being absent in the lives of their children.

Male Bonding, Weight Lifting, and Patriarchy

My criticism of the class-biased gaze with which White intellectuals often view the aspirations of working-class families is not meant to imply that problems of hypermasculinity, sexism, and patriarchy do not exist among my informants. They do, and in the end these perspectives held by the boys (and by most of the girls) contribute to their destruction in the "criminal justice system."

In the spring, there was a group of African-American boys who were particularly fond of using a weight machine in the detention center. They would press weights on the machine whenever they could, would ask staff for permission to lift weights during every free period, and would comply with staff for the reward of lifting weights. It was an expensive machine and the type of equipment that the boys were unlikely to have had access to previously.

One of the boys who had come to accept my presence and who helped me to introduce my work to others, telling them, "he's ah ight" [he's alright], had taught the other boys to use the machine. Though smaller than most of the others, John was strong and determined at this task. He had learned from older brothers and boys in the neighborhood to lift weights. Unfortunately, John had also learned from these boys to hold disparaging views of girls. He would often make insulting comments towards the girls in detention, encouraging the other boys to do so as well. When I was present for these comments I would try to intervene. At the same time, I was afraid to criticize their attitudes so strongly as to alienate them from myself.

John was in the detention center because of a rape charge. He was the youngest of several boys who had been involved. The others were being held upstairs, charged as adults. I came to feel that the attitudes that he and some of the other boys expressed towards women may have been related to their behavior that brought them to the detention center. Whether John was directly involved in the assault for which he was charged or not, he was being mentored by the older boys towards engaging in this sort of behavior.

It was in the midst of this conflicted relationship with this group of boys, in which I both wanted to continue to talk with them and wanted to encourage them to question their attitudes and behaviors, that John decided to teach me to lift weights as well. Though I was larger than the boys, they were all stronger than I and were able to lift much more than I could. Even Scott, the smallest boy in the center, could lift more than I could.

This was my initiation, in the dynamics of their group, as an honorary member. With this taste of their male bonding I began to understand the relationship between the powerlessness these boys experience in their lives as they suffer with poverty and school failure, physical strength, and attacks on women. Despite the large body of literature in which men who rape speak of the desire to have power as the motivation for their violence, at least in stranger rapes, I have no doubt that in some cases, and in John's case, that this violence was also mixed up with feelings of inadequacy, anger at a life of desperation, and a desire to be accepted by other men. I do not know the extent to which John was involved in the rape he was associated with or even whether the charges were true, but I did come to understand how this friendly and helpful boy, motivated by his relationships with other males, might have been capable of such conduct.

Some months later I arranged to have one of my students at the university come to talk with this group of boys. It took some time to find an evening when he was available given his work schedule as a personal trainer. My student had used his interest in working out to motivate himself to overcome an inadequate high school education and had worked his way into college. He used his influence with these boys to encourage them to find the discipline and focus they needed if they were to have any hope of changing their situations. John, unfortunately, had already been sent to a state juvenile prison by the time we arranged the visit. I saw the position of personal trainer as a realistic career choice for him in his future. His sentencing judge reported later that he was doing well in jail; that means he was not getting in more trouble. I wonder if he received counseling and if he ever confronted the world of peers that was leading him to such behaviors.

The role of sexism and hypermasculinity in the behaviors of boys and men has been documented by other researchers (Cunningham & Meunier, 2004; Pleck, Sonenstein, & Ku, 2004). The bonding among boys is often tied to the denigration of girls and women, and it often enforces a strict expectation of heterosexuality with the threat of violence. We must be careful, however, not to overstate this phenomenon, or attempt to give it explanatory power beyond its actual impact. Feguson (2000), for example, has written a compelling book about the making of "bad boys" by our school systems and the role of sexism and hypersexuality as forms of opposition among Black boys. But I fear that she has overstated somewhat the meaning of her observations. She tells the story of an 11-year-old boy who wrote on school property, "Write 20 times. I will stop fucking 10 cent teachers and this five cent class. Fuck you. Ho! Ho! Yes Baby." She describes the meaning of his words as follows:

> An alternative reading looks at the content of the message itself and the form that Alain's anger takes at being sent to the Punishment Room. Alain's anger is being vented against his teacher and the school itself, expressing his rejection, his disidentification with school that he devalues as monetarily virtually worthless. His message expresses his anger through an assertion of sexual power — to fuck or not to fuck — one sure way that a male can conjure up the fantasmatic as well as the physical specter of domination over a female of any age. His assertion of this power mocks the authority of the teacher to give him orders to write lines. His use of "baby" reverses the relations of power, teacher to pupil, adult to child; Alain allies himself through and with power as the school/teacher becomes "female," positioned as a sex object, as powerless, passive, infantilized. He positions himself as powerful

through identification with and as the embodiment of male power as he disidentifies with school. At this moment, Alain is not just a child, a young boy, but taking the position of "male" as a strategic resource for enacting power, for being powerful. At the same time, this positioning draws the admiring, titillated attention of his peers. (p. 174)

Alain is 11 years old. He doesn't fully understand what it means to fuck or to say fuck. He's just repeating things that he has heard in our culture that are considered insulting. Ferguson's observations about this language in general are very interesting and may well reveal the attitudes of adult males when used by them, but Alain is a child. I fear that we can all, however well intentioned, too easily fall into the trap of sexualizing and criminalizing children of color, in our gaze, in the ways that we interpret their behavior.

Changing Perspectives on Race, Class, and Gender

The young people in my study were there because of their race, class, and gender. The young people of color tended to see race as the overarching explanation for their troubles, but would often describe class dynamics when asked to explain how racism worked in their lives. They actually provided little analysis that we would associate with critiques of racism in the literature, though they had many examples of racism to draw upon. The young people did not name gender as the primary issue in their lives. But it was dramatically important nonetheless. Some boys may have come to the detention center in part because of their attitudes towards women and girls, which may have contributed to acts of violence. They also came to the center because they engaged in fighting at times to maintain their macho image, or even to impress girls. (Gang membership is in part, after all, a way to hook up with girls.) They may have sold drugs in order to fulfill their gendered obligation to be the bread winner. Girls, on the other hand, tended to get in trouble when their behavior differed or rebelled against the feminized expectations that society places on them, as are described so well by Ferguson (2000). To some extent they got in trouble when they rejected gendered expectations that girls should not fight, or talk back, and so forth.

In the course of conducting my research I encountered no students who were openly gay or confided in me that they were gay or lesbian. The extent to which heterosexuality is enforced among young people of all races and ethnicities is very troubling indeed. Homosexual youth are targeted, drop out of school, and commit suicide at rates that surpass all other demographics. I did not have the opportunity, and perhaps did not have the courage, to confront this issue with these young people as directly as is needed. To do so would have almost certainly alienated me from them. The almost complete silence (aside from the constant use of insults like "gay" among the young people) about sexual orientation — something that impacts on all of our lives every day — is frightening. The level of fear that keeps this topic in the closet must be immense.

As a scholar, I was often irritated by the blurring of defined categories in the words and actions of my informants. The categories that we use (race, class, and gender) are constructed on evidence and go a long way towards explaining the critical problems with which we have grappled. It may be the case, however, that we can learn something from these young people about race, class, and gender analysis. At the very least we should ask ourselves why these categories get jumbled and redefined as they try to make sense of their lives. We should also try to develop a more holistic way of looking at these categories and the issues that they represent. What may look to us like hypermasculine drug dealing by violent macho types may actually be the actions of a dedicated father who is doing the wrong things for all the right reasons. Even the sexist language directed at girls by some boys (which was only used by a small number of the boys), while always hurtful, may not be intended to cause harm.

Chapter 7

Conclusion

Using the methodology of critical ethnography (and more specifically a type of Freirean-inspired critical ethnography I call advocacy ethnography), in the tradition of critical theory, I have recorded and then compared the perspectives and voices of my informants with those of theory. In particular, I have attempted to illuminate the relationship between the political economy, education, and the prison industrial complex. The preceding chapters have sorted, sifted, and winnowed, in an attempt to better understand why the young people in my study, and the demographic they are a part of, are so likely to leave school, die or go to prison, at an increasingly young age. I have attempted to remind us that the statistical links between education, poverty, and incarceration represent human lives. I have endeavored to convey the voices and perspectives of my informants, because society should listen to what they have to say, and also because their insights can be quite illuminating. In this process I have also struggled to hold on to the complexity of forces and issues that affect my informants.

In this chapter I will first review the findings from each of the preceding chapters. Next, I will discuss my ideas that emerge concerning the causes of educational failure and incarceration of my informants, and young people like them in other communities, and the resulting devastation this has caused nationally. Finally, I will argue for a liberatory movement, joining schools, intellectuals, and larger community movements; which I believe holds potential for improving the lives of young people like those in my study, and the lives of their families, and which is part of a larger struggle towards a more just social and economic order.

A Summary

In the introduction, I discussed my motivations for the research, the reasons for the general approach that I took, and my commitment to advocacy research, which can be seen in the orientation of my ethnography towards the scholarship of Paulo Freire. I put the reader on notice, as it were, that my purposes were not simply to document my observations and perspective, but to help the communities from which my informants come, and other communities like them, to find solutions to their collective problems of poverty, educational failure, incarceration, and high mortality rates.

In the historical chapter I argued that modern schooling in the United States and the prison industrial complex evolved in an intertwined and interdependent manner through various historical periods. A number of related notions about punishment, responsibility, opportunity, and social obligation held positions of differing prominence in different periods, but none of these notions (in their various manifestations) ever completely disappeared. These various positions on the continuum between compassion towards, or the condemnation of poor people (and between the understanding that children are not fully formed socially and psychology and the idea that children are little adults or worse), seem to have percolated to the surface of political discourse recently in a manner that allows these contradictory positions to exist simultaneously.

In our current historical period society is generally compassionate towards the children of privilege, who enjoy extended periods of adolescence, and are valued and forgiven. Poor children, and children of color in particular, on the other hand, are viewed with a racially charged gaze that defies known human biology in an effort to conceive of them as adults, evil in their motives, and threatening like giant and dark creatures of the night. It is in the imaginations of White people, still dreaming of that savage and dark jungle, that children of color are constructed, ignored in school, condemned, and convicted by juries. This construction of children of color in the imaginations of dominant White society is exploited, promoted, and at times shared by the professions and industries that benefit from their destruction. The history discussed in this chapter documents not only the growth and evolution of the relevant professions and industries that have become the prison industrial complex but also the rationalizations (in science, political discourse, and psychology) that the privileged classes employ to justify their exploitation of and violence towards poor people, and poor people of color in particular.

In the pedagogy chapter I examined the attitudes of the young people in my study towards the education that they had received in public schools. I described my observations of them in educational settings, compared the educational practices of the center school with their memories of public schools (and my general knowledge of these schools), and raised critiques about an approach to education that is Eurocentric, boring, decontextualized, lacks relevance in the lives of most young people, and is increasingly competitive. Drawing upon the ideas and perspectives of my informants, I made suggestions for improving education that would involve project work with an explicit focus on exposing community problems and improving the lives of students and their families. I also stressed the importance of having teachers who are caring and who accommodate the need of young people to socialize and move about from time to time.

The public schools in Coldville have adequate resources, well-trained teachers, with safe and well-maintained buildings compared to public schools across much of the country, both urban and rural. Teachers have access to curricular materials that are current and innovative. The system as a whole is informed by research in the field of education and has been flexible in its efforts to meet the needs of an evermore diverse student population. The vast majority of teachers in Coldville sincerely desire to see all of their students learn and be successful.[1] Many of the glaring problems that are so often identified in the literature, and rightly so, are absent or less pronounced in Coldville. My comments here are not meant to minimize, for example, the need for a more equitable distribution of resources to schools in low-income communities. Students cannot learn in classrooms that flood when it rains. Teachers cannot help students learn without curricular materials. For students in the sort of school environments described by authors such as Jonathan Kozol (1991) and Tom Hayden (2004) it may be necessary to infuse the schools with more resources before any progress can be made. Coldville, however, demonstrates that adequate funding of schools does not automatically result in improved outcomes for students who are struggling academically and economically.

Given the presence of concerned teachers and adequate resources, I looked carefully at the role that students might have had in their own educational failure. What I found was that students had not given up entirely on learning, so that personal inadequacy or family attitudes towards education could not explain their educational difficulties. I found that the curriculum and pedagogy they experienced, as well as the perceived lack of caring on the part of teachers, often alienated students from their educations. Even in classrooms where students reported having teachers who supported and cared for them in ways that were effective, students often continued to struggle. Part of this is explained by their already being behind in an increasingly competitive environment. Part is explained by the distraction of economic and psychological difficulties in their lives. Ultimately, and despite the complexity of the problem of school failure for my informants, I argued for an approach that I believe could help young people like those in my study. Rather than ignore their lived experience, curriculum and pedagogy must be designed to help students investigate and challenge the injustice in their lives. Such an approach in schools (see Tewksbury & Sher, 1998) can both contribute to better educational outcomes for these students while producing a generation of young people with the analytical skills and organizational savvy to build political movements in their communities.

In "Perspectives on the Economy and Hopes for the Future" I placed the development of the economy and educational system in the proper historical context, with attention to both the history of the United States and of the theories that inform critical theory. I argued that my informants are too busy trying to survive, too confused, and too overwhelmed by the competition in schools to engage in any organized resistance to school. They fail in school, for a complex range of reasons, which are as varied as there are young people. The young people in my study were shown to have few hopes for the future. Some had fantasies about being famous performers, athletes, or, as a backup plan, successful drug dealers. Others, who had engaged in the drug trade, saw themselves dead or in prison in the future. While there were exceptions and the young people seemed to change their minds or be confused about the economic prospects for their future, the world view of my informants was generally bleak, more so than earlier ethnographies have reported.

The educational failure of working-class students has been described in the critical literature as either being the inevitable result of structural factors in the capitalist economy, or else as a process of active endorsement of a working-class counterculture. This counterculture rejects intellectualism as effeminate and the aspiration towards professional work as both a rejection of where one comes from and a risky investment of time and energy. Resistance, or cultural-productive theory, is the dominant explanation as to why working class children remain in the working class; a theory that has influence outside of critical circles as well. My study, though, does not support either reproductive theory or resistance theory as primarily explanations for the educational failure of my informants. I did document reproductive moments, such as racial profiling (by teachers and police officers alike), where the actions and attitudes of my informants seemed to have little impact on their getting caught up in the justice system. I also documented both oppositional behavior and politically conscious resistance on the part of my informants. These tended to be moments that passed like moods, and these passing moods were related to their mixed feelings, or confusion, as to the economic viability of graduating from high school or attending college. My informants told me that they struggled in school, skipped school, dropped out, or were expelled from school, for a complex and quite varied range of reasons, including pregnancy, boredom, poverty, homelessness, and alcohol addiction. Their critiques of schooling were not, in their views, primary among the actual reasons that they ultimately failed in school or got in trouble with the legal system.

The mixed feelings and confusion of my informants, though understand-able and even logical, can increase their educational and legal troubles. For young people like those in my study, who start the competitive educational race behind the wealthier students in their classrooms, they could not afford to stumble, hesitate, or doubt. The pace of our current high stakes educa-tional system makes it almost impossible for them to catch up with their wealthier peers.

In "Corruption and Racism in the Legal System" high rates of incarcera-tion were shown to be related to the structural needs of late capitalism and tied to the actions of wealthier and Whiter members of society, perpetuated against poor people and people of color in order to maintain inequalities in society. The claims of my informants that they are illegally and/or unjustly targeted by the police for surveillance, harassment, coerced and illegal searches, were documented. I discussed the ever-widening range of behav-iors that are used to criminalize young people of color. The bias in the justice system on the part of judges, prosecutors, social workers, and juries was also documented. The relationship between the media, rightwing intellectuals, and the boom in incarceration were also discussed.

This chapter documents instances of and discusses the frequency of po-lice perjury to secure convictions. It also presents evidence that young people were abused, if not tortured, in a neighboring county where they were held short term due to crowded conditions. The attitudes of my informants to-wards drug use, and the frequency of their use of alcohol and drugs were dis-cussed. Ultimately, I argued that the gaze with which young people of color are viewed and the manner in which they are treated by authorities, both in schools and in the community, actually contributes to their school failure, skipping, dropping out, and engaging in illegal activities. In short, it is often the indignity of harassment by the police that pushes young people, who have tried to cling to hope for their futures, over the edge towards destructive and illegal activities. This harassment and their treatment in the juvenile jus-tice system serve to convince them that there is little point in staying out of trouble or focusing on their schooling. It teaches them that they will always be targeted based on their skin color, lack of economic power, and address.

In the chapter "Race, Class, and Gender" I discussed the impact of ra-cism on my informants and the racist ways that they are constructed in the public sphere. The class bias inherent in this gaze, and the patriarchal orien-tation of some of the young people in my study that contributes to their legal troubles, were also discussed. I noted in particular that most of the young people in my study were disconnected from the history of struggle for racial equality and also lacked an analysis of racism that could help them to confront it effectively. Instead, racism was experienced as an immutable force in their lives that would always limit their potentials. The racism in the community, policing, and the legal system made them targets. Once in the system, they were not treated in a fair or compassionate manner, leaving them either more angry or with more feelings of self-loathing, or both. This chapter concluded by suggesting that race, class, and gender should be considered outside of the categories and understandings that have been developed in the scholarly literature, at least tentatively, so that we might better understand the perspectives of our informants.

A Word of Theoretical Caution

Critical theory, more than most approaches to social inquiry, has a tradition of considering the complexity of social problems. Drawing on the best aspects of Marxism, sociology, anthropology, and psychology, critical theory attempts to understand human interaction as occurring in a mix of individualism, socialization, and structures. Embracing its interdisciplinary nature, the field strives to take a broad view.[2]

Despite taking such a broad view of social problems, however, there has been a tendency in the field (as in other fields of inquiry) to look for overarching theoretical explanations that likewise imply their own and unitary solutions. Reproductive theory, as advanced by Bowles and Gintis, and resistance theory, as advanced by Willis, are equally guilty of this tendency. I am, of course, over simplifying to some extent. Bowles and Gintis acknowledged the phenomenon of resistance just as Willis acknowledged that there are reproductive motives, mitigated by his notion of cultural production and resistance. Likewise, few critical scholars would claim that there is only one problem in our society or that there is one solution that will solve all the problems in society. I believe there has been a tendency, nonetheless, to look for a primary theoretical explanation.

Jonathan Kozol seems to hold the view that the first thing to be done is to address the funding inequalities between schools. Bowles and Gintis argue that the structural limitations of capitalism must be removed before schools can truly allow all students to succeed. For Willis reproduction is a cycle that occurs, ironically, in the efforts of working-class students to maintain their dignity through their counterculture, against an economic system that denigrates them. Feminist orientations tend to focus on the need to eliminate patriarchy and discrimination against women. Then there is the classic battle between some Marxists and race-based theorists over which of these best explains the oppression of working people. All of these theoretical orientations hold value, but none are primary or complete.[3]

I worry that the well-meaning impulse to make sense of our data, to understand what it all means and what has to be done to fix social problems, may have caused critical theory to fixate on particular explanations instead of focusing on the interplay of various contributing factors.[4] Worse yet, I worry that this may have resulted in a tendency to look for and to find exactly what our theoretical orientation would lead us to expect. I am thinking mostly of resistance theory. In my study I expected to find that resistance explained, in broad terms at least, the educational failure and incarceration of my informants. Given that I did find some indicators that would be consistent with resistance theory (as defined by MacLeod rather than Willis), I might have concluded that my study was yet another confirmation of the theory that Willis gave us. I essentially stumbled upon what is one of the major theoretical findings in my study, that resistance does not explain the outcomes of my informants. This matters to the extent that we believe our understanding of social phenomena can help us to improve lives and create a more just society. If we don't see the true nature of a problem, our resulting proposed solutions may be ineffective.

The Case for Pragmatism

Instead of the constant search for the perfect theory, the constant struggle to "refine theory," the leap frogging from one academic fetish to the next, I propose the adoption of a pragmatic position related to theory. As Thomas Skrtic argues in *Disability and Democracy*:

> As a pragmatist, of course, I do not expect to construct the ultimate, "true" theory of school organization and change. Given the antifoundational epistemology of pragmatism, I am interested in selecting theories that are useful for reconciling the institutional practice of special education – and ultimately the institution of public education itself – with the ideal of serving the best educational and political interests of education consumers and the democratic needs of society. (1995, pp. 196–197; see also, Skrtic, 1991, p. 124).

John Dewey described the logic of his notion of pragmatism as a means of scientific inquiry as follows:

> One cannot climb a number of different mountains simultaneously, but the views had when different mountains are ascended supplement one another: they do not set up incompatible, competing worlds... (1944/1966, p. 110)

Theories can be understood as tools, each revealing certain aspects of social reality, but simultaneously concealing others. The task, then, is to take what is useful from each theoretical position and, collectively, to form a general understanding of the world.[5]

It can be seen, then, that when Willis states that, "the notion of correspondence omits the possibility of resistance" (1981, p. 53), what he is really saying is that reproduction theory, that focuses more on macroeconomic factors, and theories that focus more on the cultural level do not fit together perfectly. Though I have argued that there are serious problems with the resistance theory articulated by Willis, I continue to believe that a theory of conscious resistance like that articulated by MacLeod remains useful; though I have also argued (given other evidence) that it cannot serve as an overarching theory of school failure and economic reproduction. I can see the value in both the work of Bowles and Gintis and that of MacLeod because I am not attempting to find the perfect theory, or even to synthesize the two theories, but rather because I take each of them for what they offer to the general and collective view of the valley (that is social reality). I am arguing, in a way, that Critical Theory be more serious about its interdisciplinary nature. Freire's work continues to be one of the best models for this.

What Is to be Done?

The immediate suggestions for improving the educational outcomes of the students in my study, and those like them around the country, are those in the chapters. Curriculum and pedagogy should relate to the lives of these students and help them, in a meaningful way, to improve their own lives and the neighborhoods in which they live. Classroom practices should move at a pace they can handle, include opportunities for social interaction, include hands on learning, and students should learn in the larger community (rather than the classroom) on occasion. Every student should have a mentor. Interested students should be released from school part of the time to engage in paid internships in business or in non-profits. There should be after-school programs in every community and in as many neighborhoods as possible. With these changes more of the students in my study will want to stay in school.

These changes will not protect students from problems at home and police harassment. Therefore, their parents should be provided with safe, meaningful jobs, that pay well. Their family should be provided with quality health care and childcare. Police harassment and racial profiling must end. There must be a decriminalization of marijuana use and fighting. Draconian sentencing must end. The concept of adolescence must hold sway in juvenile cases. Guidance, addiction counseling, psychological counseling, and healthy activities should be provided instead, for the entire family. With these changes fewer students like those in my study will get in trouble at home or with the law.

These changes will not be sufficient, however, to allow them to out compete students from wealthier families, in most cases. These families will find new ways to advantage their own children in the competition related to the educational system and economy. Even if they were the new "winners" in the competitive educational system and economy they would simply create new "losers." These changes, likewise, won't protect them from racism. If we exorcized racism from our policies and hearts, we might eliminate the racial bias in unemployment and incarcerations rates, but a newly constituted working class (containing fewer people of color) would continue to struggle for the crumbs that the larger and more affluent in society drop from their tables. So, ultimately, we must redistribute wealth and income, and therefore power, in society. This is essential, but not sufficient, to improve the educational and life chances of my informants.

Taken as a whole the voices, evidence, and analysis in this book speak to the complexity of the problems in the lives of young people like those in my study. The common thread in their stories is economic depravation and their (realistic) lack of hope for the future. But the ways that these structural forces play out in the lives of individuals is more varied, in form and explanation, than most earlier studies indicated. We cannot reverse the educational failure and trends towards incarceration for poor students by encouraging them to stop acting as agents of their own destruction (as Willis might suggest) when the forces at play in their lives (like false arrest) are beyond their control. Even if we adopt policies that result in short-term improvements for poor students, by allocating significant resources towards their immediate economic needs and educational needs and away from wars and the prison economy, their very educational success would devalue the economic benefits of an education. It would not result in the elimination of inequality, resulting poverty, or even group/class mobility. What is needed are sophisticated long-term strategies, tied to social movements for social justice, culminating in revolutionary change away from capitalism towards socialism and meaningful grassroots democracy.

As Bowles and Gintis (1976) argued 31 years ago, the inequality in society will only be corrected by revolutionary change that produces a socialist economy within a truly democratic form of government. A more equitable distribution of wealth can mediate pain among the poor, but ultimately, the needs of capitalism, the declining rate of returns, and the greed of the upper classes will continue to compel the poor to work for less and live on less, and this will continue to lead to desperation, despair, hunger, and death (not to mention environmental devastation resulting from capitalist production). Willis said that his study with the lads was not so much a study of how work-ing-class youth get working-class jobs, but of why they let themselves be reproduced into their class position. My study is not just a study of why working-class youth of color end up in detention (and jails or prisons), though it is that as well, but also of why they let us do this to them.

Where Willis (1977/81) argued that working-class lads continue to have working-class jobs, at least in part, because they allow themselves to be rele-gated to those jobs, the working-class kids in my study, especially the young people of color, will be lucky to find any job at all, and those jobs that they find will not pay them enough to live on. In the long term, those who fight for social justice must work to build a revolutionary consciousness among the working class and among those who will fight with them (Freire, 1970/93). It is not enough to argue that resources should be returned from prisons to schools or to support for the poor; although this must happen, it is not sufficient.

Critical theory has given us the tools to understand, though imperfectly, the workings of culture, power, and economy in the perpetuation of an unjust social order. Sociology and anthropology have given us the tools to docu-ment the perspectives and experiences of people. Historical, statistical, and other approaches to analysis and research have contributed as well. Critical pedagogy, following the path begun by Paulo Freire, has given us a way to approach teaching and learning that will encourage students to question, think freely, and act to change the world. The work of John Dewey taught us to make our classrooms meaningful and exciting places where learning re-lates to experience. Revolutionary fighters and singers (like Paul Robeson) alike, have, through their examples, taught us the meaning of commitment. Critical theory is a mature field with connections to a long history of strug-gling for social justice.

My book refines critical theory. It looks at it anew in an evolving histori-cal context. It does not start from scratch or reinvent the wheel. As I con-clude this book writing in the year 2007 I can attest to the fact that I stand on many shoulders. We know a great deal now. The disciplines are well estab-lished, though controversies remain, and the terrain has been mapped. One of the things we know, especially in the field of critical theory, is that our knowledge must be applied in the real world as praxis (Freire, 1970/94; Lather, 1986; Willis, 1977/81), working with, instead of for, flesh and blood human beings. We know what must happen to change the unjust social order in which we live; an order that transfers the resources needed to sustain the world population into the hands of a small minority of elites. We know how to organize. But in the years since the publication of *Schooling in Capitalist*

America, and despite the tireless efforts of many courageous teachers, scholars, and activists, we have not reversed the downward spiral of life under late
capitalism. These valiant efforts have not failed because the forces organized
against change were too strong, though they are powerful. They have not
failed because the tools of organizing and collective action are ineffective.
Rather, I believe that we have failed to reverse the course of the wildfire that
is capitalist, even though we may have slowed its pace, because too few of us
have joined the fight. We have failed to take seriously the importance of
praxis. We have spent too much time watching television. We have spent
too much time reading and writing books. We have been too preoccupied
with the quest for tenure, or with our careers in general.

I am picking on intellectuals here (the professors, school teachers, and
college students who are likely to read this book) because they have a special
opportunity, given their role in the educational system and economy, to serve
as revolutionary leaders. To work in the educational system at any level and
acquiesce to the demands that we leave children behind, to restrict our arguments to those topics that are "safe" or else to use such vague language as to
avoid being understood, to think in terms of saving a few students, to priori-
tize our own career aspirations for our responsibility to hold a mirror to society, is to be a part of the problem. Lately I see very little that is critical, much
less radical, in critical theory. To my liberal friends who hold to the futile
dream that capitalism can be reconciled with economic and social justice, I
cannot expect that you would accept all of what I am arguing for here. But I
must ask, what have you done, given your espoused liberal ideals, to actually
prevent the targeting of poor people of color in our "criminal justice system?" Intellectuals (professors or teachers) who espouse politically liberal or
radical positions who have not marched for justice, since say 1968 (or contributed in some other concrete manner), must, in my opinion, ask themselves if they are truly involved in the struggle for social justice, or if, rather,
they have simply found a niche for themselves in the economy of ideas.

My conclusion is that the complexity of the social problems that I examined in this book — the relationship among education, the political economy,
and the prison industrial complex — cannot be fixed by any one means
alone. The structural limits within late capitalism that devalue the purchasing
power of an education as more students graduate with degrees do nothing to
devalue the true benefits of genuine education; in learning to read, to reason,
and to see one's self as contributing to the making of history. The more successful marginalized students can become in our educational systems, the
more fully they can expose the nature of economic inequalities; by removing
the opportunity to blame poverty on the poor themselves, due to their alleged

lack of merit. But our strategy must work inside and outside of the system (Freire, 1970/93). Our efforts to expose the contradictions within the existing order will cause those who advocate for the status quo to respond in a dynamic manner. We must be ready for this dance.

It is far more important, in my view, for teachers to love their students and to help them come to better understand both the nature of oppression in their lives as well as to teach them the tools for defending themselves — intelligence and collective action — rather than simply teaching basic skills. Teachers must conceive of their responsibility to their students as reaching beyond the classrooms walls. We must be advocates for students and families who live in the economic margins of society. When our students are targeted by the police for walking home, we should provide opportunities for them to reflect on this problem, then we should teach them to read, write, and do mathematics in the process of working with them to expose the injustice, and demand that it stop. When Scott was portrayed in the press as a large menacing Black man, larger than his petite lawyer, and as guilty as sin, I called the editor to confront her for this and for using his real name. She informed me that I "did not know what I was talking about." Let her get hundreds of calls like mine and she may learn to be more responsible.

In taking on this larger leadership role, educators can join with communities in creating new and effective social movements. As individuals and communities, we can demand change, we can confront officers who harass young people, we can listen to the young people who complain that no one will believe them, and we can refuse to convict people for minor offenses like smoking marijuana.

Like Bowles and Gintis, like Freire, I conclude this book by arguing that the solutions for the myriad problems identified herein are to be found through love and collective action, working towards a goal of a just and better world. Moreover, I am arguing that we must abandon our fears and our flowery language that we hide behind. Rather, as academics, we should speak out more bluntly, more loudly, more often, and we should better coordinate our efforts, targeting our research to highlight social issues, as right-wing think tanks have. But we must take the initiative, not be reactive. Seemingly simple acts, like encouraging our students to volunteer in the community and giving them course credit for writing about their experiences, if coordinated by a large network of faculty across the nation, could make a difference in the lives of young people, could draw attention to crucial problems, and could mentor our students into a life of reflection and action, as scholars and social activists or community organizers. As teachers we must not only help students to be successful in terms of content learning, but must also teach in such a manner that we are also teaching the skills of critical reflection and activism. Most importantly, we must model for our students the example of an engaged and passionate life dedicated to social justice. It is not enough to speak or write of justice. Social justice must be demanded and taken. In other words, we must take seriously our responsibility as privileged intellectuals to serve as revolutionary leaders, standing with, but not speaking for, the oppressed.

Notes

Chapter One

[1] The focus that Willis (1977/81) placed on culture is a notable exception to this general statement, though his notion of culture is not that of most anthropologists.

[2] The very word *system* can serve in this capacity, e.g., arguments that claim it is not individual police officers but the system of policing that is racist, as if these systems are not made up of individuals.

[3] The difficulties that I describe with the human subjects review process are part of a growing trend, encouraged in part by recent legislation (see also Cumiskey, in Weis & Fine, 2000, p. 80; Mayers, 2001, p. 26; Burton-Rose, 1998). Increasingly academics are unable to conduct research with populations deemed vulnerable. Access is also more difficult for journalists. The Society of Professional Journalists has attempted to document this trend to restrict access, and its research may be accessed on a state-by-state basis on their web site. Edward Humes (1996), a journalist, obtained a court order to gain access to the juvenile court where he conducted his research. Ted Conover (2001) went undercover as a prison guard to gain access for the researching of his book *New Jack*. Academics would not be able to obtain access this way, but journalists can. If the goal of the review process and laws is to protect informants, then I would argue that the form that the scrutiny of research is taking is in fact backfiring. How are informants better protected by journalists who, for example, frequently name their informants, than in research by academics in other fields who are trained to hide identities?

[4] Some citations that would reveal the location of my research site or the identity of my informants are mentioned in the text, but not included in the bibliography.

Chapter Two

[1] In 1983 Graeme Newman published a disgusting book entitled *Just and Painful: A Case for the Corporal Punishment of Criminals*, in which he argued for the return to a system of punishment like that in the early colonial example, using such modern tortures as electric shock. As he writes, "The solution lies in the rediscovery of punishment in all its variety, for there are many punishments that do not need the expensive apparatus of prison and which will do the job of administering pain so much better than prison. The answer is really so simple, yet in this century has been lost. We must take seriously what the advocates of retribution have been saying for a long time, but not truly understanding: Punishment must, above all else, be painful" (p. 6). His argument is that the infliction of physical punishment is effective, short in duration, and ultimately more humane that incarceration.

[2] Debtors were jailed by virtue of having entered into a contract with their lender to provide "a pound of flesh" if repayment was not made.

[3] During this four-year period beginning in 1841 a fungus killed successive crops of potatoes, the staple diet of Irish sharecroppers. While other crops flourished and were sold in England, Irish peasant farmers were forbidden by law from growing anything but potatoes. The population in Ireland was reduced from 8 million to 5 million during this period, with at least 1 million peasants dying from disease and starvation, while the remaining depopulation was the result of immigration, primarily to England and the United States. It was common for families to sell off all of their possessions to buy passage for as many of their children as they could, which often would be the oldest boy alone. This all but assured that the remaining family would perish as they would be left with no farming implements for the next season of planting. This forced famine was used opportunistically by Irish and English land owners to switch from the farming of their land to the lucrative grazing of sheep. The great exodus of Irish people continued until approximately 1851, by which time the population had been reduced to approximately 4 million.

[4] Most lower-court judges run for state office unopposed, while federal judges are appointed. It cannot be accurately claimed that they are only responding to the public will when they lay down harsh sentences. In fact, surveys suggest that the public prefers treatment and rehabilitation to harsh sentences for nonviolent offenders. Often judges first take the bench when they are appointed to fill a vacancy, frequently as a reward for their "tough" prosecutions, after which they are reelected in unopposed races. The district attorney in Coldville made a name for herself at the time of my fieldwork by prosecuting and threatening to prosecute juveniles as adults, and was rewarded with such an appointment. One of the sitting judges who was widely known for giving the strictest possible sentences to juveniles of color and adults with drug problems was rewarded with an appointment to the Appeals Court.

Chapter Three

[1] An article in a local paper reported allegations of abuse in the detention center. I was present on the day in question. I spoke to the reporter on the condition that my name and research role not be mentioned and assured him that I had never witnessed any physical abuse of the young people at the center. I was disappointed that rather than questioning the honesty of the single young person who made these statements, the reporter suggested that young people being held in detention are not to be trusted in general.

[2] The theme of boredom is one that has been repeatedly observed by critical ethnographers, going back to Willis in 1977.

[3] For a powerful discussion of the hidden lessons of mainstream instruction, see Gatto, 1992.

[4] The students also complained about instruction in the larger room, but given the greater level of supervision in the space, they tended to express their opposition in nonverbal ways.

[5] I gave my informants juice, soda, and snack food on occasion.

[6] The annual reports published by the Juvenile Court state that around six percent of juveniles referred self-reported that they were not enrolled in any educational programming. The data are not organized by grade level to show if dropout and truancy rates increased in higher

grades, as other studies have found. The data also do not get at students who are attending, but are frequently skipping school. I do not have definitive numbers but my research suggests that closer to 20 percent of the young people held in detention were not attending school at the time of their arrest, and that around 50 percent of the young people held in detention had ditched school at some point during the year. My estimates are not necessarily in contradiction to the self-reported numbers provided by the Juvenile Court. Keep in mind that the young people in my study were those held in detention for longer periods of time and were more economically challenged, facing a range of difficulties in life and school, while the annual report was a sampling of all young people, even those who were held for very short periods of time and might come from more economically stable neighborhoods.

[7] I do not use the word utopian disparagingly or to suggest that a better world is *pie in the sky*. Rather, I am attempting to reclaim the word, as one of promise and real possibility for actual and concrete improvements in our world, born of dreams.

[8] Perhaps the best example of policy informed by this reasoning are the high-stakes tests that aspire, at least in rhetoric, to motivate students and their teachers by threatening to fail students and close schools where students do not score well. If motivation is the solution, so the theory goes, then lack of motivation must have been the problem.

[9] I note with interest that the desire on the part of students to have a laugh was reported by Willis in 1977, with the very language to "have a laff" (p. 29) being so similar. He also observed complaints about boredom.

[10] It merits mentioning that grade schools and middle schools in Coldville have made significant efforts, including purchasing expensive curricular materials, to make instruction, particularly in the area of science, more hands-on and engaging. It is common to witness a mix of instructional approaches, including the use of stations, discussions, and group work, so that students do, by and large, have an opportunity to stretch their legs.

[11] A recent study that looks at the educational failure of Black students in the face of the success of many White students in medium-sized and relatively affluent communities found that students of color spend as much time on their homework and studying as do their White peers. This may be true when looking across all students of color in a community such as Coldville, but it was not true of most of my informants who were people of color, based on what they themselves told me.

Chapter Four

[1] A more traditionally Marxist analysis would argue that prisons emerge to contain *surplus labor* (poor people who cannot find jobs) and to create jobs for some segments of the working class, while at the same time dividing segments of the proletariat by race and income. There is certainly some truth to this perspective, as prisons do serve these purposes, in part. Although I haven't the space for a thorough treatment of this topic at this time, I would argue that the economic and political motivators in the development of the prison industrial complex are bigger drivers of the boom in incarceration, at this time, than the related need to contain surplus labor. The upper class benefits from surplus labor in that real wages have been driven

down sharply. They also benefit from racism among Whites in the working class. Campaign contributions pour in from the powerful prison guard and police unions, which also mount vicious campaigns against any attempt to soften the worst effects of the war on drugs (Hayden, 2004, p. 335). These are all factors that complicate the impulse to remove surplus labor from the market. Moreover, with current trends in corporate globalization of trade policies and the outsourcing of jobs, the entire proletariat in the United States runs the risk of becoming surplus labor. Because the majority of the population cannot be housed in prisons, intensified forms of control become necessary to prevent rebellion, such as more complete hegemonic control, manipulation of the electoral process, and the steady march towards authoritarianism.

[2] By 1981 when his book was released in the United States, Willis noted in a new Afterword that the economic situation in England had already begun to change, so that the jobs that the working-class Lads could have counted on in the past were no longer available to them. This situation has only worsened over time (Willis, 2004).

[3] I would argue that the higher expectations of the Brothers vis-à-vis the Hallway Hangers might have been related in part to their having greater access than did earlier generations to the full range of universities, rather than only to African-American universities alone.

[4] In their later book, *Democracy and Capitalism* (1986), Bowles and Gintis clarify their position on the interplay of structure and agency, stating, for example, that: "We ... embrace the fundamental tenet of structural theories – that individual action is highly regulated — in a framework that insists that the historical dynamics of the structures regulating choice are themselves the result, however indirect and unintended, of individual action" (p. 96).

[5] Though their failure to understand the similarities between his view on reproduction and that of Bowles and Gintis would seem to indicate that either they don't understand his arguments related to the nature of power or else selectively ignore them.

[6] My current position on what constitutes resistance differs from the position that I held in the past, which is documented in my master's thesis *The Pedagogy and Politics of Paulo Freire*. At that time I viewed resistance as any attempt to express autonomy by people from oppressed classes (Freire, 1989). I believe now that I was confusing opposition with resistance; a moment of confusion that I do not believe Freire shared.

[7] Frantz Fanon (1963/68) and Paulo Freire (1970/93) articulated psychological processes by which people internalize a view of themselves and the world that tends to prevent them from imagining better possibilities for themselves and for the world.

[8] There are also a variety of reasons that a young person might associate with a subculture, some being politically potent, but others as basic as the need to have some place to sit in the school lunch room, given social cliques.

[9] This author wore a backwards Mohawk haircut for several years, in a deliberate attempt, along with identification with a subculture, to engage in symbolic politics. Later on, as the shock and impact of the symbolic protest in punk rock softened; they became fashion for

many young people who were no longer attempting to differentiate themselves from bourgeois culture, and were not, therefore, engaged in symbolic politics.

[10] My critique of the concept of culture described by Willis as well as my view that his well-documented counterculture of the Lads does not translate into a form of resistance should not be taken as an unfriendly rejection of the value of his work overall.

[11] There is, of course, a tradition of radical critique in Rap and Hip Hop that significantly contributes to the development of knowledge and analysis. I am not knocking Hip Hop in its more positive forms. The music of KRS One and Public Enemy are the classic and foundational examples of this critical tradition in Rap.

[12] There was great concern that computer programs lacking a four-digit reference to the year might become confused and crash or result in other significant problems when the programs were unable to record a year beyond 99.

[13] This was certainly the case in earlier historical periods as well, but at those times, rates of incarceration were not as high, nor was education credentialing so essential to the ability to make a reasonable living.

[14] The confusion and mixed feelings of my informants on the economic viability of a high school or college degree, given racism and general economic conditions, is not meant to imply that they were unsophisticated in their thinking on these issues. Though my informants often lacked the vocabulary to describe their thoughts in the language of academics, and despite lacking the skills of logic and analysis that academic training develops, I was often impressed with the thoughtful manner in which the young people attempted to weigh and sift what evidence they had at their disposal for sorting out these complex questions.

[15] The doctor who comes to the center to treat the young people, while careful not to breech confidentiality, told me in general terms that many of the young people have untreated medical problems, most common among these being tooth decay (see also Kozol, 1991).

[16] To define resistance more loosely is to engage, in part, in a leap of faith towards a theoretical explanation that, as far as I can tell, cannot be documented. We can document young people who engage in resistance as a conscious act as I have defined it, but how can we document a notion of resistance that takes place outside of consciousness, becoming at once everything and nothing at all?

[17] I note that many of my informants expressed an interest in academic subjects that one might pursue in college, and yet were doing nothing to pursue these interests. I take this as additional evidence that young people like those in my study do have a desire to learn. Follow-up questions hinted that their interest in particular academic subjects were kindled in the earlier grades, but dampened in junior high and especially in high school.

[18] It is possible, of course, that the young people I count as outside of organized gangs and the illegal drug trade industry, may have sold some quantities of illegal substances (particularly marijuana) on a small scale.

[19] In Coldville, for example, landlords could require that tenants earn three times the monthly rent or have ideal credit. These requirements were disproportionately applied to applicants who were people of color. The outcome of this discrimination was that people of color of modest means in Coldville were ghettoized into a few neighborhoods where the rents were almost as high as rents in the rest of the community.

[20] The future that my informants long for is not pie in the sky. Rather, they dream of interesting work that pays well, allows them time for leisure, and of having a loving family life. Supporting their view that this modest dream, and human right, is denied to them, we should not be surprised to learn that 90 percent of people who are arrested for violent crimes are unemployed, underemployed, or living below the poverty line (Lang, 1994).

[21] This member of the staff had a tendency to get into conflicts with young people at the center, and these conflicts tended to escalate. The other members of the staff were forced to discipline the young people and support her, but often commented to me in passing that they felt that she created these conflicts through her style of interaction with the young people.

[22] Although arrest data are always suspect and can reflect bias in policing priorities more than variations in actual rates of crime.

[23] Boys aspiring to sell drugs and girls aspiring to raise families is perhaps related to the "rights of passage" for many young people of color discussed in Tom Hayden's book *Street Wars* (2004), in which going to jail is the passage to adulthood for boys, while becoming pregnant is the right of passage for girls (p. 313).

[24] The conflicted roles of and formation of gangs are discussed by Mike Davis (1990/2006) and Kontos, Brotherton, & Barrios (Eds.) (2003).

[25] A sloppy and biased news report was published in a local paper in Coldville. In the article the perspective of people who worked in the school system and who stated that there was no real gang problem in the schools, as well as the voices of students who denied that gangs presented a danger to them in their schools, were discounted while the voices of law enforcement personnel were favored, in bold print and tone, when they stated that the gang problem was out of hand, and that the very distinction between serious gang involvement and wannabes was a false one. What is most disturbing about the article is that shocking photos (later admitted to be stock photos not even of youth in Coldville) were intermixed with the text, photos of a young person discharging a gun, another giving a gang sign, others fighting, or standing around on a public street. This article is not a serious challenge to my position.

[26] Unlike some larger cities, as reported by ethnographers such as Terry Williams (1992) and Philippe Bourgois (2003), dealing in poor neighborhoods in Coldville takes place on the street rather than in store fronts.

[27] This attitude towards legitimate work and the drug economy, which I recorded, is consistent with what Bourgois (2003) reported.

[28] Classrooms in public schools in Coldville are integrated, especially in the early grades, though advanced classes are populated with kids from privileged families.

Chapter Five

[1] A report released by the Federal Bureau of Investigation in 1998 revealed that there were more arrests on marijuana-related charges in 1997 than any previous year in U.S. history, with 695,201 people arrested on marijuana-related charges, 87 percent of which were for possession.

[2] My findings that marijuana use may be higher among poor Blacks in particular neighborhoods in Coldville should not be interpreted as a justification for the racially biased arrest rates of young people in impoverished neighborhoods. The means by which the young people of color are caught with marijuana reveals a racial bias. If White youth were searched by the police as are Black youth, their arrest rates for marijuana possession would be much higher.

[3] I did not ask and do not know the extent to which the parents of my informants are using alcohol or other illegal substances. When I asked one boy why kids get in trouble he told me "because their parents may do drugs." This is an area of inquiry that could have been fruitful, but I was not comfortable asking questions about illegal activities on the part of their parents in this setting because it might have scared them from speaking honestly with me and because their answers might have been overheard.

[4] Many jurisdictions, lacking juvenile facilities, routinely hold juveniles in adult jails.

[5] Community policing, which is trumpeted as an approach to policing that will reduce racism and build better relations with the police by having officers stationed in a given area, is often described by my informants (and by members of the Black community whom I met at community meetings) as a stricter form of surveillance, with individual officers targeting people against whom they have held a grudge, often for beating earlier charges.

[6] Having consent for this interview also gave me consent to see his file.

[7] James Q. Wilson and George L. Kelling developed a "theory" that a broken window left unattended would result in higher rates of serious crime when people saw the window and concluded that no one cared about the neighborhood. Their argument was one for maximum surveillance and control, and it was used by Mayor Guliani to justify the imposition of a regime of police control in New York City. This has been emulated by police departments around the country. Of course, this theory did not hold up to scrutiny and arguments against it that were supported by actual evidence (Miller, 2001). But, as I hope to systematically defend in the future, the theory was never about evidence or broken windows. It was about fascism, the notion that human beings must be controlled, for their own good, and the good of an orderly society. It was about the exercise of arbitrary power, brute force, and conformity. The actions of the police, described by my informants and in other research, were supported by the proponents of this neofascist movement and the police culture that embraces "law," when it serves their interests, but mostly "order."

[8] Ayers (1997), for example, documents the case of a boy named Jesus who was picked up as a juvenile under false pretences and allegedly signed a confession, after reading it, even though Ayers had tutored the boy and knew for a fact that the boy could not read.

[9] Whether he can actually land a job selling drugs or make the kind of money that he might imagine, it is his belief that he can, or his resignation to the idea that this is his only option, that sets the stage for this fateful decision, which is encouraged by police misconduct.

[10] Adolescence referring to the idea that children enter a state before adulthood in which they are not fully formed and are not fully responsible for their actions as an adult would be, or even if they are equally responsible are still malleable and changeable.

[11] It should be noted that, unlike the findings of Ferguson (2000), the girls in my study did engage in all-out fistfights with other girls, and occasionally with boys as well. This discrepancy may be explained by age differences between the populations with which we were working, differences in socioeconomic status, or in geography.

[12] One of the most extreme examples of the ambition of prosecutors to target young children took place in Chicago, where the police coerced confessions from two African-American boys, ages 7 and 8, for the rape and murder of an older girl in their neighborhood. The subsequent media coverage claimed among other things that one of the boys was a member of a notoriously violent black gang. The charges were eventually dropped, however, when semen was found on the girl's clothing. Boys that young couldn't have produced semen (Hancock, 2000). Even after the charges were dropped against these boys and an adult was charged with the rape and murder, the police and state's attorney refused to exonerate the boys (*Chicago Tribune,* April 23, 1999).

[13] There is little hope of hiding the identity of this boy from anyone who digs deeply, because his name and image were widely published in the media, at the urging of the police. Nonetheless, I am using a false name for him. His physical description, which is important to understanding the issues around his case, has not been altered.

[14] It should be noted that the death rate related to guns has dropped in recent years, and was already lower in 1999 than it had been previously (*Wisconsin State Journal,* November 19, 1999).

Chapter Six

[1] In fairness I should note that the young people were often all together too verbal about the things they had done. On many occasions I told them that it would be better if they spoke with their attorneys before admitting to anything that they might have done. Open and honest as always, they would continue to tell anyone who would ask what they had done, and would occasionally volunteer this information without being asked.

Chapter Seven

¹ Most critical scholarship has tended to focus on examples of teachers who have low expectations for their students of color, hold racist views, are abusive, uncaring, or at a minimum turn cultural conflicts into power struggles with their students. My observations of teachers in Coldville, and what my students tell me about their teachers, leave me with a much higher opinion of the practice and potential of the average teacher in the system. My research demonstrates that most teachers, in *Coldville* at least, are dedicated to the success of all of their students. This is not to say that I am satisfied with what goes on in most classrooms. I have observed an appalling lack of expectations related to students with special education labels in some classrooms, for example, and as my pedagogy chapter discussed, I believe that most classrooms fail to develop an approach to teaching that adequately understands the needs of students of color and students from poor families.

² This is not to imply that critical theory is the only theoretical orientation that strives for a broad view of social problems. John Dewey's notion of pragmatism, for example, is an orientation in the politically liberal tradition that takes a broad view, and he was an author who wrestled with similar social problems as those addressed by Marxists.

³ I am not denying the importance of strategic decisions on priorities. I am also not denying that some situations or particular historical periods may best be understood by emphasizing a particular theoretical orientation.

⁴ Professor Gloria Ladson-Billings helped me to sort out my thoughts on this issue in a private conversation in which she compared the complicated nature of a car with the complexity of a reef aquarium. A car is complicated, but not complex. An aquarium contains an ecosystem that is living and not simply reducible to the sum of its parts. The explanation of the failure of one of my informants, then, is the result of his interaction with the interpersonal and social forces in his life. Certain categories of experiences are shared by groups in society, such as the experience of racism or poverty, and may affect people in similar ways, but each person's experience is unique. Just as there are personality types but no two personalities are identical.

⁵ I should note that Abowitz (2000) has also advocated for a notion of pragmatism to replace resistance theory. His notion of pragmatism seems unrelated to what I am advocating here.

References

Abowitz, K. K. (2000). A pragmatist revisioning of resistance theory. *American Educational Research Journal, 37*, 877–907.

Adler, P., & Adler, P. (1987). The past and the future of ethnography. *Journal of Contemporary Ethnography, 16* (1), 4–24.

Aggleton, P. J. & Whitty, G. (1985). Rebels without a cause? Socialization and subcultural style among the children of the new middle classes. *Sociology of Education, 58*, 60–72.

Albelda, R. (1999, January/February). What welfare reform has wrought. *Dollars & Sense.*

Ambrosio, T. J., & Schiraldi, V. (1997). *From classrooms to cell blocks: A national perspective.* Washington, DC: The Justice Policy Institute.

Anderson, G. (1989, Fall). Critical ethnography in education: Origins, current status, and new directions. *Review of Educational Research, 59*(3), 249–170.

American Civil Liberties Union (1999). *Driving while black: Racial profiling on our nation's highways.* New York: American Civil Liberties Union.

Annual Report on School Safety. (1998, October). U.S. Department of Education and U.S. Department of Justice.

Anyon, J. (2005). *Radical possiblities: Public policy, urban education, and a new social movement.* New York: Routledge.

Apple, M. W. (1971). The hidden curriculum and the nature of conflict. *Interchange 2*(4), 27–34.

Apple, M. W. (1980). Analyzing determinations: Understanding and evaluating the production of social outcomes in schools. *Curriculum Inquiry, 10*(1), 55–76.

Apple, M. W. (1982). *Education and power.* Boston: Routledge & Kegan Paul.

Apple, M. W. (1990). *Ideology and curriculum.* New York: Routledge.

Apple, M. W. (1996). *Cultural politics and education*. New York: Teachers College.

Apple, M. W. (2000) *Official knowledge* (2nd ed.). New York: Routledge.

Apple, M. W., & Beane, J. (Eds.). (1995). *Democratic schools*. Alexandria, VA: Association for Supervision and Curriculum Development.

Apple, M. W. & Weis, L. (Eds.). (1983). *Ideology and practice in schooling*. Philadelphia, PA: Temple University Press.

Ayers, W. (1997). *A kind and just parent*. Boston: Beacon Press.

Bradsher K. (1995, April 17). Gap in wealth in U.S. called widest in west. *New York Times*.

Beatty, P., Holman, B., & Schiraldi, V. (2000). *Poor prescription: The costs of imprisoning drug offenders in the United States*. San Francisco: Center on Juvenile and Criminal Justice.

Beck, A. J., Karberg, J. C., & Harrison, P. M. (2002). *Prison and jail inmates at midyear 2001*. Washington, DC: U.S. Bureau of Justice Statistics.

Bernard, T. J. (1992). *The cycle of juvenile justice*. New York: Oxford University Press.

Betraying the young: Children in the US justice system. (1998, November). Retrieved from http://web.amnesty.org/library/ Index/ engAMR 510601998.

Biddiscombe, P. (1995). The enemy of our enemy: A view of the Edelweiss Piraten from the British and American Archives. *Journal of Contemporary History. 30*(1), 37–63.

Bloom, B., & Steinhart, D. (1993, January). *Why punish the children: A reappraisal of the children of incarcerated mothers in America*. Oakland, CA: National Council on Crime and Delinquency.

Bourgois, P. (2003). *In search of respect: Selling crack in el barrio*. San Fransico: Cambridge University Press.

Bowles, S., & Gintis, H. (1976). *Schooling in capitalist America*. New York: Basic Books.

Bowles, S., & Gintis, H. (1986). *Democracy & capitalism: Property, community, and the contradictions of modern social thought.* New York: Basic Books.

Breggin, P. (1991). *Toxic psychiatry.* New York: St. Martin's Press.

Breggin, P., & Breggin, G. (1998). *The war against children of color: Psychiatry targets inner city youth.* Monroe, ME: Common Courage Press.

Brown, C. (1974, July). Literacy in thirty hours: Paulo Freire's process. *The Urban Review, 7*(3).

Burton-Rose, D. (1998). *The celling of America.* Monroe, ME: Common Courage Press.

Carspecken, P.F., & Apple, M. (1992). Critical qualitative research: Theory, methodology, and practice. In M. D. Lecompte, W. L. Millroy, & J. Preissle (Eds.), *The handbook of qualitative research in education* (448–505). San Diego, CA: Academic Press.

Cass, C. (2004, May 28). *Report: 1 of every 75 U.S. men in prison.* Associated Press.

Cho, M. K. (1997). *School, work and subjectivity: An ethnographic study of two South Korean commercial high schools.* Doctoral dissertation, University of Wisconsin, Madison, 1997.

Coles, G. (1978, August). The learning disabilities test battery: Empirical and social issues. *Harvard Educational Review, 48*(3), pp. 313–40.

Coles, G. (1987). *The learning mystique: A critical look at "learning disabilities."* New York: Ballantine Books.

Connell, R. W. (1993). *Schools and social justice.* Philadelphia: Temple University Press.

Conover, T. (2001). *Newjack: Guarding Sing Sing.* New York: Vintage Books.

Cremin, L. (1951). *The American common school: An historic conception.* New York: Teachers College Press.

Cunningham, M., & Meunier, L. (2004). The influence of peer experiences on bravado attitudes among African American males. In N. Way, & J.

Chu (Eds.), *Adolescent boys: Exploring diverse cultures of boyhood* (219–234). New York: University Press.

Currie, E. (1985). *Confronting crime: An American challenge*. New York: Pantheon Books.

Driving while black: Racial profiling on our nation's highways. (1999). New York: American Civil Liberties Union.

Dance, L. J. (2002). *Tough fronts: The impact of street culture on schooling*. New York: RoutledgeFalmer.

Davies, S. (1995). Reproduction and resistance in Canadian high schools: An empirical examination of the Willis thesis. *The British Journal of Sociology, 46*, 662–687.

Davis, M. (1990/2006). *City of quartz: Excavating the future in Los Angeles*. New York: Verso.

Dei, G., Zine, J., Mazucca, J., & McIsaac, E. (1997). *Reconstructing 'drop-out': A critical ethnography of the dynamics of black students' disengagement from school*. Toronto: University of Toronto Press.

Dershowitz, A. (1998, December 1). *Testimony before the House of Representatives Judiciary Committee, regarding the impeachment of President Clinton*.

Dewey, J. (1916/44). *Democracy and education*. New York: The Free Press.

Dohrn, B. (2000). 'Look out kid, it's something you did': The criminalization of children. In V. Polakow (Ed.), *The public assault on America's children: Poverty violence and juvenile injustice* (157–187). New York: Teachers College Press.

Dolby, N., & Dimitriadis, G. with Willis, P. (2004). *Learning to labor in new times*. New York: RoutledgeFalmer.

Everhart, R. (1983). *Reading, writing, and resistance: Adolescence and labor in a junior high school*. London: Routledge and Kegan Paul.

Ex-Minneapolis cop throws the book at police culture. (2004, October, 28). *Minneapolis Star Tribune*.

Fanon, F. (1963/68). *The wretched of the earth*. New York: Grove Press.

Feld, B. (1999). *Bad kids: Race and the transformation of the juvenile court*. New York: Oxford University Press.

Ferguson, A. (2000). *Bad boys: Public school in the making of black masculinity*. Ann Arbor: University of Michigan Press.

Fine, M. (1991). *Framing dropouts: Notes on the politics of an urban public high school*. Albany: State University of New York Press.

Fine, M., & Weis, L. (1998). *The unknown city: The lives of poor and working-class young adults*. Boston: Beacon Press.

Foley, D. (1990). *Learning capitalist culture: Deep in the heart of Texas*. Philadelphia: University of Pennsylvania Press.

Fordham, S. (1996). *Blacked out: Dilemmas of race, identity, and success at capital high*. Chicago: The University of Chicago Press.

Freire, P. (1970/93). *Pedagogy of the oppressed*. New York: Continuum.

Freire, P. (1970a). *Cultural action for freedom*. Cambridge, MA: Harvard Educational Review and Center for the Study of Development and Social Change.

Freire, P. (1989). *Learning to question*. New York: Continuum.

Freire, P. (1998). *Pedagogy of freedom: Ethics, democracy, and civic courage*. Lanham: Rowman & Littlefield Publishers.

Fuentes, A. (1998, June 15). The crackdown on kids: The new mood of meanness toward children — to be young is to be suspect. *Nation*.

Gatto, J. T. (1992). *Dumbing us down: The hidden curriculum of compulsory schooling*. Philadelphia: New Society Publishers.

Gee, J. P. (1987). What is literacy? *Teaching and Learning, 2,* 3–11.

Gibson, M. A. & Ogbu, J. U. (1991). *Minority status and schooling: A comparative study of immigrant and involuntary minorities*. New York: Garland Publishing.

Gilligan, J. (1996). *Violence: Our deadly epidemic and its causes*. New York: Putnam.

Giroux, H. A. (1981). *Ideology, culture, and the process of schooling*. Philadelphia: Temple University Press.

Giroux, H. A. (1983). *Theory and resistance in education.* South Hadley, MA: Bergin and Garvey.

Giroux, H. A. (1983, August). Theories of reproduction and resistance in the new sociology of education: A critical analysis. *Harvard Educational Review, 53,* 257–293.

Gordon, L. (1984). Paul Willis: Education, cultural production and social reproduction. *British Journal of Sociology of Education, 5,* 105–115.

Hancock, L. (2000). Framing children in the news: The face and color of youth crime in America. In V. Polakow (Ed.), *The public assault on America's children,* (78–100). New York: Teachers College Press.

Hawes, J. (1971). *Children in urban society: Juvenile delinquency in nineteenth-century America.* New York: Oxford University Press.

Hargreaves, A. (1982). Resistance and relative autonomy theories: Problems of distortion and incoherence in recent Marxist analyses of education. *British Journal of Sociology of Education, 3*(2), 107–126.

Hayden, T. (2004). *Street wars: Gangs and the future of violence.* New York: The New Press.

Heaviside, S., Rowand, C., Williams, C., Farris, E., Burns, S., & McArthur, E. (1998, February). *Violence and discipline problems in U.S. public schools: 1996–97.* National Center for Education Statistics, U.S. Department of Education.

hooks, bell (1989). *Talking back: Thinking feminist, thinking black.* Boston: South End Press.

Horn, D. (1973). Youth resistance in the Third Reich: A social portrait. *Journal of Social History 7*(1), 26–50.

Human Rights Watch (1989). *Shielded from justice: Police brutality and accountability in the United States.* New York: Human Rights Watch.

Humes, E. (1996). *No matter how loud I shout: A year in the life of juvenile court.* New York: Simon & Schuster.

Juarez, J. A. (2004). *Brotherhood of corruption: A cop breaks the silence on police abuse, brutality, and racial profiling.* Chicago, IL: Chicago Review Press.

Justice Policy Institute. (2002). *Cellblocks or classrooms? The funding of higher education and corrections and its impact on African American men.* Washington, DC.

Kaufman, P., Chandler, & K., Rand, M. (1998, October). *Indicators of school crime and safety, 1998.* National Center for Education Statistics and Bureau of Justice Statistics, U.S. Department of Education and U.S. Department of Justice.

Kingston, P. (1986). Resistance Theory: How Marxists interpret student life. *Sociological Forum, 1,* 717–725.

Kliebard, H. (1995). *The struggle for the American curriculum.* New York: Routledge.

Kohl, H. (1994). *I won't learn from you and other thoughts on creative maladjustment.* New York: The New Press.

Kohn, S. (1994). *American political prisoners: Prosecutions under the espionage and sedition acts.* New York: Praeger Publishers.

Kontos, L., Brotherton, D., & Barrios, L. (Eds.). (2003). *Gangs and society: Alternative perspectives.* New York: Columbia University Press.

Kozol, J. (1991). *Savage inequalities: Children in America's schools.* New York: Crown Publishing.

Ladson-Billings, G. (1994). *The dreamkeepers: Successful teachers of African American children.* San Francisco: Jossey-Bass.

Lang, S. S. (1994). *Teen violence.* New York: Franklin Watts.

Lather, P. (1986, August). Research as praxis. *Harvard Educational Review, 56* (3), 257–277.

Lee, L. (1939/1999). *World War II.* Westport, CN: Greenwood Press.

Lee, S. J. (1996). *Unraveling the "model minority" stereotype.* New York: Teachers College Press.

Lee, S. J. (2001, Fall). More than "model minorities" or "delinquents": A look at Hmong American high school students. *Harvard Educational Review, 71*(2), 505–528.

Lee, S. J. (2004). Hmong American masculinities: Creating new identities in the United States. In N. Way & J. Chu (Eds.), *Adolescent boys: Ex-*

ploring diverse cultures of boyhood, (13–30). New York: New York University Press.

Lee, S. J. (2005). *Up against whiteness: Race, school, and immigrant youth.* New York: Teachers College Press.

Leondar-Wright, B. (2004, May/June). Black job loss déjà vu. *Dollars & Sense*.

Levy, G. (1970). *Ghetto school: Class warfare in an elementary school.* New York: Pegasus.

Lopez, N. (2003). *Hopeful girls, troubled boys: Race and gender disparity in urban education.* New York: Routledge.

Luttrell, W. (1997). *School-smart and mother-wise: Working-class women's identity and schooling.* New York: Routledge.

MacLeod, J. (1987/95). *Ain't no makin' it: Aspirations & attainment in a low-income neighborhood.* Boulder, CO: Westview Press.

Males, M., & Docuyanan, F. (1996). Crackdown on kids: Giving up on the young. *Progressive Magazine, 60*(2), 24–26.

Marx, K., & Engels, F. (1848/1964). *The communist manifesto.* New York: Washington Square Press.

Maas, Peter (2005). *Serpico.* New York: Harpertorch.

Mayers, M. (2001). *Street kids & streetscapes: Panhandling, politics, & prophecies.* New York: Peter Lang.

McFadden, M. G. (1995). Resistance to schooling and educational outcomes: Questions of structure and agency. *British Journal of Sociology of Education, 16,* 293–308.

McGrew, K. (2004, Summer). Last page commentary. *Dissent Magazine*.

McLaren, P. (1993). *Schooling as a ritual performance.* London: Routledge and Kegan Paul.

McLaren, P., & Scatamburlo-D'Annibale, V. (2004). Paul Willis, class consciousness, and critical pedagogy: Toward a socialist future. In N. Dolby, G. Dimitriadis, & P. Willis (Eds.), *Learning to labor in new times* (61–82). New York: Routledge.

McNeil, L. M. (1988). *Contradictions of control: School structure and school knowledge*. New York: Routlege.

Metz, M. (1992). *Different by design: The context and character of three magnet schools*. New York: Routledge.

Metz, M. (2000, Spring). Sociology and qualitative methodologies in educational research. *Harvard Educational Review, 70*(1), 60–74.

Miller, D. W. (2001, February 9). Poking holes in the theory of 'broken window's. *Chronicle of Higher Education*.

Miller, J. (2004, March/April). High and dry: The economic recovery fails to deliver. *Dollars and Sense*.

Mollen Report (1994). *The city of New York Commission to Investigate Allegations of Police Corruption and the Anti-Corruptuion Procedure of the Police Department*, Milton Mollen, Chair. New York: City of New York.

Morrow, R., & Torres, C. (1995). *Social theory and education: A critique of theories of social and cultural reproduction*. Albany: State University of New York Press.

Nasaw, D. (1984). *Schooled to order: A social history of public schooling in the United States*. New York: Oxford University Press.

Navarro, V. (1991, September). Class and race: Life and death situations. *Review of the Month, 43*(4), 1–13.

Newman, G. (1983). *Just and painful: A case for the corporal punishment of criminals.* New York: The Free Press

Noguera, P. (2000). Listen first: How student perspectives on violence can be used to create safer schools. In V. Polakow (Ed.), *The public assault on America's children: Poverty, violence and juvenile injustice* (130–156). New York: Teachers College Press.

Noguera, P. & Cannella, C. M. (2006). Youth agency, resistance, and civic activism: The public commitment to social justice. In S. Ginwright, P. Noguera, & J. Cammarota (Eds.), *Beyond resistance! Youth activism and community change* (333–348). New York: Routledge.

Nolan, K., & Anyon, J. (2004). Learning to do time: Willis's model of cultural reproduction in an era of postindustrialism, globalization, and mass incarceration. In N. Dolby & G. Dimitriadis (Eds.), *Learning to labor in new times* (133–149). New York: RoutledgeFalmer.

Oakes, J. (1985/2005). *Keeping track: How schools structure inequality.* New Haven, CN: Yale University Press.

October 22 Coalition (1999). *Stolen Lives — Killed by Law Enforcement (2nd edition).* New York: October 22nd Coalition.

Ogbu, J. U. (1978). *Minority education and caste: The American system in cross-cultural perspective.* New York: Academic Press.

Ogbu, J. U. (1992). Foreword. In P. Solomon (Ed.), *Black resistance in high school: Forging a separatist culture* (vii–x). Albany: State University of New York Press.

Oppenheimer, T. (2003). *The flickering mind: The false promise of technology in the classroom and how learning can be saved.* New York: Random House.

Parenti, C. (2000). *Lockdown America: Police and prisons in the age of crisis.* New York: Verso.

Win at all costs. (1998, November 22 – December 13). *Pittsburgh Post-Gazette.*

Pleck, J., Sonenstein, F., & Ku, L. (2004). Adolescent boys' heterosexual behavior. In N. Way & J. Chu, (Eds.), *Adolescent boys: Exploring diverse cultures of boyhood* (256–270). New York: New York University Press.

Polakow, V. (2000). *The public assault on America's Children: Poverty, violence and juvenile injustice.* New York: Teachers College Press.

President's Commission on Higher Education. (1947). *Higher education for American democracy, 6.* Washington, DC: Government Printing Office.

Quinn, M. (2004). *Walking with the devil: The police code of silence.* Self-published.

Reiman, J. (1990). *The rich get richer and the poor get prison.* Boston: Allyn and Bacon.

Rikowski, G. (1997). Scorched earth: Prelude to rebuilding Marxist educational theory. *British Journal of Sociology of Education, 18,* 551–574.

Rist, R. (1970). Student social class and teacher expectations: The self-fullfilling prophecy in ghetto education. *Harvard Educational Review, 40,* 3, pp. 411–451.

Robinson, C. C. (2007). *From the classroom to the corner.* New York: Peter Lang Publishing, Inc.

Sapon-Shevin, M. (1994). *Playing favorites.* Albany: State University of New York Press.

Schultz, S. (1973). *The culture factory: Boston public schools 1789–1860.* New York: Oxford University Press.

Second chances — 100 years of the children's court: Giving kids a chance to make a better choice. (1999). Washington, DC: Justice Policy Institute.

Sennett, R., & Cobb, J. (1972). *The hidden injuries of class.* New York: Vintage Books.

Shor, I. (1980/87). *Critical teaching and everyday life.* Boston: South End Press.

Shor, I. & Freire, P. (1987). *A pedagogy for liberation: Dialogues on transforming education.* South Hadley, MA: Bergin and Garvey.

Skrtic, T. M. (1991). *Behind special education: A critical analysis of professional culture and school organization.* Denver: Love Publishing Company.

Skrtic, T. M. (Ed.). (1995). *Disability and democracy: Reconstructing [special] education for postmodernity.* New York: Teachers College Press.

Solomon, P. (1992). *Black resistance in high school: Forging a separatist culture.* Albany: State University of New York Press.

Stack, M. & Kelly, D. M. (2006). Popular media, education, and resistance. *Canadian Journal of Edcucation, 29*(1), 5–26.

Stamper, Norm (2005). *Breaking rank: a top cop's expose of the dark side of American policing.* New York: Nation Books.

Streitfeld, D. (2003, December 29). Jobless count skips millions. *Los Angeles Times.*

Tavares, H. (1996). Classroom management and subjectivity: A genealogy of Educational identities. *Educational Theory, 46*(2), 189–202.

Tewksbury, G., & Scher, A. (1998, March/April). To raise a village: Education for the community. *Dollars and Sense.*

Tewksbury, G. & Uhl, M. (1986). An interview with Paulo Freire. *Old West Review, 1*(1).

Thurow, L. (1975). *Generating inequality.* New York: Basic Books.

Torres, A., & Freire, P. (1994). Twenty years after *Pedagogy of the Oppressed*: Paulo Freire in conversation with Carlos Alberto Torres. In P. L. McLaren & C. Lankshear (Eds.), *Politics of liberation: Paths from Freire* (100–107). New York: Routledge.

Turner, G. (1979). Review of the book *Learning to Labor*: How working class kids get working class jobs. *Sociology, 13*(2), 336–338.

Valenzuela, A. (1999). *Subtractive schooling: U.S. — Mexican youth and the politics of caring.* Albany: State University of New York Press.

Valli, L. (1983). Becoming clerical workers: Business education and the culture of feminity. In M. W. Apple & L. Weis (Eds.), *Ideology and practice in schooling* (213–234). Philadelphia: Temple University Press.

Violence Policy Center (1997). *Who dies? A look at firearms death and injury in America* (Revised Edition).

Vorrasi, J. & Garbarino, J. (2000). Not all risk factors are created equal. In V. Polakow (Ed.), *The public assault on America's children: Poverty, violence and juvenile injustic*e (59–77). New York: Teachers College Press.

Walker, J. C. (1986). Romanticizing resistance, romanticizing culture: Problems in Willis's theory of cultural production. *British Journal of Sociology of Education, 7*(1), 59–80.

Waller, W. (1965). *The sociology of teaching.* New York: J. Wiley.

Weiler, K. (1988). *Women teaching for change: Gender, class & power.* South Hadley, MA: Bergin & Garvey Publishing.

Weis, L. (1983). Schooling and cultural production: A comparison of black and white lived culture. In M. W. Apple & L. Weis (Eds.), *Ideology and practice in schooling* (135–261). Philadelphia: Temple University Press.

Weis, L. (1990). *Working class without work: High school students in a deindustrializing economy.* New York: Routledge.

Weis, L. (2004). *Class reunion: The remaking of the American white working class.* New York: Routledge.

Weis, L., & Fine, M. (2000). *Speed bumps: A student-friendly guide to qualitative research.* New York: Teachers College Press.

Welsh, S. (2001). Resistance theory and illegitimate reproduction. *College Composition and Communication 52*(4), 553–573.

Willis, P. (1977/81). *Learning to labor: How working class kids get working class jobs.* New York: Columbia University Press.

Williams, T. (1992). *Crackhouse.* New York: Penguin Books.

Willis, P. (1981). Cultural production is different from cultural reproduction is different from social reproduction is different from reproduction. *Interchange on Educational Policy, 12*(2–3), 48–67.

Willis, P. (2000). *The ethnographic imagination.* Malden, MA: Blackwell Publishers.

Willis, P. (2003). Foot soldiers of modernity. *Harvard Educational Review, 73*(3), 390–415.

Willis, P. (2004). Twenty-five years on: Old books, new times. In N. Dolby & G. Dimitriadis (Eds.), *Learning to Labor in New Times* (167–196). New York: RoutledgeFalmer.

A Teacher Killed by His Pupil. (1886, April). *Wisconsin Journal of Education.*

Zimring, F. (1998). *American youth violence.* New York: Oxford University Press.

Zinn, H. (1999). *People's history of the United States: 1492 – present.* New York: HarperCollins.

Index

Studies in Criticality

General Editor
Shirley R. Steinberg

Counterpoints publishes the most compelling and imaginative books being written in education today. Grounded on the theoretical advances in criticalism, feminism, and postmodernism in the last two decades of the twentieth century, Counterpoints engages the meaning of these innovations in various forms of educational expression. Committed to the proposition that theoretical literature should be accessible to a variety of audiences, the series insists that its authors avoid esoteric and jargonistic languages that transform educational scholarship into an elite discourse for the initiated. Scholarly work matters only to the degree it affects consciousness and practice at multiple sites. Counterpoints' editorial policy is based on these principles and the ability of scholars to break new ground, to open new conversations, to go where educators have never gone before.

For additional information about this series or for the submission of manuscripts, please contact:

Shirley R. Steinberg
c/o Peter Lang Publishing, Inc.
29 Broadway, 18th floor
New York, New York 10006

To order other books in this series, please contact our Customer Service Department:

(800) 770-LANG (within the U.S.)
(212) 647-7706 (outside the U.S.)
(212) 647-7707 FAX

Or browse online by series:
www.peterlang.com